DATE DUE			

HIGHSMITH #45114

Michael Smith

FINE ENGLISH COOKERY

Foreword by Geraldene Holt
Decorations by Benedicte Barford

Serif
London

This edition first published 1998 by
Serif
47 Strahan Road
London E3 5DA

Originally published, in a slightly different form, by
Faber and Faber in 1973

British Library Cataloguing-in-Publication Data.
A catalogue record for this book is available from the British Library.

Library of Congress Cataloging in Publication Data.
A catalog record for this book is available from
the Library of Congress.

ISBN 1 897959 36 2

Designed by Sue Lamble.
Typeset in North Wales by
Derek Doyle & Associates, Mold, Flintshire.
Printed and bound in Ireland by
ColourBooks Ltd, Dublin.

CONTENTS

FOREWORD

It may strike you as odd that there are some cookery writers who do not, indeed cannot, cook. Michael Smith was assuredly not one of them. Everything he did, said and wrote about food and cooking revealed his deep understanding and experience of the craft. His knowledge and insight were gained as much from years spent over the searing heat of the stove as from his abiding respect for what cooking reveals about a person or a place.

For Michael Smith did not collect recipes like postage stamps – stuck in an album according to colour or theme. He cared about provenance; he researched the origins of a dish, such as A Ragoo of Lamb or Flummery, and relished exactly how it would have been prepared in the past and – just as important – how it could be interpreted most honourably today.

His intention was always to maintain the spirit of a dish rather than betray it with needless but trendy additions or fussy ideas. He revered the character and distinctiveness of English food, and was well ahead of his time in seeing that any national cuisine can all too easily lose its identity in the modern climate of globalisation, resulting in immense cultural losses when the same drab, *déraciné* food is available in every continent.

Nor would Michael's work have lasted so well had he belonged to the school of food historians who, in attempting to recreate the cooking of the past, subject us to almost inedible dishes prepared on the altar of authenticity. He realised that to do so offends the first rule of good cooking – that food should give pleasure.

Look at his recipe for English Cucumber Soup – a beautiful, subtly flavoured dish rarely encountered today, on the page or the table. Simple and elegant, light and delicious – the soup is enjoyable either hot or chilled. Yet using easily available home-grown ingredients, the recipe can be followed by the shakiest novice because Michael never forgets the reader in the kitchen: he points out possible pitfalls here, alerts the cook to exactly the right colour or consistency there and, most helpfully of all, offers guidance on how to correct any mistakes along the way.

His sheer professionalism – I defy anyone to better his instructions for Hollandaise Sauce – makes Michael Smith a cook's cook, and moreover a cookery writer's cookery writer: 'Of the many books on our food, his is my favourite, the one I use most,' wrote Jane Grigson, a fellow champion of our native food.

I first met Michael during the early 1980s when he and I were writing for the same magazine, a monthly 'glossy' with heavy paper and lots of photographs. We talked regularly as colleagues and I soon discovered that he was one of the most generous and warmly sympathetic people one could meet, always supportive, and blessed with a gift for true friendship. One of his most attractive qualities was his talent for delighting in the enjoyment and happiness of others. When he died he was writing his autobiography which would, I think, have been as witty and amusing as any conversation with him.

A Yorkshireman and proud of it, he was brought up in a prosperous household of eleven women representing three generations. He felt he'd inherited from his grandmother a shrewd assessment of people and a respect for excellence wherever one finds it. No one I know would travel further than Michael to hear good music or eat good food. It may well have been his extended family that sowed the seeds of his empathy with the cooks of the past. For Michael always expressed his admiration for anyone who cooks, he appreciated that this life-enhancing skill is ever under threat as it competes for our time and he pays tribute to the work of the thirteen women and eight men whose cooking in earlier centuries has inspired him. How well I remember his despair when an editor banned his giving the attribution or original inspiration of his recipes during the neophiliac 1980s when everything had to appear ridiculously innovative.

What a brave beacon this book was when it first appeared a generation ago and our love affair with foreign flavours was getting into its stride. And few indeed were the loyal voices who defended our own tradition of good food. Even today, the term fine English cookery is regarded by some as an oxymoron. Yet, even though Michael can no longer refute such charges in person by calmly and skilfully preparing one of his highly accomplished meals, we are most fortunate to see the re-issue of this, his best book. Michael Smith's discriminating collection of superb recipes sends a confident message of hope. It is sure to endure well into the next century and continue to inspire all of us who care passionately that English food should never lose its unique and delicious place in the world.

Geraldene Holt

CREDITS

My eternal thanks to the ladies and gentlemen of the past, many of them listed here – cooks and mastercooks, who recorded their kitchen happenings for posterity and gave me hints and advice, no matter how elaborate or obtuse, which all helped to stimulate my own imagination and urged me on to prove a point.

Hannah Glasse, Elizabeth Raffald, Eliza Smith, Ann Peckham, Mrs Frazer, Elizabeth Cromwell, Mary Kettilby, Anne Blencowe, Elizabeth Moxon, Mrs Rundell, Isabella Beeton, Eliza Acton, Agnes Marshall, Patrick Lamb, John Middleton, John Farley, John Evelyn, William Parkes, Charles Elmé Francatelli, Robert May, John Gay.

INTRODUCTION

Fine English Cookery is part of a collection of recipes which I have amassed over the many years that I have been cooking both professionally and as a hobby. I have sifted and sorted them with the intention of showing that there is a great number of delicate, subtle and remarkably interesting dishes which, if not in our repertoire today, ought to be; for somewhere at some time in our history they have had pride of place on the tables of our great houses.

After the French Revolution many of the great French chefs fled to England, and the fashion to employ them in English kitchens grew. Their style, with their 'tricks and kickshaws', rapidly eclipsed the simple elegance so unmistakable in English cookery then. About the same time our own Industrial Revolution, responsible for so many social changes in this country, was creating a period of enormous wealth amongst the upper and middle classes, who were only too happy to jump on the bandwagon of French cookery. It was this, together with the new 'below-stairs' attitude to cooks and cooking fostered by the Victorians and the Edwardians, as well as two world wars and periods of depression, which brought English cooking into disrepute.

We are guilt-ridden to this day at the mere thought of half a pint of thick, thick cream or half a pound of rich butter which, together with a Victorian hangover of nursery food and the birth of home economics, has done little to help us regain our indigenous style. Why, even I can remember what a social crime it was to discuss food at the table; the very word was almost as taboo as the word sex! It is tempting to go into long arguments and delve further into our social history and even to doubt Isabella Beeton's efficacy. But this would bog us down and most certainly destroy any spontaneous enjoyment of the recipes.

There will be those who perhaps find my choice arbitrary. There will also be some who only think well of dishes from the 'stoves of France' and to whom anything not from the French kitchen is anathema. But I feel sure there are enough chauvinistic English men and women who, like myself, enjoy showing what our great country has to offer, but may have a somewhat damp wicket when the batting is at the kitchen end and feel they must resort to 'foreign' parts for a worthy dish.

Regional dishes, as we call them, have not suffered the fate of the many richer and more elegant English recipes. But even these are somewhat difficult to link with their origin at times, so much have they changed face. I have used some few of these and, where necessary, have restored them to one version of their original content – I say one version, for opinions have always differed on minor points, as is healthy, justifiable and regional!

I have deliberately fluctuated in the naming of the dishes, changing these when I felt the original title was dull and did not encourage me at first to continue, as in 'Stew'd Pears' or 'Another way to Dress Pease'. Reading on, I saw that the pears were 'stewed' in red wine and spiced with cinnamon or cloves, their colour heightened with real cochineal and the jars filled up with brandy before being 'stopped close'. The 'pease' were to be young and tender, tossed in cream, thickened with 'butter roll'd in flour' and scented with delicate herbs.

'Good Melted Butter' was a deceptive little title if ever there was one. After reading through many sixteenth-, seventeenth- and eighteenth-century cookery books, it gradually became clear that in the best kitchens this meant a very rich butter sauce as near in character and quality to the French *Sauce Hollandaise* as you could wish. And think of Crackling Crust, a delectable, crisp, biscuity pastry made with ground almonds, sugar and egg-whites, which is no longer one of our standard daily pastries.

I have written brief notes at the beginning of some of the recipes where I feel these will help to identify the dish with England. Otherwise I think they stand worthily with their heads held high, dusted, refurbished and ready to be reinstated. We should certainly feel somewhat abashed that we ever let them go!

My choices are not necessarily from one particular period, although there is an obvious leaning towards the eighteenth century when elegance in this country was at an all-time high in everything – architecture, furniture, dress, music, painting, literature, china, glass and silver. Surely food would have been presented in a manner which complemented the rest of the way of life at that time?

Just how to list the dishes for the twentieth-century table posed a minor problem, as our eating habits are now different, for we have yet again been influenced by our Continental neighbours. But soups have *always* been a first course in the English home and I have left these as the only first courses. The 'Side Dishes' and 'Corner Dishes' of the seventeenth and eighteenth centuries I have moved into a new group of 'Principal Dishes' or put them into a 'medley' of other things which can be served as, where and when you will; first courses, savoury, buffet, lunch, supper, picnic and so on. The Tudor and pre-Tudor 'Sallets' and the Victorian affected 'Entrées' and 'Relevées' have been listed similarly. All the fish dishes come into the category of 'Principal Dishes' and anything sweet is to be a 'Pudding'! In this way I hope it will be easy to compile a totally new-looking and exciting English formula for eating.

The small section of sauces, chutneys and so forth appears separately, if only to prove, thoughbeit posthumously, to one Signor Francesco Caraccioli that there no longer exists in England 'sixty different religious sects but only one sauce'. Nor as far as I can see was that ever true.

Michael Smith
Kingston-upon-Thames
April 1973

GENERAL NOTES

QUANTITIES

Most of the recipes given here are for four to five servings, but when it comes to quantities we are touching on very personal ground, for it is up to the reader to decide just how generous the portions served are going to be. The cook will have to make his or her own decisions in many cases and these will depend on several factors. Is the dish being served as a main course? Is the starter to be a substantial dish followed by a more modest main course, or vice versa? Is it to be a two-, three- or four-course meal? How much meat is on the actual joint or bird purchased? Will you give two, three, or perhaps only one fillet of fish to each person? Will you expect your pint of soup to serve two, three, or even four? It is on factors such as these that you will base your estimate of quantities.

A little imagination and an assessment of the main ingredients of a recipe should give the reader a fairly good idea of what to expect. Game Soup is a good example of this and I would not make this recipe unless a minimum of, say, eight people are going to be served.

So far as the sweet recipes are concerned, some will serve rather more than four to five people: I would not, for instance, make Chocolate Pye, Pippin Pie or Rich Old English Sherry Trifle in smaller quantities than I have given in my recipes, for not only are they extremely rich, but it would not be worth the time and trouble involved to make them in smaller quantities.

CONSISTENCY

As a cookery writer cannot actually be at the side of the reader when he or she is cooking, it is sometimes difficult to convey the writer's *exact* intention when it comes to consistency. Only a guide can be given, as there are so many factors which govern the finished consistency of a dish - strength of flour used, actual size of cups and spoons, actual fat content of cream (which varies from county to county), and so on. It is therefore left to the cook to make adjustments at the end of the cooking time with soups, sauces, casseroles, ragouts and the like. When a sauce is somewhat too thick, one can quite simply add a little of the appropriate stock, or a little thin cream or milk. In the case of a dish ending up with a sauce that is too runny or not completely cohered - due perhaps to oven temperature variation and reduction not taking place at the expected rate - a little *beurre-manié* or, as this is a book about English cooking, 'rolled butter' (2 parts butter to 1 part flour, mixed to a paste), whisked in in small pieces, will soon put things right. Slaked potato flour is also a good last-minute rectifier.

SEASONINGS

Remember when making pale-coloured soups and sauces that black pepper will show and, whilst this will not impair the flavour of the soup, freshly ground white pepper should be used if possible: its flavour is more subtle than that of black pepper, yet not so hot as regular white pepper. In recipes where I have not indicated whether black or white pepper should be used, then the choice is yours. I would, however, always recommend that freshly ground salt and pepper be used, as their flavour is preferable.

VARIATIONS

In a number of recipes I have suggested some variations, but it is a cook's right, after first trying a recipe, to develop on the basic ingredients and method to suit his or her own taste and to experiment and be inventive. I hope my own suggestions will serve as a guide as to how one can ring the changes.

EQUIPMENT

There is no real necessity for a large battery of pans, casseroles, oven dishes, sauté pans, etc. in most kitchens, nor is it essential to have a whole regiment of knives. A good deal of thought must, however, be given to the equipment you buy and this must be geared to the individual household, taking into account both family needs and entertaining. Buy only top quality items and let these be as versatile as possible. It is far better to have a few first class pieces than a whole range of cheap, and in many cases inadequate, equipment.

Pots, Pans, Casseroles and the Like

These are generally made of one of the following: aluminium, enamelled cast-iron, enamelled steel, stainless steel, copper, ceramic (by this I mean the whole range of earthenware, stoneware, porcelain and flameware) and heat-resistant glass. Manufacturers do not always clearly indicate major points to be watched when buying these goods. They are more often taken up with the aesthetics of design - by no means to be ignored - but leave the average housewife with a great gap in her knowledge and understanding of what each particular vessel will or will not do. The following information should help you to make your choice.

(1) *Steel (Stainless and/or Enamelled)*
This is a poor conductor of heat, whether used on top of or inside a cooker, but good steel pans will have a bonded ground steel or copper base which ensures even heat distribution, thus making the pan much more satisfactory to use. Steel will not, of course, break when dropped, even on a stone floor, but enamelled steel can chip badly and may dent.

(2) *Cast-iron (Usually Enamelled)*
This will break if dropped onto any very hard surface. It will also chip if struck with some other hard substance, but it does have in its favour that which steel lacks - it is a good conductor of heat and also a good retainer of heat. Thus a lower heat is required when cooking with cast-iron enamelled pans and casseroles, or you will get undue sticking and burning.

Both these metals need constant attention when long slow cooking is called for, stirring and clearing the bottom of the pan at regular intervals with a straight-edged wooden spatula (metal spoons tend to scratch an enamel surface). If foods do become unduly stuck, making the pans very dirty, soak them overnight in an ordinary soap-based detergent. This will eliminate any harsh scouring with wire wool or other abrasives. If enamel linings become very discoloured through constant use, soak overnight with a modicum of domestic bleach in the water. Always rinse the pan well in plenty of water after this treatment, and dry thoroughly, as the metal bases will rust if left wet or stored in a damp place. If rust does occur, wire wool will be necessary to clean the raw metal base. Some 'couture' pans have an added extra luxury - the ground bases are overcoated with a layer of stove enamel, making them easier to maintain. Usually this is evident, because the enamel at this point will be black, as opposed to the multi-colours of the pans themselves. They are, of course, relatively more costly.

(3 *Ceramics*

These are breakable, so be very careful not to handle them carelessly or risk dropping them. Attention must also be paid to rapid changes of temperature, and this applies particularly to flameware - where the manufacturers claim the pot can sit directly on top of the stove. It can, so long as the pot hasn't been in a very cold place, and in the case of a gas cooker it is wise to use a heat-diffuser to deflect the sharp points of the living flame. Most other ceramics are for oven use only. One other point to watch for is the lead content of the glaze. It is advisable to ask the retailer to tell you if a particular brand meets the standards of the British Standards Institution for, say, cadmium content. (This also applies to enamelled ware.) He should know this fact, and on the whole British-manufactured goods are perfectly safe in this respect.

(4) *Copper*

Much is said by the old pundits about the merits of this metal as a good medium for pans. When it is of heavy gauge it is one of the best metals used, but it entails a great deal of maintenance and is very heavy: if a copper pan is light - forget it! It is also necessary to have the linings re-tinned at regular intervals and this is not always an easy job to get done these days, particularly in the provinces, so do take this into account. Copper can look extremely decorative, but unless one is lucky enough to have a bevy of servants, it is best to have it laquered to maintain its attractive shimmering appearance. Both lacquered and unlacquered copper will go black immediately when they are in contact with heat. In restaurants where an abundance of copper is evident in the 'front of the house', food has usually been transferred at the last minute, unless the establishment has an enormous staff and its charges are equally gigantic!

Storage of cookware is important, particularly in the case of enamel ware, which will readily chip if care is not taken. Metal lids will bend and buckle if thrown casually into some cupboard. All these points will impair the efficiency of a pan or casserole.

Cooks' Knives, etc.

The following pointers will help you to choose and preserve your knives.

Knives today should be of stainless steel with fully ground blades. Watch that they are not of the type where the blade is stamped out of sheet steel, being ground at the edges only. These may be cheaper, but they are virtually useless. Further, note that all blades should extend right through the wooden handle and be held firm with rivets for maximum strength.

Care must be taken at all times to protect the delicate blade, either by having an individual sheath for each knife, or by storing them in a knife-slot or suspending them from a hook or magnetic knife-holder. Never leave knives with their blades unguarded in a drawer. Protect their delicate tips with a piece of cork.

Never, never chop or cut on a hard surface such as formica, glass or tile - this spells sure death to any knife blade. Always use a wooden chopping board.

A knife should be sharpened or buffed up before each use and not allowed to become so blunt that heavy handling is necessary to resharpen the blade. This leads to undue wear and is often the cause of unevenness in a blade, which will impair efficient working technique.

A good palette knife will be flexible at its tip, where the metal should be well tempered and thin. If it bends only near the shaft of the handle, it has been made from poorly tempered metal and will be of little real use, as it will not have maximum flexibility.

A cooks' fork should have long straight points for piercing and lifting. A carving fork should have a guard suitably placed for protection of the hands.

Select your equipment with care, treat it with respect, and it will serve you well!

SOUPS

Many of the soups which follow can be served either hot or chilled: a great advantage of the latter is, of course, that they involve no last-minute preparation. Remember to serve chilled soup in chilled cups.

Often, where a filling menu is to follow, it is good practice with chilled soups to abandon the more traditional soup cup or plates and serve in teacups, providing good old-fashioned large teaspoons with which to eat it.

ALMOND SOUP (Chilled)

I well remember the time, years ago, when a customer sent for me and remarked, 'This soup is stone cold, I swear it has never seen the sight of a pan!'

Those were the days when a cold soup near caused a revolution!

1 litre/2 pints chicken stock
175 g/6 oz sweet flaked almonds
60 ml/2 fl oz nut oil
30 g/1 oz plain flour
175 ml/⅓ pint single cream
Salt and freshly ground white pepper
Flaked almonds for garnish

Simmer the almonds and stock together for 20 minutes. Squeeze them hard through a clean, unstarched linen towel.

Heat the oil over a very low heat in a heavy-bottomed pan. Stir in the flour away from the heat. Gradually add the strained almond stock and bring to the boil, stirring continuously to avoid lumping. Season lightly with salt and pepper and cook for a further 10 minutes over a low heat.

Strain again through a fine sieve and put aside to cool in a bowl. Cover with an oiled paper cut to fit the surface area of the soup. (If you use a buttered paper, the butter will harden when the soup is cold.) When cold, transfer to the refrigerator and chill well.

Before serving, whip the cream until the whisk leaves an obvious trail which takes a few seconds to subside. Fold the cream into the soup. Garnish with a sprinkling of fresh flaked almonds.

An alternative and equally good way of making this soup is to put the stock and almonds through the blender. This will give you a slightly thicker soup than the original recipe, so have a little more clear chicken stock chilled and at the ready to thin it down if you so wish. The finished soup should well coat the back of a dessert-spoon – not a wooden spoon, as liquid clings too readily to the wood and is not a good indication of consistency.

APPLE AND CABBAGE SOUP

Half a large white cabbage
3 medium-sized onions
1 crushed clove garlic
4 large green apples
60 g/2 oz butter
1½ litres/3 pints vegetable or chicken stock
1 tsp castor sugar
Salt and freshly ground pepper
1 tbsp green ginger

Finely shred the cabbage and slice the onions. Peel and core the apples and cut into even-sized pieces.

Melt the butter in a heavy-bottomed pan, taking care not to let it colour. Add the cabbage, onions and apples and sweat over a low heat, tossing the pan frequently. Add the garlic and cover with the cold stock.

Simmer until the cabbage is just tender. Pass through a blender or Mouli. Season with salt, pepper and the sugar.

Re-heat the soup and serve with a little chopped green ginger in each bowl.

———————

ASPARAGUS SOUP (Chilled)

An extravagant soup unless you are in the habit of visiting back-street markets on Saturdays when this sort of luxury can often be found cheaply.

A bundle of fresh asparagus (about 500 g/1 lb)
1 small onion
400 ml/¾ pint chicken stock
125 g/4 oz butter
60 g/2 oz flour
400 ml/¾ pint extra chicken stock (double-strength)
Salt and freshly ground white pepper
¼ litre/½ pint double cream
Grated rind of 1 lime

First slice the onion. Remove the asparagus tips and reserve for garnishing. Cut away the tough ends of the asparagus, scrape the stems clean and cut these into inch-long pieces.

Melt the butter over a low heat, add the asparagus pieces and the sliced onions and sweat them until they are tender, tossing the pan at regular and frequent intervals. Add the ordinary stock and simmer until the stalks are really tender.

Add the flour and stir in well. Add the double-strength stock and stir until the soup boils. Season to taste at this stage.

Pass the soup through a hair sieve or Mouli, as asparagus tends to be stringy like celery and strings get left behind with most blenders.

Cool the soup before putting in the refrigerator and chilling well.

Steam the asparagus tips until tender. Cool, then chill. Half-whip the cream until it is just beginning to stand in peaks. Finally fold in the cream, leaving it to 'marble' the soup. Top with a little grated lime rind and serve garnished with the asparagus tips.

BEETROOT SOUP (Hot or Chilled)

This is not meant to be in any way like Borscht. The soup should be a good bright red colour and it is essential that the beetroots are well washed of any soil before use or a stale favour will permeate.

500 g/1 lb cooked beetroots
250 g/8 oz chopped onion
60 g/2 oz butter (or 4 tbsp olive oil if the soup is to be chilled)
1 stick celery
2 crushed cloves garlic
Juice and rind of 1 orange
½ litre/1 pint chicken stock
½ tsp powdered rosemary
1 tsp sugar
Salt and freshly ground black pepper

Melt the butter in a heavy-bottomed pan. Add the onion and cook without browning until it is transparent. Add the garlic, celery and stock and simmer gently for 15 minutes.

Meanwhile peel the beetroots and cut them into even-sized pieces, then add them to the stock and cook for 5 minutes only. Add the orange juice and rind and seasonings.

Remove the celery before passing the soup through a blender or Mouli; check the seasoning and serve.

If served chilled, a good teaspoon of freshly chopped chives can be added, together with a little grated orange rind, to each cup, and a segment of orange can be slipped over the rim.

BEETROOT AND CUCUMBER SOUP
(Chilled)

Whilst I am very fond of beetroot, I have never been totally satisfied with the average recipe for beetroot soup in this country. I have therefore devised a soup using two popular vegetables, with orange, as these are vegetables and a fruit that have been popular here for centuries.

375 g/¾ lb cooked beetroot
1 large cucumber

10 medium-sized spring onions
A handful of fresh parsley
2 oranges
1 tbsp red wine vinegar
400 ml/¾ pint cold chicken stock
1 tbsp olive oil
Salt and freshly ground black pepper

Peel the beetroots and grate them on the coarse side of a grater. Peel the cucumber, cut it in half lengthways and scrape out all the seeds with a teaspoon. Grate this also on the coarse side of a grater.

Cut off the coarsest part of the green of the onions, but retain as much as you can. Clean them well and slice them very finely. Grate the rind of the oranges and squeeze the juice. Chop the parsley.

Put all these ingredients into a large bowl, add the vinegar and two-thirds of the cold chicken stock and season well. Retain one-third of the stock so that you can adjust the consistency of the soup. Chill well before serving, adding the olive oil at the last minute to give the soup a bright colour.

With a soup of this nature there is little need to serve breads or crackers as there is a deal of body about it. A twist of orange peel or a segment of orange, slotted onto the edge of the cup, is a good luxurious touch.

CREAM OF CARROT SOUP

Often pretentiously called Crécy after the battle of that name. The carrot has been with us in England since Charles I's days and is still a popular vegetable and soup, not to be missed out of any English recipe book.

300 g/10 oz carrots (peeled weight)
175 g/6 oz onion
2 crushed cloves garlic
¾ litre/1½ pints chicken stock
100 g/3 oz butter
¼ litre/½ pint single cream
1 tsp castor sugar
30 g/1 oz plain flour
Salt and freshly ground pepper

Grate the carrots and onion on the coarse side of a grater.

Melt one-third of the butter in a heavy-bottomed pan. Put in the grated onion and cook until transparent. Add the carrot and the garlic. Cover with a lid, reduce the heat and sweat for 10 minutes.

Pour on the stock and cream and bring to the boil. Reduce the heat and simmer for half an hour. Towards the end of the simmering period add the seasoning and sugar.

Gently melt the rest of the butter in a smaller pan and stir in the flour. Bit by bit whisk this mixture into the simmering soup until the required thickness is achieved.

Do not strain. For extra richness, add an egg-yolk beaten with a little cream.

CARROT AND ORANGE SOUP
(Hot or Chilled)

Root vegetables are often wrongly put into a social class beneath their status; this soup is refreshingly tasty and colourful and is also delicious when served chilled; olive oil is then used instead of butter as the latter has a tendency, even when emulsified, to set hard.

375 g/12 oz carrots (peeled weight)
175 g/6 oz onion
The white part of 1 large leek
2 oranges with the grated rind of one and juice of both
1 litre/2 pints chicken stock
As much curry powder as will cover a new halfpenny
1 crushed clove garlic
Salt and freshly ground black pepper
1 tsp brown sugar
60 g/2 oz butter (or 4 tbsp olive oil if the soup is to be served · chilled)

Coarsely chop the vegetables. Gently heat the butter (or oil) in a heavy-bottomed pan. Add the vegetables and gently sweat them for 10 minutes, keeping the pan covered with a lid. Take care not to let the vegetables get the slightest bit brown – this would add an unwanted flavour.

Add the curry powder, garlic, orange rind, stock and juice. Season lightly. Continue to cook until the carrots are *just* tender. Pass the soup through a blender or Mouli.

The finished soup should be full-bodied but not too thick. Reheat and add the sugar. Chill well if serving cold.

CAULIFLOWER SOUP

Everybody has his or her own special version of a dish; this is mine, as it leaves the florets intact and makes a more interesting soup, completely without the odious smell so often associated with it when badly made. The addition to each bowl of a poached or lightly boiled egg, whichever is easier, makes this a splendid soup for a soup and cheese lunch.

1 medium-sized very white and firm cauliflower
½ litre/1 pint chicken stock
½ litre/1 pint milk
30 g/1 oz plain flour
60 g/2 oz butter
Grated nutmeg
Salt
1 poached or lightly boiled egg per person (optional)

Divide the cauliflower into fingertip-sized florets. Patience at this stage will prove to be very rewarding.

Bring the stock to the boil. Drop in the florets and poach gently for 7 minutes, no longer, for the secret of this soup is to have the florets cooked but firm. Lift out the florets and place on one side.

Add the milk to the stock and bring to the boil.

In a second small pan, melt the butter, stir in the flour and blend well. Whisk this mixture into the now gently boiling milk and stock. Simmer the soup over a low heat for 5 minutes.

Season with salt and a little grated nutmeg, about the tip of a teaspoon at first. Add more if you like the combination.

Strain the soup into a clean pan, add the florets and re-heat carefully. Serve with poached or lightly boiled eggs if liked.

CHESTNUT SOUP

I cannot remember a Christmas in my home when this richest of soups was not served, but I think it should come into our repertoire earlier in the season.

The chestnut came to us with the Romans and there is said to be a tree in Gloucestershire which has been there since around 1100 AD.

At Christmastime the soup can be made two days before and kept in the refrigerator.

4 dozen peeled chestnuts (or 250 g/8 oz dried chestnuts,
covered with boiling water and left to soak overnight)
125 g/4 oz potatoes (the floury sort that collapse easily are ideal)
175 g/6 oz carrots
1 stick celery
2 rashers good-flavoured green bacon
125 g/4 oz onion
60 g/2 oz butter
1½ litres/3 pints chicken stock
¼ tsp powdered mace
1 teacup dry Madeira
Salt and freshly ground black pepper
Crisp-fried bacon rolls to garnish

Cut the de-rinded bacon into striplets and fry in the butter until crisp. Chop the onion roughly and add to the bacon, cooking until soft and golden coloured. Add the celery, carrot and potato cut into even-sized pieces. Add the chestnuts. Toss these around in the pan and cover with the cold stock. Simmer until the chestnuts are tender. (Allow at least 1½ hours for this.)

Pass soup through a blender or Mouli and add the Madeira. Adjust the seasoning with salt, pepper and mace. If the soup is too solid, add more chicken stock.

Garnish with miniature crisply fried bacon rolls.

CREAM OF CHICKEN SOUP

A rich English chicken soup surpasses any of its Continental rivals, but take care, for it can be a meal in itself.

1 roasting chicken, 1¼ kg/2½ lb dressed weight
1 onion
1 leek
1 large carrot
1 good blade of mace
Water to cover
125 g/4 oz butter
100 g/3 oz flour
Juice of half a lemon
¼ litre/½ pint single cream
Salt and freshly ground pepper
1 tbsp freshly chopped parsley

Peel, wash and cut all the vegetables into even-sized pieces. Fit the chicken into a pan and cover with cold water, add the vegetables, mace, salt and pepper and bring to the boil *slowly*. Simmer until the bird is tender. This should not take much longer than 45 minutes. Strain the liquid, cool and skim off the fat.

In a second pan large enough to contain the finished soup, melt the butter and stir in the flour. Gradually add 1¼ litres/2½ pints of the strained chicken stock until a smooth soup is arrived at.

Save the chicken legs for sandwiches, etc. Cut the breasts into ¼-inch dice.

Add the cream to the soup, and then the lemon juice. Finally, add the diced meat, sprinkle with fresh parsley and serve.

For a very special occasion, mix a couple of egg-yolks with the cream and stir in at the last minute.

CITIZEN'S SOUP (Hot or Chilled)

If sophistication means the disguising of basics with elegance, style and many-faceted tastes, then this soup is very sophisticated, with its bitter-sweet back taste, its unusual olive-green colour and its 'tweedy' texture. It scores high as an appetiser and for this reason alone I commend it to the guest table. It is good served chilled, garnished when cold with plenty of chopped chives and parsley.

In the seventeenth century there were two versions of this soup, a winter and a spring version. I have based my recipe on the latter.

1 cucumber
60 g/2 oz unsalted butter
1 medium-sized onion
1 small head celery (about 150 g/5 oz when cleaned and
stripped of its outside stalks)
1 small head chicory
60 g/2 oz small frozen peas
1 small round lettuce
¼ litre/1 pint chicken stock
A sprig of basil
Salt and freshly ground pepper
Chopped chives and parsley to garnish
(when the soup is served cold)

De-seed the cucumber by cutting it in half lengthways after peel-ing, then drawing a teaspoon down the centre, thus removing the seeds and pulp. Cut the cucumber into 1-inch cubes.

Roughly chop the onion, celery and chicory and shred the lettuce.

Melt the butter in a heavy-bottomed pan without letting it brown. Add the onions and celery, cover with a lid and sweat over a low heat until they are softened but not brown.

Add the cucumber and chicory, cover with a lid and cook for 5 more minutes, tossing the pan occasionally to prevent colouring. Add the stock and cook, uncovered, for 20 minutes. The soup will give off scum so remove this with a skimmer or tablespoon.

Add the shredded lettuce, peas and basil and cook for just 5 more minutes; any longer and you will lose the bright green colour.

Pass the whole contents of the pan through a blender or Mouli. (If a blender is used, take care not to over-emulsify the soup, as a fairly coarse texture is preferable.) Re-heat and serve.

If old celery is used there may be a tendency for this to leave strings when puréed. The celery should be carefully peeled as you would do with rhubarb, or a Mouli used instead of a blender.

EGG AND CHEESE SOUP

This soup was popular as far back as the sixteenth century. It is light and tasty and a good way of using up chicken stock. It is also so quick and easy to make that I give the ingredients for individual portions.

For each serving you will need:
175 ml/⅓ pint well seasoned, strong-flavoured fresh
chicken stock
Half an egg
1 dessertspoon tiny cubes of Cheddar
1 tsp chopped chives or parsley

Bring the stock to the boil and skim well. Beat the eggs and whisk into the soup.

Pour the soup into heated bowls, add the cheese and chives to each bowl and serve the soup whilst the cheese is still melting.

ENGLISH CUCUMBER SOUP
(Hot or Chilled)

The cucumber has been with us since Roman times, but its uses have diminished somewhat and until recent years it rarely made an appearance other than in an English salad. Over the centuries it was frequently used in soups in this country.

2 large cucumbers
125 g/4 oz chopped onion
60 g/2 oz butter
30 g/1 oz plain flour
1 tsp castor sugar
1 litre/2 pints chicken stock
Juice and zest of half a lemon
400 ml/¾ pint single cream
1 dessertspoon chopped mint (peppermint for preference)
Salt and freshly ground white pepper

Peel and de-seed the cucumber and cut into ½-inch cubes. Grate just the yellow part (zest) of the half lemon and squeeze the juice into a cup.

Melt the butter slowly in a heavy-bottomed pan. Add the onion and soften it without colouring. Add the cucumber pieces, cover the pan with a lid and sweat the two vegetables together until the cucumber is tender but not over-cooked.

Sprinkle the flour over the contents of the pan and stir in well; allow the steam to escape before doing this to avoid lumping. Add the stock and cook slowly for 15 minutes.

Pass through a blender or Mouli until a creamy consistency is obtained. Add the lemon juice and rind and season lightly with the salt, pepper and sugar. Add the cream and bring the soup to boiling point, but do not let it boil as this will discolour it and a scum will form.

Add the freshly chopped mint just before serving.

If the soup looks rather 'beige' due to possible over-cooking, add a little parsley juice made by chopping the parsley when wet and then squeezing the liquid out through the corner of a clean tea-towel.

FENNEL AND COURGETTE SOUP

Fennel was one of the most used herbs in the Middle Ages, but it has fallen into disuse. I find that it is a most suitable partner for courgettes when used in its seed form.

500 g/1 lb courgettes
60 g/2 oz butter
1 small onion
½ litre/1 pint mild chicken stock
1 crushed clove garlic
125 ml/¼ pint single cream
1 egg-yolk
1 level tsp castor sugar
A screw of freshly ground white pepper
Salt
½ tsp fennel seeds or the green tops
of 1 large fennel
¼ tsp potato flour
Chopped fennel herb or diced courgettes to garnish

Melt the butter but do not let it brown. Roughly chop the onions and sweat in the butter until soft but not coloured. Half-peel the courgettes, cut into 1-inch cubes and add to the pan.

Add the garlic to the pan, stir well and add the cold stock. Bring to the boil and add the fennel seeds, tied in a piece of muslin, and simmer until the courgettes are just tender. Season lightly. Remove the fennel seeds half-way through the cooking time (after approximately 10 minutes).

Pass the soup through a blender or Mouli, return to the pan and add the sugar.

Slake the potato flour with the egg-yolk and cream. Bring the soup back to the boil, remove the pan from the heat, add the egg and cream liaison, stirring briskly all the time. Do not boil again.

Serve with a garnish of finely chopped fennel herb if it is available, or ¼-inch courgette dice tossed for a few minutes in hot butter until they are tender.

GAME SOUP

A good game soup cannot be made without good ingredients (nor can anything for that matter), so assuming that you have decided to make the soup, the quantity I give is for upwards of eight servings. It is rich and gamey, and worth every ounce of effort you put into it.

Half a hare, fresh or frozen
An old grouse or pheasant, fresh or frozen
250 g/½ lb lean ham
250 g/½ lb stewing steak, weighed without fat
60 g/2 oz butter
100 g/3 oz flour
4 tbsps olive oil
2 large carrots
1 large onion
250 g/½ lb field mushrooms
2 sticks celery
2 litres/4 pints game stock made from the bones (see below)
3 tbsps tomato purée
½ litre/1 pint red wine
8 cloves
3 bay leaves
1 tsp thyme

1 wine glass tawny port
Salt and freshly ground pepper
The breasts and liver of the grouse or pheasant for garnish

Clean, peel and cube the carrots, onion and celery. Slice the mushrooms.

Strip the raw meat off the hare and the grouse or pheasant.
Cover the bones with cold water (about 2 litres/4 pints), bring to
the boil, skim well and simmer for 2 hours, adding an extra
¼ litre/½ pint of water after the first hour. Do not season. Strain
and reserve the stock.

Cut all the meat, except the grouse or pheasant breasts and liver,
into cubes. Take a large plastic bag, put in the flour, salt and pepper
and shake the cubes of meat in this until they are thoroughly
coated.

Melt the butter and oil together in a large pan. Gradually add
the vegetables (except the mushrooms) and fry them over a good
heat, taking care to brown them without burning. Stir them
constantly.

Remove the browned vegetables to a platter and brown all the
meat cubes in the remaining fat. Add the uncut breasts and vegetables to the pan and shake any remaining flour over them.

Add the tomato purée and the mushrooms. Lower the heat and,
stirring all the while, let all this acquire a good brown colour. Pour
over 1½ litres/3 pints of strained stock and the red wine. Add all the
seasonings.

The breasts of the grouse or pheasant will be cooked in 15
minutes. Remove these and allow them to cool before cutting them
into ¼-inch dice. Set aside for the garnish.

Cook the rest of the soup very slowly for 2½ to 3 hours, occasionally stirring well to ensure that nothing is sticking to the
bottom. Strain the soup and check the seasoning. Bring the quantity up to approximately 2 litres/4 pints, depending on how thick
you like it, using the remaining stock. Skim off any fat that has risen
to the surface.

If great care has been taken with the frying at all the different
stages, the soup should be rich, brown and glossy.

Quickly fry the liver in a knob of butter and cut into dice. Re-
heat the soup and, just before serving, add the diced breasts and liver
and the port.

LEEK SOUP

8 medium-sized leeks
1 crushed or chopped clove garlic
125 g/4 oz butter
1 litre/2 pints chicken stock
30 g/1 oz flour
¼ litre/½ pint single cream
Salt and freshly ground pepper

Cut off the root and coarse dark green part of the leeks. Cut right down the leeks lengthways, stopping at the centre, open them out flat, lay them on a board and carefully slice crossways into the thinnest strips possible. Plunge them into a large sink of cold water and leave for 15 minutes, after which any dirt will have sunk to the bottom. Carefully lift the floating shredded leeks into a colander to drain or shake them dry in a clean towel.

Slowly melt the butter in a heavy-bottomed pan. Add the leeks and the garlic. Cover the pan with a lid and lower the heat until the leeks just simmer in the butter and start to soften.

Sprinkle on the flour and seasoning and stir in well. Add the stock and bring to the boil. Cook until the leeks are tender — for about 35 minutes — then add the cream.

Do not strain this soup.

COLD LENTIL SOUP

250 g/8 oz red or yellow lentils
½ litre/1 pint chicken stock
1 tbsp olive oil
4 cloves garlic
½ head of celery
½ tsp carraway seeds
1 tbsp mild curry powder
125 ml/¼ pint single cream
1 tbsp castor sugar
Salt and freshly ground black pepper
125 ml/¼ pint yoghurt
Freshly chopped chives (or raisins) to garnish

Cover the lentils with boiling water and soak overnight. Drain them, re-cover with cold water and bring to the boil. Drain them again and rinse them in a sieve under plenty of cold running water.

Cut the celery into 1-inch pieces and put into a pan with the drained lentils. Cover with the stock, add the carraway seeds and oil and simmer for 2 hours. Remember to stir from time to time to prevent sticking.

After 1½ hours crush the garlic and add to the pan, season with salt, pepper and the sugar. Add the cream gradually to the curry powder until you have a smooth paste; add this to the soup and cook for 10 minutes.

Allow the soup to cool and then pass it through a blender or Mouli. Cut a circle of grease-proof paper to fit the surface of the soup, oil this and lay it over the soup before putting the bowl into the refrigerator to chill – this will prevent a skin forming.

Before serving, add a spoonful of yoghurt to each bowl and sprinkle with freshly chopped chives, or raisins which have been plumped up in a tablespoon of port.

MARROW SOUP (Hot or Chilled)

What to do with a zeppelin-sized marrow can be somewhat of a prob-lem. Your treatment of it need by no means be restricted to presenting it with a blanket of white sauce. It makes a good soup and I also serve it as a starter with a vinaigrette dressing. The soup is good served chilled, when cubes of cantaloupe or honeydew melon can be added as a garnish.

A green-skinned marrow weighing 2 kg/4 lb
¼ litre/½ pint chicken stock
1 coffeespoon grated nutmeg
60 g/2 oz butter
125 ml/¼ pint single cream
1 tsp castor sugar
Juice of half a lemon
Salt and freshly ground black pepper
Cubes of cantaloupe or honeydew melon to garnish

Peel and de-seed the marrow. Cut into 2-inch cubes.

Melt the butter in a largeish pan, add the marrow cubes, cover with a lid and toss over a low heat until the pieces begin to draw. Let the marrow stew for 10 minutes.

Add half the grated nutmeg and the stock, sugar and lemon juice. Simmer until the marrow is tender but has not fallen into a mush. Pass the contents of the pan through a blender or Mouli. Add the cream, half-whipped, and more seasoning of nutmeg, salt and pepper if necessary.

MULLIGATAWNY SOUP

That it comes from India cannot be in doubt, for 'mulagutannir' was a pepper water that formed the base of this soup.

There was a time when this form of curry soup, much loved by our friends in other parts of the then Empire, was very fashionable and rarely was it missed from a menu. It is still a good warming broth. The British Raj's insistence on soup was to be obeyed, hence our possession of the recipe to this day.

250 g/½ lb lentils
2 medium-sized onions
250 g/½ lb tomatoes
1 tbsp strong tomato purée
1½ litres/3 pints chicken stock
4 cloves
1 red pepper
3 chillies
3 crushed cloves garlic
1 tbsp mild curry powder
1 tsp brown sugar
60 g/2 oz seedless raisins
60 g/2 oz butter, *ghee*
or olive oil
Freshly milled salt and freshly ground black pepper
Saffron rice (see below) and lemon segments to garnish

Cover the lentils with boiling water and soak them overnight. Skin and de-seed the tomatoes.

Chop the onion finely and fry until golden brown in the butter or oil. Drain the lentils and add to the onions, stirring well.

Add the curry powder and the garlic. De-seed the pepper and chillies, cut into smallish pieces and add to the pan. Add all the other ingredients, cover with the stock and simmer for 1½ hours.

Pass the soup through a Mouli or blender – leaving it rather rough-textured. Re-heat, check the seasoning and serve with a spoonful of cooked rice, mixed with a little melted butter and a sprinkling of saffron.

The lemon segments are passed separately.

MUSHROOM SOUP WITH MADEIRA

A really good rich mushroom soup, this is always well received as a starter to any meal.

500 g/1 lb button mushrooms
125 g/4 oz onion
45 g/1½ oz white flour
125 g/4 oz butter
¾ litre/1½ pints chicken stock
¼ litre/½ pint double cream
125 ml/¼ pint dryish Madeira
Salt and freshly ground black pepper

Wipe, but do not wash or peel, the mushrooms and chop them and the onion – the fineness of the chopping will add greatly to the finish of this soup.

Melt the butter in a heavy pan until it starts to foam and acquire a nutty flavour. Add the onions and fry until golden brown – stirring frequently to ensure that you get even colouring and no burnt edges!

Add the mushrooms and fry for 1 minute at a higher temperature. Reduce the heat back to simmering point and stir in the flour. Add the seasoning and the stock, bring to the boil and simmer for no more than 10 minutes or the mushrooms will become like bits of tough leather.

Add the Madeira and stir well. Half-whip the cream, stir into the soup and bring to the boil, stirring continually. Serve immediately.

MUSHROOM AND MUSTARD SOUP

This is one of those soups which just happened and has remained a firm favourite ever since. It really has great style. There is no flour thickening in it.

250 g/½ lb button mushrooms
60 g/2 oz butter
¼ litre/½ pint chicken stock
125 ml/¼ pint double cream
2 tbsps dry sherry
1 dessertspoon French mustard
Salt and freshly ground black pepper

Wipe, but do not wash or peel, the mushrooms and chop them roughly.

Melt the butter in a heavy-bottomed pan until it takes on a nutty colour and flavour. Add the mushrooms and toss them in the butter until they are just tender but still fairly crisp. Add the stock and sherry, bring to the boil and add the mustard.

Pass the soup immediately through a Mouli or blender. Add the cream, adjust the seasoning, re-heat and serve.

MUSTARD SOUP

'His wit is as thick as Tewkesbury mustard'
Shakespeare. Henry IV, Part II

Mustard has been with us a long time, certainly since the Romans came. Perhaps we think of it today more as a relish than as it was formerly used, in sauces, with herrings, pork and suchlike. The mustard soup I have made has always drawn comments about 'foreigners', but I doubt it has ever left our shores.

60 g/2 oz unsalted butter
60 g/2 oz made-up English mustard
60 g/2 oz plain flour
½ litre/1 pint chicken stock
1 small onion
¼ litre/½ pint single cream
2 egg-yolks
1 lettuce
Salt and freshly ground pepper

Grate the onion finely. Melt the butter in a pan and stir in the flour.
Gradually incorporate the stock until a smooth soup is achieved.

Add the onion, with its juice, and the salt and pepper. Simmer
slowly for a quarter of an hour. Whisk in the mustard thoroughly.

Remove the pan from the heat. Whisk the egg-yolks with the
cream and add gently to the soup, stirring briskly.

Add the lettuce, which should be shredded as finely as vermicelli!

ONION SOUP

*My own recipe for what is a most popular soup – I served it frequently
in my restaurant and often to the staff for lunch on a cold day, for it
appealed to their 'foreign' natures, even though a basic onion soup has
been in the English repertoire since Domesday. A good tasty variation of
this soup is to omit the curry powder and add two crushed cloves of garlic
at the last minute.*

2 very large onions
60 g/2 oz butter
1 level tsp curry powder
45 g/1½ oz flour
1 litre/2 pints chicken stock
125 ml/¼ pint single cream
Salt and freshly ground black pepper
A pinch of nutmeg

Peel the onions, cut them in half and slice them as finely as possible.

Melt the butter, without letting it brown, in a heavy-bottomed
pan. Add the onions. Cover the pan with a lid and sweat them until

they are tender and transparent. Toss the pan from time to time to ensure that the onions do not brown.

Sprinkle the flour and curry powder over the onions and stir in well. Add the chicken stock, bring to the boil and simmer for 20 minutes. Season with salt, pepper and a modicum of nutmeg.

Do *not* strain, but add the cream when the soup has boiled and serve straight away. (Milk will 'split' in onion soup, so if economy is called for, omit the cream or use top of the milk.)

OXTAIL SOUP

We are so brainwashed by the tinned and pre-packed varieties of this soup that the original subtle flavour is probably unknown to most of us.

First Stage
1 whole oxtail
60 g/2 oz brown flour
125 g/4 oz butter
2 litres/4 pints water

Second Stage
2 large carrots
1 head celery
A small piece of turnip (125 g/4 oz)
1 tsp thyme
2 bay leaves
6 cloves
1 dessertspoon Barbados sugar
60 g/2 oz tomato purée
1 wine glass Madeira or Marsala
About 3 tbsps oil for frying
Salt and freshly ground pepper
Croûtons of brown bread and grated orange rind
to garnish (optional)

First Stage

Have your butcher cut the oxtail into small joints, or chop it yourself, through the obvious sections, with a cleaver. Cut off any surplus fat, rinse in cold water and pat dry with a clean towel. Roll each piece in the flour.

Melt the butter in a heavy-bottomed frying pan and fry the pieces a few at a time until they are a good brown colour. This will take patience; do not fry them all together or they will not acquire a colour.

Cover with the water and simmer for 2 hours, skimming when necessary. Meanwhile proceed with second stage.

Second Stage

Clean, peel and dice all the vegetables.

Heat the oil in a second pan until it smokes, add the diced vegetables and fry them until they are evenly browned, stirring to ensure this even colouring and so that they don't burn.

Add the tomato purée and reduce the heat *immediately*, for purée burns at a very low temperature. Add the sugar and seasonings.

When the oxtail has simmered for 2 hours, add to it the vegetable mixture and continue cooking gently for a further hour.

Take out the pieces of oxtail, allow them to cool and then strip off the lean meat. Cut this into small dice and reserve for the finished soup.

Strain the rest of the soup – let it stand to see if any fat rises to the surface and, if it does, skim well. Re-heat the soup and add the Marsala or Madeira, check the seasonings, add the diced oxtail and serve with croûtons of brown bread.

The grated rind of an orange added before serving is a complement to this soup.

PARSLEY SOUP

We used to get a good bunch of profusely-leaved parsley with every half pound of cod, but no longer. We have paid for it ever since the plastic variety made its advent on to the slabs of butchers and fishmongers where it appears as a medieval-type border to their wares. Parsley still does grow, in abundance, and this soup is fast returning to popularity, though great care must be taken to use only the freshest and youngest parsley possible. Old parsley will give a 'hay-like' flavour to any dish.

8 tbsps chopped parsley
1 large onion
½ litre/1 pint chicken stock
½ litre/1 pint cold milk
A little olive oil
30 g/1 oz butter
30 g/1 oz flour
½ tsp grated lemon rind
Salt and freshly ground white pepper
Garlic butter to garnish (p. 242)

Chop the onion very finely. Gently heat the oil and fry the onion until it is soft but not coloured.

Add the butter and, when it is melted, sprinkle on the flour and work this in. Add the stock and bring to the boil, stirring to ensure a smooth texture. Add the parsley and the milk and bring back to boiling point.

Simmer gently for 5 minutes. Season with salt, pepper and the lemon rind and serve as soon as possible. This soup will 'split' and go dark if kept hot for long.

As a garnish, serve lumps of garlic butter in a bowl of crushed ice for guests to help themselves.

PEASE SOUP

This is a very understated title for what must be the most elegant of pea soups. Apart from my choice of the actual proportions (and of frozen peas), this recipe is exactly as it was served back in the seventeenth century. It also appears in an eighteenth-century recipe book of mine from my adopted home town of Leeds.

I recommend frozen peas because they are *better unless you can get really fresh young peas.*

60 g/2 oz frozen peas
¾ litre/1½ pints chicken stock
1 small rasher bacon
30 g/1 oz butter
100 g/3 oz onion

2 small sticks celery
30 g/1 oz plain flour
½ tsp fresh rosemary leaves
½ lettuce

For the Special Garnish
4 rashers good-flavoured green bacon
Enough fresh mint leaves to cover these rashers
Minuscule triangular croûtons white bread fried in butter
(not more than ½-inch wide at base)

Slice the onions and chop the celery, shred the lettuce and cut the first bacon rasher into striplets.

Bring the cold stock and frozen peas to the boil. Simmer for a few minutes until the peas are just tender.

Melt the butter in a second pan and fry the onions and bacon until they are a pale golden colour. Add the celery, cover and sweat until soft. Stir in the flour and add the rosemary leaves.

Bring the contents of the two pans together and add the shredded lettuce. Simmer for 10 minutes.

Pass through a Mouli or blender – as a coarse-textured soup is preferable, the former is recommended. If you use a blender, take care to ensure that the soup is not over-puréed.

Make the bacon rolls, which must be minuscule: de-rind each rasher and spread the meat out with the wetted flat of a knife. Lay the mint leaves to cover completely the surface of the rasher and roll up tightly. Secure with a cocktail stick and fry gently until you are sure the bacon is cooked inside. Remove the sticks and cut each roll into small pieces. This garnish is an integral part of the soup and ugly or clumsy preparation at this stage will spoil an otherwise delectable start to a meal.

Re-heat the soup, check the seasoning and add croûtons and bacon rolls to each bowl just before serving.

PINEAPPLE AND CURRY SOUP (Chilled)

During the Age of Elegance the pineapple was a symbol of wealth and luxury. Today this delicious fruit is within the reach of most pockets in this country.

375 g/12 oz fresh pineapple
1 large onion
2 courgettes
2 tbsps olive oil
1 dessertspoon curry powder
1 dessertspoon mango chutney
½ litre/1 pint chicken stock
Juice and rind of 1 lemon
¼ litre/½ pint cream
¼ litre/½ pint pineapple juice
Salt and freshly ground white pepper
30 g/1 oz toasted almonds to garnish

Finely chop the onion and roughly slice the courgettes.

Heat the oil in a heavy-bottomed pan and add the chopped onion. Add the curry powder and fry gently for a few moments.

Add the chopped pineapple and cover with the stock and pineapple juice. Bring to the boil and add the courgettes; simmer for 8 minutes or until they are tender.

Stir in the chutney. Pass the soup through a blender, leaving it rather coarse.

Return the soup to the pan and re-heat, seasoning with salt and freshly ground pepper. Cool the soup before putting in the refrigerator to chill.

Add the lemon juice and rind. Half-whip the cream and fold into the soup, leaving it to 'marble' rather than stirring it in completely.

Fill chilled soup cups and scatter toasted almonds on each serving.

POTATO AND ONION SOUP

This is one soup where I give way to convenience foods and use dehydrated potato, when I want a refined soup rather than the chunky soup I used to get at home; this was very good, but more of a meal than a first course.

4 large onions
125 g/4 oz butter
1 litre/2 pints chicken stock

2 bay leaves
Dehydrated potato (see below)
¼ litre/½ pint single cream
Salt and plenty of freshly ground black pepper
1 dessertspoon of fresh dill (optional)
or 1 crushed clove garlic to garnish

Peel and slice the onions very thinly. Melt the butter in a pan, add the sliced onions, cover with a lid and sweat until they are transparent but not coloured.

Add the stock and bay leaf, bring to the boil and cook until the onions are completely tender. Gradually rain in the potato powder, allowing it to thicken the soup before you add more. Add just enough to achieve required thickness. Cook the soup for a further 10 minutes.

Remove the bay leaves and season. Half-whip the cream and stir into the soup. Chop the dill and sprinkle it, or the garlic, onto the soup.

PUREE OF FRESH VEGETABLES

125 g/4 oz chopped onion
125 g/4 oz leeks
125 g/4 oz carrots
125 g/4 oz cauliflower
125 g/4 oz turnip
125 g/4 oz green cabbage
125 g/4 oz celery
125 g/4 oz potato
1 litre/2 pints chicken stock
1 bay leaf
A sprig of parsley
4 cloves
1 tbsp tomato purée
Salt and freshly ground black pepper
Garlic butter (p. 242) and parsley
or other herbs to garnish

Clean and prepare all the vegetables. Cut them all into pieces of roughly the same size.

Bring the stock to the boil, add the root vegetables and cook for 15 minutes. Add the tomato purée and the seasonings. Add the rest of the vegetables and cook for a further 20 minutes.

Put the soup through a sieve, Mouli or blender. If the latter is used, endeavour to keep a fairly coarse texture. Check the seasoning.

Serve with knobs of garlic butter rolled in parsley or any chopped fresh herbs. Allow a small ball for each serving.

The soup should be robust, but if the purée is too heavy add more stock or water.

SPINACH SOUP

1 kg/2 lb fresh spinach
125 g/4 oz butter
½ litre/1 pint chicken stock
½ tsp castor sugar
Juice and grated rind of half a lemon
Salt and freshly ground white pepper

Melt the butter in a heavy-bottomed pan. Add the washed, picked over and roughly cut spinach leaves (see Note). Cover the pan with a lid and over sweat the spinach over a low heat until just tender.

Add the lemon juice, sugar, seasoning and stock. Pass through the blender until a fine purée is produced.

Re-heat quickly and serve immediately. If this soup is kept hot for long it will lose its colour and go dark. It should be bright, bright green.

An optional garnish is to serve a teaspoon of sour cream floated on the top of each bowl.

Note: Spinach is usually very sandy and needs washing in oodles of cold water. The main part of the stalk must be taken away. This is easiest done if the leaf part is drawn away from the stalk by pulling the stalk through the prongs of a table fork.

TOMATO AND CURRY SOUP

This is a robust soup based on tomato purée, but is most men's idea of tomato soup, whilst still a good pace away from the commercial variety.

175 g/6 oz tomato purée
1 large onion
1 large carrot
2 crushed cloves garlic
1 dessertspoon curry powder
60 g/2 oz butter
60 g/2 oz flour
1 litre/2 pints chicken stock
1 glass sherry
1 dessertspoon apricot jam
Salt and freshly ground black pepper
2 tomatoes to garnish

Clean, peel and slice the vegetables.

Melt the butter in a heavy-bottomed pan. Add the onions and let them acquire a good brown colour. Add the carrots, garlic and curry powder – fry for a few seconds.

Add the purée, stir in the flour and reduce the heat. Over a very low heat, let a crust form on the bottom of the pan. Remove the contents of the pan to a plate, leaving the crust behind. Pour the sherry into the pan and work the crust into this – if there is not sufficient liquid, add a little stock, or more sherry.

Return the vegetables to the pan and add the stock. Slowly bring the soup to the boil, stirring frequently, and add the jam. Reduce the heat and simmer for 1 hour.

Strain, check the seasoning and re-heat. Skin and de-seed the 2 tomatoes, cut the flesh into ¼-inch dice and add to the soup just before serving.

TOMATO AND ROSEMARY SOUP

This tomato soup of mine is gently edged with rosemary; it is delicate in flavour, not the usual robust type as in the preceding recipe. I serve it with tiny triangles of hot brown toast liberally spread with lemon-flavoured butter.

60 g/2 oz finely chopped onion
A healthy sprig of rosemary
60 g/2 oz butter
45 g/1½ oz flour
60 g/2 oz tomato purée
½ litre/1 pint tomato juice
2 tsps castor sugar
400 ml/¾ pint chicken stock
175 ml/⅓ pint double cream
Juice of half a lemon
2 tomatoes to garnish

Melt the butter in a heavy-bottomed pan, add the onion, put a lid on the pan and sweet the onion until transparent. Add the rosemary and the flour and stir in well.

Add the stock, either hot or cold, gradually working the soup with a whisk until all is smooth. Stir in the tomato purée, sugar and tomato juice.

Cook gently for 20 minutes, strain and serve, or, if it is to be used later, strain into a clean pan and cover with an oiled paper cut to fit the surface of the soup.

Re-heat the soup, add the cream and, just before serving, add the lemon juice and garnish.

To Make the Garnish

Dip the 2 tomatoes into boiling water and count to ten in seconds. Plunge the tomatoes immediately into a bowl of cold water.

Peel off the skins. Cut out the little stalky bit. Cut them across 'equatorwise' and press out the seeds with your thumb. Cut the tomato flesh into ¼-inch dice, heat at the side of the stove in a nut of butter and add to the soup just before serving.

TURNIP SOUP

You must certainly not arch your nostrils before trying this delicious soup, and if you have nervous guests the name turnip ought not to cross your lips until after the first mouthful! Its rich nutty favour and amber colour quickly win people over.

750 g/1½ lb turnip (peeled weight)
60 g/2 oz butter
1 litre/2 pints veal or chicken stock
60 g/2 oz dry (but not stale) brown bread
60 g/2 oz onion
1 tbsp olive oil
½ level tsp nutmeg
Salt and freshly ground black pepper
Watercress to garnish

Chop the onion; peel and cut the turnip into 1-inch cubes.

Melt the butter in a heavy-bottomed pan, swirling it round until it is foaming and giving off a delicious nutty flavour. Add the onions and the turnip. Cover with a lid and sweat the vegetables gently over a low heat until they are tender. This will take about 25 minutes.

Cut the brown bread, crusts and all, into ½-inch cubes. In a separate frying pan, heat the olive oil and fry the bread cubes until crisp and evenly browned – move them about constantly to achieve this even colouring.

Add the fried bread to the turnip. Add the cold stock and cook gently for a further 20 minutes.

Season with the salt, pepper and nutmeg. Pass through a blender or Mouli.

Serve with sprigs of watercress on a side plate.

CRAB SOUP

Now that frozen crab meat is easily available there is no reason to dismiss this delightful fish soup as only for those living on the coast.

250 g/½ lb crab meat (half dark and half white)
1 large onion
1 clove garlic
1 litre/2 pints fish stock (made as for the following recipe)
60 g/2 oz butter
30 g/1 oz white flour
Grated rind of 1 orange

¼ litre/½ pint double cream
1 glass dry sherry
Salt and freshly ground white pepper

Slice the onion and crush the garlic.

Melt the butter in a heavy-bottomed pan. When just foaming, but not coloured, add the onion and garlic. Cover with a lid and soften the onion without colouring.

Add the dark crab meat and work in well. Add the flour, stirring in well to avoid lumping. Slowly add the fish stock, stirring all the time until the soup boils.

Simmer for half an hour. Strain the soup into a clean pan. Season with salt and pepper; add the cream, sherry and orange rind.

Chop the white crab meat and remove any skin or 'blades'. Add the fish to the soup, re-heat and serve immediately.

LOBSTER SOUP

There are two types of lobster soup in England, the pale creamy variety or the red-brown type often mistaken for the French lobster Bisque — which is called this because it is thickened with a type of biscuit crumb, and indeed could well have been made thus in England. In view of the astronomical price of lobsters, the basic soup is usually made with the crushed lobster shells only, to give the flavouring; fresh, frozen or canned lobster meat is often used as garnish. Mine is a very personal recipe which I hope you will enjoy; I don't use lobster shells and though I recommend a lobster garnish, the soup is so delicious that you can even omit the garnish — you can then call the soup something different if you really want to!

1 kg/2 lb washed sole bones
1 large onion, roughly chopped
1 large carrot, cut into even-sized pieces
125 g/¼ lb field mushrooms, cut into even-sized pieces
2 tbsps brandy
1 tbsp Madeira
2 crushed cloves garlic
1 heaped tsp sweet paprika

2 tbsps tomato purée
75 g/2½ oz flour
1 bay leaf
Salt and freshly ground black pepper
½ tsp rubbed thyme
A pinch of powdered saffron
½ tsp castor sugar
½ bottle red wine
1 teacup rich first-pressing olive oil
½ litre/1 pint water
1 litre/2 pints fish stock
¼ litre/½ pint double cream (optional)
Lobster meat to garnish (optional)

First of all make a fish stock by simmering the washed sole bones in 1 litre/2 pints of cold water. (There is little gain in ever simmering fish bones for more than 25 minutes to half an hour.) Drain this stock through a fine muslin and put aside for use.

Heat the oil in a large pan. Add the onions and let them become golden brown. Add the carrots and brown these, then add the mushrooms.

Lower the heat under the pan and add the seasoning – garlic, saffron, paprika, bay, thyme – and work these into the browned vegetables. Add the tomato purée and then the flour. Reduce the heat and allow a crust to form on the bottom of the pan – don't let it burn.

Remove the contents of the pan (but not the crust) to a basin. Increase the heat slightly and add the brandy and Madeira. Ignite this with a taper – or if you use gas, tip the pan to the flame.

Briskly work in the crust from the bottom of the pan, using red wine as you need more liquid. Replace the other contents, cover with cold fish stock and the pint of water, add a little salt and pepper and the sugar and simmer for 1 hour.

Strain all this through a fine strainer and then through a muslin, preferably arranged inside a conical strainer to support it. Bring the soup back to the boil, adjust the seasoning and thickness by adding a little stock if it is too thick.

To obtain a creamier soup, simply add ¼ litre/½ pint of thick cream, half-whipped.

Add chopped lobster meat as a garnish.

Note: Reduce ½ litre/1 pint of this soup to ¼ litre/½ pint, add 2 tablespoons thick cream – and a little Madeira or water if it looks somewhat oily – and you have a good lobster sauce!

MUSSEL SOUP

3 litres/6 pints mussels
2 medium-sized onions
125 g/4 oz butter
60 g/2 oz flour
½ bottle Burgundy-type dry white wine
¼ litre/½ pint double cream
¼ litre/½ pint water
3 tbsps finely chopped fresh parsley
1 finely crushed clove garlic
Salt and freshly ground white pepper
Juice of half a lemon

Sort the mussels into open and closed ones, discarding the open ones, as they are dead! Wash them well in an abundance of cold water, letting the grit sink to the bottom, take them out and drain them.

Take a large enamel pan of the modern variety – put in the mussels, cover with the wine and put on a lid. Bring to the boil, shaking the pan from time to time. When all the mussels have opened under this treatment (discard any that haven't), strain them and reserve the cooking liquor. Scrape out the mussels from their shells and remove and discard the dark grey beards.

Melt the butter in another heavy pan. When it is foaming, add the onion and garlic, cover with a lid, reduce the heat and soften the onions. Stir in the flour and gradually add the cooking liquor, stirring all the time to ensure that you have a smooth soup.

Add sufficient water, depending on how thick you want the finished dish – soup or stew? Season well with salt, pepper and lemon juice.

Add the cream and finally, just before serving, add the mussels and freshly chopped parsley. Do not let the soup boil again or the mussels will shrivel up into tough pieces.

OYSTER SOUP

This ancient of English soups was served every Christmas Day in my restaurant for ten years and was always a winner.

2 dozen oysters (frozen will suffice)
1 litre/2 pints fish stock (made with bones from about 6 soles,
stewed for half an hour in water only)
125 g/4 oz unsalted butter
60 g/2 oz flour
¼ litre/½ pint single cream
Juice of half a lemon or a small glass of white Burgundy
2 egg-yolks
Cayenne pepper
Salt and freshly ground white pepper

Melt the butter in a heavy-bottomed pan, but do not let it get hot. Stir in the flour. Add the strained fish stock and bring this to the boil, stirring all the time.

Add the cream (reserving a little to mix with the egg-yolks) and the juice from the oysters if you are using fresh ones. Adjust the seasoning, and gradually add the lemon juice or wine to your taste. Bring to the boil and strain.

Add the oysters just before you are ready to serve the soup – no sooner or they will toughen.

At the last minute, when the soup is in the tureen, mix the egg-yolks with the reserved cream and stir briskly into the hot soup. Sprinkle just a dash of cayenne pepper on the surface of the soup before serving.

SHRIMP SOUP

125 g/4 oz frozen shrimps
125 g/4 oz Morecambe Bay or other potted shrimps
1 litre/2 pints fish stock (made as in the previous recipe)
125 g/4 oz butter
60 g/2 oz flour
¼ litre/½ pint single cream

1 crushed clove garlic
Juice of half a lemon
2 egg-yolks
½ tsp ground mace
Salt and freshly ground white pepper

Melt the butter in a heavy-bottomed pan. Stir in the flour. Add the fish stock and cook for 15 minutes.

Add the mace, cream (reserving a little to mix with the egg-yolks), garlic and seasonings. The soup should be pale, pale pink.

Mince the defrosted shrimps and add to the soup. Season again with a little lemon juice.

Just before serving, re-heat, whisk in the egg-yolk and reserved cream mixture and add the potted shrimps as garnish.

SMOKED HADDOCK SOUP

Do make this soup with genuine smoked haddock and not coloured imitations that do not have the subtle oaky flavour.

500 g/1 lb smoked haddocks or 'finnies'
1 onion
2 cloves garlic
¾ litre/1½ pints cold water
¼ litre/½ pint single cream
100 g/3 oz butter
50 g/1½ oz flour
A screw of black pepper
Chopped chives, parsley or basil to garnish

Slice the onion and crush the garlic. Melt one-third of the butter in a heavy-bottomed pan. Add the sliced onion and soften it without colouring.

Cut the haddock into pieces and add to the pan. Cover with the water. Simmer for half an hour.

Melt the remaining butter and mix with the flour. Strain the stock into this second pan. Bring the soup to the boil and check the seasoning; it will probably be salty enough.

Remove the fish from the bones and put on one side for fish cakes another day.

Add the cream, re-heat and serve with plenty of freshly chopped chives, parsley or basil, or all three.

A MEDLEY *of* SAVOURY *and* VEGETABLE DISHES

Eggs

CLARY OMELETTE

Clary was a much-used herb of the sage family (it is today used in the making of vermouths) and appears frequently in old recipe books with different combinations of other ingredients.

Often a large open-faced 'amulet' would be made and a hand-salamander employed to brown the surface of the omelette.

3 eggs
3 tbsps thick cream
30 g/1 oz butter
1 tbsp minced cooked ham
1 tbsp freshly chopped parsley
1 tbsp freshly chopped chives
1 tsp chopped sage leaves (unless you are lucky
and have clary growing in a pot)
A pinch of nutmeg
Salt and freshly ground pepper

Beat the eggs and cream together. Add all the other ingredients except the butter.

Melt the butter in a heavy-bottomed frying pan which is not too big to slip under the grill. Pour in the mixture and, after it has initially seized, reduce the heat and cook slowly until it is almost set but still wet on top.

Slide the pan under a hot grill just long enough to set the surface but leaving the omelette moist.

Serve as quickly as possible whole or in half on large heated dinner plates.

EGGS IN CASES

This harmless little title has carried some cooks to endless results and with a little imagination your creative powers can bring you to many pastures new. At one time the case was sometimes made of paper, which would act as the container for what is now a baked egg, but pastry shells add an interesting dimension. (They deep-freeze very successfully and are a good thing to have in stock. They should be at least 1 inch deep and 3 inches in diameter.)

250 g/8 oz rich shortcrust pastry (for 6 cases)
125 g/4 oz boiled ham
1 heaped tbsp chopped chives, basil or parsley
12 eggs
6 tbsps single cream
A little butter
Salt and freshly ground white pepper

Roll the pastry as thinly as possible and line the tins. Cut small circles of foil to fit inside the lined tins and bake the cases at 200°C/400°F/gas mark 6 for about 10 minutes. (They should be slightly under-baked.)

Remove the foil and leave the cases to cool a little and then carefully remove them from the tins and stand them on a wire rack until ready for use.

Mince the ham and mix it with the herbs and about half an ounce of soft butter; season the mixture lightly. Divide it into 6 portions and spread evenly over the bottom of each pastry case; make a slight hollow for the eggs to sit in.

Reduce the oven temperature to 180°C/350°F/gas mark 4.

Stand the cases on a baking sheet. Carefully break each egg first into a cup to ensure that it is whole and that there are no bits of shell in it, and then slide 2 eggs carefully into each pastry case.

Season lightly with salt and pepper and pour 1 tablespoon of cream over the top. Return the filled cases to the oven and bake for a further 15 minutes or until the eggs are set but the yolks are still soft.

Serve immediately.

EGGS DRESSED WITH SPINACH AND PARMESAN

We tend to know this dish by the now more popular name of Eggs Florentine. Originally the English version did not have cheese on top, nor was it made with a cheese sauce, as cheeses were not used nearly so much in cookery as they are today; but the idea of combining eggs and spinach is a very old one, and if it can be improved upon, as indeed adding Parmesan cheese does, then we must do so in the natural course of events.

8 eggs
1 kg/2 lb leaf spinach (or 500 g/1 lb frozen)
¼ litre/½ pint cheese sauce (p. 217)
Grated Parmesan cheese
Butter
A little thick cream
Nutmeg
Salt and freshly ground pepper

Wash and strip the spinach and boil in salted water until just tender. Drain well; chop very finely and mix with a little butter, a table-spoon of thick cream and season with salt, pepper and nutmeg.

Poach the eggs in lightly salted and acidulated water – let the water just simmer, so that the eggs do not break up and you can keep them a good shape. Do not over-poach the eggs.

Butter individual oven-proof dishes big enough to hold spinach, sauce and 2 eggs. Arrange a layer of the hot spinach in each dish and gently place 2 poached eggs on top of this. Cover with hot cheese sauce. Sprinkle well with freshly grated Parmesan cheese and slip the dishes under a medium hot grill until the cheese has browned nicely.

FRICASSEE OF EGGS WITH CREAM

The word fricassee has been Anglicised for many centuries and was at one time a very popular way of cooking in this country.

Usually it implies that the finished dish will be white or pale in colour, and it is a common way of dealing with veal and chicken.

A fricassee of eggs is not quite so usual, but it does make a cheap and effective beginning to any dinner party.

6 eggs
125 ml/¼ pint milk
125 ml/¼ pint single cream
30 g/1 oz flour
45 g/1½ oz butter
1 small onion
1 tbsp fresh chives
Salt and freshly ground white pepper
3 slices white bread
Butter for frying

Cut 6 rounds of bread, no bigger than 2 to 2½ inches across and ¼ inch thick.

Melt some butter in a frying pan and carefully fry these rounds until they are golden brown and evenly coloured. This will be easily achieved if you watch the frying process carefully and frequently turn and move the bread about in the pan.

Drain the rounds of fried bread on crumpled kitchen paper and put them to keep warm. You can make them in advance and warm them up in the oven to 140°C/275°F/gas mark 2 just before you need them.

Chop the onion very finely. Make a sauce by melting the butter in a small pan. Add the onion and sweat it until it is transparent but not coloured at all.

Stir in the flour and gradually incorporate the milk and then the cream, beating all the time to ensure that the sauce is smooth.

Season well with salt and pepper, cover with a buttered paper and stand the pan in a second pan of boiling water to keep hot until you are ready to use it.

If you make the sauce in the morning, cover with an oiled paper and re-heat by standing the pan in a second pan of boiling water (or use a double boiler), stirring from time to time until the sauce is quite hot.

To ensure that this dish is really good it is better not to cook the eggs too far in advance, as the whites when completely cold to tend to get a bit rubbery.

Have the eggs at room temperature and gently lower them into the simmering water. Bring the water back to the boil and boil them for 8 minutes. Put the pan under running cold water for 10 minutes or so, and then roll the eggs, gently pressing with the palm of the hand, on a hard top to loosen the shell. Peel them under the running water. This way you should not have any difficulty in having perfect hard-boiled eggs, where the yolk is not rock hard, but just has that touch of moisture right in the centre, making it a joy to eat and not a green-rimmed sulphur-like abomination.

Now cut the eggs in half lengthways. Take out the yolks and mash these before beating them into the sauce. Cut the white into 8 inch-long striplets. Fold into the hot sauce together with the freshly chopped chives. The sauce will heat the eggs through.

Pile the fricassee onto the hot bread rounds and serve immediately.

FRICASSEE OF EGGS, MUSHROOMS AND ONIONS

3 eggs
125 g/4 oz mushrooms
2 medium onions
30 g/1 oz butter
1 heaped tsp plain flour
125 ml/¼ pint single cream
2 tbsps water
1 tbsp lemon juice
1 tbsp chopped parsley or chives
1 clove garlic
Salt and freshly ground black pepper
Hot buttered toast or boiled rice to serve

Put the eggs into cold water and bring to the boil, allowing 12 minutes from cold. Run under cold water, shell and cut the eggs into quarters.

Slice the onions, wipe and quarter the mushrooms and crush the garlic.

Melt the butter in a heavy-bottomed pan, add the onions, cover with a lid and soften the onions over a low heat until they are transparent but not coloured. Add the quartered mushrooms and the garlic and continue to simmer these in the covered pan for a further 5 minutes, tossing regularly. Sprinkle the flour over the onions and mushrooms and stir in well.

Add the cream and water and bring the sauce to the boil. Simmer for 2 or 3 minutes. If the sauce is too thick or buttery add a little more water. Season well with salt and pepper and add the lemon juice.

Just before serving, carefully fold in the quartered eggs without breaking them, add the chopped parsley and then allow to heat through, which will only take a minute or so.

Serve this fricassee with hot buttered toast or with plain boiled rice.

Cheese

CHEESE PIE

When making this type of flan I always use a deep flan ring and a baking sheet, which means I can remove the ring to permit the sides of the pastry shell to brown nicely. I can then return the ring when the shell is filled to prevent the walls collapsing. The pastry will be crisp and buttery and the filling light and creamy. The original recipe used cheese, but I use many other fillings.

250 g/8 oz plain flour
150 g/5 oz unsalted butter
1 egg-yolk beaten with a little iced water
400 ml/¾ pint single cream
6 eggs
Salt and freshly ground pepper or nutmeg
Fillings (see below)

Make up the pastry for an 8-inch diameter, 1½-inch deep pastry shell without over-kneading it. Let it rest for at least half an hour. Form into a flat circle and gently roll into the size for your ring. Line the ring carefully, pressing away any unwanted thickness at the perimeter of the base.

Trim the edge and decorate. Line the case with foil and bake blind at 200°C/400°F/gas mark 6 until cooked. Carefully remove the foil and slip off the ring, return the shell to the oven to dry out for 5 minutes.

Replace the ring round the pastry and it is ready for filling with the basic custard.

Beat the eggs and add a little salt and pepper or nutmeg. Bring the cream to the boil, pour onto the beaten eggs, stirring until the two are combined thoroughly.

Place your chosen filling in the baked pastry shell and pour this liquid gently over it; bake in the centre of a pre-heated oven at 170°C/325°F/gas mark 3 until the custard is set (for about 25 to 30 minutes).

The fillings are a purely personal matter, but here are my suggestions for a pie of this size:

250 g/8 oz of tiny cubes of Gruyère (sprinkle 30 g/1 oz fresh Parmesan cheese onto the surface when the custard is beginning to set).
250 g/8 oz dark and light crab meat.
Fried bacon snippets and onions.
Finely chopped, freshly cooked spinach, flavoured with a little grated nutmeg and with a topping of Parmesan cheese.
Prawns, lobster, mussels or scampi, either mixed or singly.
Wafer-thin slices of smoked salmon. An excellent alternative to this is to put the smoked salmon with the eggs into a blender, making a purée, before pouring on the hot cream; this gives a lighter, more subtle filling.

Squeeze bits of fresh unsalted butter onto the finished surface of any of these flans.

Note: They are at their best when served straight from the oven, but can be eaten cold or re-heated, in which latter case, leave the custard slightly under-cooked and re-heat at the original temperature – no hotter.

MACARONI CHEESE

This dish isn't just an old wartime favourite, it has been on the go for many a year and was one of the first dishes in which Parmesan cheese appeared in English cookery books.

London has had a colony of Italians for many generations and this no doubt accounts for its appearance in our repertoire before 1720.

500 g/1 lb macaroni
½ litre/1 pint rich cheese sauce (p. 217)
100 g/3 oz grated Parmesan cheese
1 crushed clove garlic
60 g/2 oz butter

Cook the macaroni in boiling salted water until it is *al dente* (firm to the bite) – don't over-cook it. Wash the cooked macaroni under plenty of hot water, drain well and pat dry with a clean tea-towel.

Melt the butter in a large frying pan, add the garlic and swirl the macaroni round in this before turning it into an oven-proof dish. Coat with cheese sauce and sprinkle liberally with the freshly grated Parmesan cheese. Bake in a hot oven until golden brown and crisp on top.

RAMEKINS

There are many versions of this cheese dish and from the evidence in many cookery books it is certain that some cooks had arrived at a type of soufflé without actually calling it by that name, for they wouldn't recognise it as such – it would be just their particular version of a ramekin.

As we do know very much what a soufflé is all about these days, I have developed one of the recipes which still has breadcrumbs in it and which can be baked in a large dish or in small oven-proof pots, as the name actually applies to the contents and is not so much the name of the container, as today's use perhaps implies.

100 g/3 oz Double Gloucester
or farmhouse Cheddar

100 g/3 oz Cheshire
(Both cheeses should be a day or two old)
2 tbsps freshly made white breadcrumbs (4 slices)
¼ litre/½ pint single cream
3 eggs
A dash of Worcester sauce
A good pinch of cayenne pepper
A pinch of powdered mace
Salt

Separate the eggs. Grate the cheeses. Soak the crumbs in the cream, add the cheese, season with the Worcester sauce, mace, cayenne and a little salt.

Beat in the egg-yolks. Beat the whites until they stand in peaks and fold carefully into the cheese mixture. This task is made easy if you beat in one spoonful first to slacken the mixture.

Pour into a large buttered oven-proof dish or into smaller individual pots. Bake at 220°C/425°F/gas mark 7 for 20 minutes (large dish), 12 to 15 minutes (individual pots).

WENSLEYDALE CHEESE SOUFFLE

This is the recipe I created for the Yorkshire Post *some years ago and it proves that English cheeses lend themselves well to soufflé making.*

30 g/1 oz plain flour
45 g/1½ oz unsalted butter
Scant ¼ litre/½ pint milk
125 g/4 oz grated Wensleydale
(buy in advance so that it can dry slightly)
4 egg-yolks
5 egg-whites
Salt and freshly ground white pepper

Gently melt the butter in a heavy-bottomed pan: do not let it get hot. Remove the pan from the heat and stir in the flour.

Warm the milk and gradually add this to the flour and butter mixture, stirring all the time and gradually letting the sauce come to the boil. Cook over a very low heat for 5 minutes, stirring to prevent sticking. Add the grated cheese and beat thoroughly until it has all dissolved into the sauce. Remove the pan from the heat.

Beat the egg-yolks in a separate basin and add these to the sauce, a little at a time, beating as you do so. Season well with salt and pepper, cover with an oiled paper and allow to cool.

Whip the egg-whites until they just stand in peaks; take care not to over-whip – you will recognise if this is happening as they will start to go flecky at the edge of the bowl.

Add a spoonful of the whipped whites to the sauce and slacken the mixture with this to ease the deft folding in and thorough incorporation of the rest of the whites. Pour into a well buttered ¾-litre/1½-pint soufflé dish.

Stand the dish on a heated baking sheet and bake in the centre of an oven pre-heated to 200°C/400°F/gas mark 6 for 40 to 45 minutes.

If your soufflé is ready before your guests are, just turn the temperature of the oven right down. It will stand for some 15 minutes – there is no reason to panic with soufflés unless they are of the steamed variety.

The basic sauce can be made a couple of hours in advance. If you do this remember to cover the surface with an oiled – not buttered – paper. Then beat the sauce before incorporating the egg-whites, as above.

Fish

GEORGIAN SALMON SALAD

This unusual way of serving salmon makes us realise that our eighteenth-century ancestors were so interested in different dressings that never did a salad appear stark naked as is the case in many places today.

Use this refreshing recipe as a first course or pack it into containers for picnic use.

250 g/½ lb middle-cut steak of salmon
Sufficient water to cover the salmon
1 tbsp white wine or cider vinegar
1 baby onion
1 carrot

The Dressing

½ tsp English mustard
½ tsp salt
Freshly ground white pepper
Juice of half a lemon
½ teacup olive oil
3 tsps chopped chives
2 crisp green eating apples
Lettuce leaves, cucumber pieces
and lemon segments to garnish

Clean the salmon.

Bring the water to the boil. Acidulate it with the wine or cider vinegar, add the onion and carrot and simmer for 15 minutes before putting in the salmon steak. Cook for 10 minutes and let the fish cool in the liquor.

When the fish is cooked, skin, bone and mash it with a fork. Peel and dice the apple and toss it in the lemon juice. Make up the dressing with the remaining ingredients, add the lemon-flavoured apples and the chives and combine with the mashed salmon.

Pile onto lettuce leaves, decorate with peeled and seeded cucumber pieces and extra lemon segments. Chill well.

SMOKED SALMON

Frozen smoked salmon is ideal for dishes calling for this fish as an integral part; it is also good for garnishing and even for sandwiches, but it will not do when it is being served in its luxurious state, in long, thin, virtually transparent slices. The Scots are the only people to produce good quality, delicately smoked salmon. The Norwegians do produce a delicate fish, but it is quite different.

A side of smoked salmon should weigh between five and seven

*pounds and is best when delicately grained with a little fat. If you use
any quantity of this fish it is well worth while buying a whole side from
one of the better firms, either in England or Scotland. Covered with an
oiled paper, it keeps for quite a time if left hanging in a cool, airy place.*

Remove any top hard skin with a thin-bladed knife. Withdraw any
bones – this is easier if you use a pair of eyebrow tweezers to catch
the tiny tips of these bones where they protrude: there will be some
thirty or so to pull from a side of salmon.

Patiently cut long, thin diagonal slices of the fish, starting at the
tail and taking care not to cut into the dark skin underneath.
Arrange the slices, tail and middle-cut mixed together, on a large
platter. Serve segments of lemon and the thinnest possible slices of
crusted and buttered brown bread. Red or black pepper are often
asked for, but lettuce, tomato segments, cress or other garnishings
should not appear on the plate.

Note: For years it has been acceptable to serve a dry white wine
with smoked salmon, smoked trout and other smoked and oily fish.
Many people will have noted, but rarely voiced their opinion, that
a none too pleasant 'cod-liver oil' flavour is left as an aftertaste when
this type of wine is served. Try serving a white wine in which there
is good evidence of some natural fruit sugar. You will find that this
type of wine marries very well with these rich foods. A light
Sauternes is extremely good and there will be no strange tastes
afterwards.

———————

MARINATED KIPPER FILLETS

*An oak-smoked kipper is the only one to use for any recipe where this
smoked fish is called for. Of course other types will do, but the delicacy
for which our kippers have rightly gained a good name will not be so
evident.*

*Smoked mackerel are also delicious when prepared in the following
way.*

4 uncooked kippers (2 pairs)
1 level tsp dry mustard
3 tbsps bland nut oil

1 tbsp red or white wine vinegar
1 tbsp finely sliced raw onion
1 dessertspoon freshly chopped parsley
Rye bread fingers and extra chopped parsley to garnish

Using your fingers and a very sharp, thin-bladed knife, carefully skin and fillet the kippers. Cut each fillet diagonally into 6 or 7 strips, following the natural grain of the fish.

Make up the dressing as you would a normal French-type dressing with the oil, vinegar, mustard, onion and parsley. Put the strips of kipper into the marinade, cover with foil, chill and marinate for at least 3 hours.

Serve with a little extra freshly chopped parsley on top and buttered rye bread fingers.

SARDINE FAVOURS

Sardines baked in this way make a good savoury or are equally interesting as a first course. As far as I know, they are Victorian in origin, but may well be a follow-on of the 'puffs' that were popular in the eighteenth century. When cold they are easily packed for taking on picnics and when made very small are ideal as a cocktail savoury.

125 g/4 oz shortcrust or puff pastry
60 g/2 oz fresh Parmesan cheese
8 large tinned sardines
A touch of cayenne
Grated lemon rind, chopped chives, or other seasoning
Salt and freshly ground pepper

Roll out the pastry and cut into 8 pieces which will conveniently enfold each sardine.

Roll the sardines in plenty of grated cheese and season with whichever combination appeals to you.

Roll them up as you would do a sausage roll; nick the tops, brush with beaten egg and bake for 20 minutes at 190°C/375°F/gas mark 5 if you are using shortcrust; for puff pastry, bake at 220°C/425°F/gas mark 7.

Meat

MARBLED VEAL

*This interesting way of cooking veal makes an unusual first course served
cold, with a fresh mint jelly or Cumberland Sauce (p. 219). As the name
implies, the dish has the appearance of marble when sliced, and was just
another of the many ways the Georgians had of dressing their foods to
look attractive on the table. Serve it straight from the pot in which you
cook it, or turn it out and serve the marbled slices arranged attractively
with, perhaps, sprigs of watercress around the platter. Like all dishes of
this type, it is better for being made a day or two in advance.*

375 g/12 oz leg of veal
375 g/12 oz very fat loin of pork
125 g/4 oz *extra* fat from the loin of pork
250 g/8 oz cooked tongue
2 eggs
1 dessertspoon chopped chives or
the green part of spring onions
1 dessertspoon freshly chopped parsley
2 tsps finely shredded lemon rind
3 tbsps cold water
Salt and freshly ground black pepper

Trim the meat of any skin or gristle. Put the veal and loin of pork
through the mincer twice. Add all the seasonings and herbs. Bind
with the eggs.

Cut the tongue into ¼-inch cubes. Cut the extra pork fat into
¼-inch cubes. Mix these together with the minced meats, adding
the water to make a softish forcemeat.

Butter a seamless loaf tin or an oven-proof pot that is just large
enough to contain the mixture. Fill the receptacle and cover with a
lid or foil. Stand it in a meat tin or dish large enough to hold
enough hot water to come half-way up the sides of your pot.

Cook in a pre-heated oven at 180°C/350°F/gas mark 4 for 1½
hours, or until the juices are quite clear. When cooked, remove the

pot from the hot water bath and leave to cool before covering with a foil-covered board and a kitchen weight to press the meat.

Put the weighted pot into the refrigerator to set.

SOLOMONGUNDY (Sallid Magundi)

Never has a dish had so many various ways of having its name spelt! This answer to France's Salade Niçoise is well enough known as a joke because of its extraordinary name. Perhaps Saladmagundi or even Salmagundi will give a better clue to what is a truly excellent salad which, once tried, will never be allowed again to sink into oblivion. This salad has been with us since Tudor times, but for reasons which no one can explain it has been forgotten for decades.

1 cold chicken (either pot-roast or boiled)
1 lettuce
250 g/8 oz whole frozen beans
60 g/2 oz anchovy fillets
125 g/¼ lb grapes, black or green
4 hard-boiled eggs
12 button onions
60 g/2 oz flaked almonds
60 g/2 oz stoned raisins
1 large cup oil and vinegar dressing
1 tbsp mixed chopped herbs
Lemon juice and rind

Skin the chicken and carve the breasts and legs into thin slices.

Wash and shred the lettuce and arrange on a large flat platter. Skin and boil the onions, leaving them somewhat crisp.

Plunge the beans into boiling salted water for 5 minutes, rinse under running cold water until they are cold and drain well on a clean cloth as beans hold the water.

Skin and de-pip the grapes. Shell and quarter the hard-boiled eggs. Season the dressing well, adding lemon juice and rind and herbs to taste.

Arrange all the salad items in attractive groups on the bed of lettuce. Pour over the dressing and, when ready to serve the salad, toss everything together.

Potted Foods

Well made potted foods are national dishes of which we should be justly proud, for they reflect our social history. To borrow from other countries is flattering to them, but ought we not to repay in kind? Two world wars have had a marked effect on many of our national dishes and economies instituted to cope with food scarcities have tended to linger on, thus causing many of our specialities to fall into disrepute. Much that England has to offer is indeed robust, but a quick glimpse beyond the obvious and present-day norms reveals many exotic things that were at one time British by right. One or two of the better versions of potted meats, fishes and cheeses ought to convert any suspicious visitor over to our side of the fence, for they are extremely tasty, and by no means need they be restricted to the tea-table. When served with hot toast or buttered fingers of rye bread, they make an excellent first course to any dinner.

Potted foods keep well when covered with clarified butter to preserve them, and can be stored in a refrigerator for a week or so.

To Clarify Butter:

Method 1

Place the butter in a dish or small pan and put in a warm place. You will see readily when it is finished, as all the sediment will have dropped to the bottom. Pour off the clear butter and allow to cool before pouring over the filled pots.

Method 2

Put the butter in a small pan, together with some water. Bring the contents to the boil and simmer until all the butter is melted. Leave to set, then take off the cleaned hard butter from the top and pat the underside free of water.

POTTED RABBIT

Don't throw up your hands in horror – rabbit is a delicacy in its own right. This recipe is very closely related to the French terrine (English tureen) and if served as a first course in thin, thin slices it makes an excellent introduction to any meal. It is better for being made two or three days in advance. Serve a home-made crab apple jelly with it and a few sprigs of watercress.

A rabbit weighing 1½–2 kg/3–4 lb
1 kg/2 lb lean pork
5 to 6 chicken livers
500 g/1 lb extra pork fat
1½ teacups dry white wine or dry cider
1½ tbsps Jamaica rum
1 egg
1 crushed clove garlic
1 tsp powdered ginger
500 g/1 lb streaky bacon for lining the pot
Salt and freshly ground black pepper
Clarified butter to cover

Take the rind of the bacon and stretch the rashers with the flat of a knife, wetting it with cold water if it pulls and tears the meat. Line an earthenware pot with these now-thin rashers. A seamless loaf tin will serve the same purpose but will have to be wrapped in a napkin when it comes to be served, as this potted meat should be served in its container.

Cut out the 2 fillets from the back of the rabbit and cut them into long, ¼-inch thick strips. Put these strips together with the chicken livers into the rum and wine to marinate. Cut the fat pork into similar-sized strips and put in with rabbit fillets.

Mince the remaining pork and the meat from the rabbit's legs, etc., and make into a forcemeat with the beaten egg, ginger, salt, pepper and garlic. Add this liquor to the forcemeat after the rabbit has soaked in the marinade for a couple of hours.

Now cut the strips into ¼-inch cubes and cut the chicken livers into similar-sized pieces. Mix with the forcemeat. Fill this into your pot, pressing it well down. Cover the dish with a lid, or foil, and stand it in a meat tin half-filled with boiling water.

Cook in the centre of the oven 180°C/350°F/gas mark 4 for 2 hours or until the juices are quite clear, which indicates that all is cooked. Remove the lid or foil half an hour before the end of the cooking time, setting your timer to remind you to do this.

Have ready a board which will just fit inside the top of the pot.

Cover this with foil. When the potted meat is cool but not set, put this foil-covered board on the top and place a heavy weight on it.

When it is quite set, take off the board, clean the edges of the dish and cover with a film of clarified butter.

POTTED HARE

This is my own recipe based on a very old Scottish method — the rum and ginger are my own additions. It should be made at least two days before you are going to need it.

1 large brown hare
1 kg/2 lb loin of pork
6 large chicken livers
(plus a few grouse livers if you can get any)
500 g/1 lb extra pork fat from the back
1½ teacups red wine
1 egg
1 glass Jamaica rum
2 cloves garlic
1 tsp powdered ginger
1 tsp thyme
500 g/1 lb thinly cut streaky bacon
Salt and freshly ground black pepper
Aspic jelly to cover

Cut the rind off the bacon and stretch the rashers with the flat of a knife so that they do not shrink. Line an oven-proof casserole or tureen with this, leaving enough to overlap across the top of the filled pot.

Cut all the meat from the hare and the pork, taking off any skin and tissue. Cut all but the leg meat into 1-inch cubes and put to marinate overnight in the rum and wine.

Mince the remaining meats and fat together with the garlic and livers through the fine blade of a mincer, adding any left-over bits of bacon. Mix this forcemeat with the egg and seasonings and add the liquor from the marinade. Mix in the cubes of meat and fill the lined pot.

Cover with a lid or foil and stand the pot in a meat tin half-filled with hot water. Bake at 180°C/350°F/gas mark 4 for 1½ to 2 hours or until the juices are quite clear. Half an hour before the estimated time of cooking is finished, remove the cover so that the top acquires a nice brown finish. To preserve its attractive appearance, cover with an aspic jelly rather than clarified butter.

POTTED BEEF

500 g/1 lb fatless rump steak
3 cups red wine
A pinch of powdered mace and powdered cloves
60 g/2 oz butter
A little salt and freshly ground pepper
Clarified butter to cover

Trim the meat of all sinew and fat, cut it into 1-inch cubes and put into a stone jar or basin. Season with salt and the spices. Cover with the wine. Cover the jar or basin with foil and stand this in a roasting tin containing boiling water.

Cook this in a slow oven, 170°C/325°F/gas mark 3, until the meats fall apart. This could take up to 4 hours. Make sure that you top up the tin with boiling water when necessary. When the meat is ready, drain the juices into a small pan and reduce these until you have only a couple of tablespoons left.

Put the meat into a blender, or pound it to a paste in a mortar. Beat in the softened butter and the reduced juices. Check the seasoning before filling into little pots or wax cartons.

Cover with a film of clarified butter.

Serve as you would a pâté.

POTTED SALMON

Newcastle carries much of the responsibility for salmon being potted, for it was often said to be done 'in the Newcastle way'. There is little mystery about this, as this city is very near salmon fishing country and of course is a major port where salmon would be in transit from Scotland on their way down to London.

Today it is an expensive fish and many will think it a sacrilege to present it in any other form than poached or grilled, but it does make a beautiful pâté and keeps for quite a while.

500 g/1 lb middle-cut salmon
1 tsp powdered mace
2 glasses Madeira
1 tbsp chopped parsley
125 g/4 oz butter
A squeeze of lemon juice
Salt and freshly ground white pepper
Clarified butter to cover

Skin the salmon whilst it is still raw. Cut the flesh into broad diagonal slices with a long-bladed sharp knife, starting at the centre of the backbone and cutting to the outer edge.

Arrange the slices of salmon in layers in a fairly narrow, deep, oven-proof pot, dotting each layer with a little of the butter and sprinkling mace, salt and pepper, a little of the parsley and a modicum of lemon juice.

When the pot is filled, pour over the Madeira and lay a circle of buttered paper directly on to the surface of the fish. Cover with a tight-fitting lid or foil and bake in a slow oven, 170°C/325°F/gas mark 3, for 1 hour.

Allow the fish to cool and remove the paper, which will have collected any scum or albumin from the fish. Strain the juices into a small pan and reduce these by boiling rapidly until only 2 tablespoons remain. Pour this back over the salmon.

Clean the edges of the pot and then fit a plate or foil-covered board over the surface and press with a kitchen weight. Put into the refrigerator complete with weight, until it has set.

Cover the surface with clarified butter.

This dish is best when cut into thin slices and eaten alone as a starter with brown bread and a segment of lemon for those who want this. It can also be served as a main course with your favourite salad.

POTTED KIPPERS

As an alternative, use 2 medium-sized smoked mackerel instead of kippers.

2 pairs oak-smoked kippers
(or 2 large packets kipper fillets)
150 g/5 oz unsalted butter
Juice of half a lemon and a very little rind
125 ml/¼ pint double cream
A little freshly ground black pepper
Clarified butter to cover
Additional double cream if required

Cook the kippers or kipper fillets in 1 ounce of the butter – real kippers are infinitely preferable. Soften the remaining butter. Then carefully skin and bone them and put through a Mouli or blender with the softened butter, lemon juice and black pepper.

Blend until you have a very smooth paste. Half-whip the cream and fold into the kipper paste. Test for seasoning before filling into an earthenware dish, pots or wax cartons.

Cover with a film of clarified butter. Set in the refrigerator.

If a very fine version is required, fold in 2 additional tablespoons of double cream, half-whipped. Serve with hot buttered toast and lemon segments.

POTTED CRAB

1 large dressed crab
(frozen crab is excellent for this)
175 ml/⅓ pint double cream
60 g/2 oz butter
A little lemon juice
1 sherry glass Madeira
Salt and freshly ground black pepper
Clarified butter to cover

Chop the white meat and pound well together with the dark meat.

Melt the butter in a pan and add the crab. Cook very slowly for 15 minutes, stirring all the time. Add the cream and continue cooking until you have the consistency of a very thick sauce. Pass through a Mouli or blender and allow to cool.

Beat in the Madeira, add a little lemon juice and seasoning to taste. Fill into little pots or wax cartons and cover with a film of clarified butter. Set in a refrigerator.

POTTED SHRIMPS

When so many other good things are lost to us for some inexplicable reason, potted shrimps are still very much a thing to eat. Morecambe Bay shrimps are the most popular as they are the tiny brown sand shrimps peculiar to that part of the country.

Try using pink shrimps or even prawns. Freshly prepared ones are delicious and are very easy to do. If you live near the coast you may prefer to boil your own shrimps, but usually these days the fishermen have already done this for you. If you are using frozen shrimps or prawns, allow them to defrost slowly at room temperature.

500 g/1 lb freshly boiled shrimps
250 g/8 oz butter
½ tsp ground mace
½ tsp ground nutmeg
½ mustardspoon cayenne pepper
Salt

Boil some water in a small pan, cut the butter into pieces and add this to the boiling water. Dissolve the butter completely, then draw the pan on one side to cool. Let the butter set on the top then lift it off and wipe away any drops of liquid that are on the underside with a clean cloth .

Put half of this butter into a large frying pan until it foams and starts to go quiet. Now add the seasonings (apart from the salt) and stir them in well.

Add the shrimps and toss in the seasoned butter until they are well coated. Don't add any salt until you have tasted the shrimps, as they can be quite salty enough without adding any more.

Spoon the coated shrimps into wax cartons or individual pots and press them down well. Allow them to cool.

Melt the rest of the clarified butter and pour this over the top to seal them. Chill well before serving.

POTTED CHEESE

60 g/2 oz farmhouse Cheshire
60 g/2 oz unsalted butter
1 glass cream sherry or port
Cayenne pepper (see below)
1 tsp Worcester sauce
Clarified butter to cover

Soften but do not melt the butter. Grate the cheese. Combine these together with all the other ingredients and pound them until you have a smooth paste, remembering that cayenne pepper is very hot.

Press into little pots or wax cartons and cover with a film of clarified butter.

This potted cheese is excellent as a stuffing for halved and peeled pears which have been rubbed over with lemon juice to keep them white.

Vegetables

ARTICHOKES

Both Jerusalem and globe artichokes have been known in England for many years, but have never achieved real glory. The Jerusalem artichoke gets its name from the old Italian word 'girasole' and has never had anything to do with the Holy City; it is a very good root vegetable and is not related to the globe artichoke at all. There is an interest today in the globe artichoke served with melted butter into which the tender leaves can be dipped, and the bitter-sweet fleshy parts sucked away from the base of the leaf. Otherwise I doubt whether there is as much use for it in our kitchens as in the flower clubs of Great Britain!

The Elizabethans had exotic recipes for globe artichoke ('artichock') pies in which they put grapes, dates, hard-boiled eggs and spices. The French use 'fonds' or artichoke bases for garnishes in their gastronomic dishes, but I wonder just how recherché they really are. Care must be taken with this rather confusing thistle – for that is the family from which it comes. The leaves of a boiled artichoke are succulent and tender, but the choke is the part sitting on top of the base and is not to be eaten. It is easily recognisable by its black hairy appearance and is evident when all the leaves have been stripped off. The actual base comes away quite easily and is obviously a separate part.

The heart is the young artichoke stripped of most of its top leaves; they are delicious stuffed and always look very attractive cut into quarters revealing the beautiful formation of the leaves. I much prefer these to any other form.

BOILED GLOBE ARTICHOKES

First wash them thoroughly in cold water. Boil them, completely covered in plenty of salted water, for 30 to 40 minutes, depending on their size. It is as well to select even-sized heads so that they are ready at the same time. Drain them well on a clean tea-towel, tipping them upside down, as water lodges in the leaves. Serve hot with melted butter or Hollandaise Sauce (p. 225).

STUFFED ARTICHOKE HEARTS

12 artichoke hearts (tinned are very good)
3 slices cooked ham
100 g/3 oz cream cheese
2 hard-boiled eggs
Juice of half a lemon
4 anchovy fillets

Freshly ground black pepper
Lettuce to garnish

Mince the ham with the anchovy fillets; mix with the cheese and season well, adding lemon juice a little at a time until you have the right balance.

It is doubtful whether any salt will be needed as the anchovies are rather salty, but add a little pepper.

Gently open the drained hearts and fill with the mixture.

Arrange the hearts on a bed of lettuce leaves and cover with a veil of hard-boiled eggs pressed through a hair sieve.

ASPARAGUS AMULET

This may seem to be an odd man out, but the 'amulet', or omelette, was a great favourite at the dinner tables of the eighteenth century, particularly when dressed with asparagus.

Toast made one of its rare early appearances with amulets and was served well buttered and hot, sometimes as a base for the egg dish and sometimes served separately.

3 eggs
2 tbsps thick cream
30 g/1 oz butter
6 green asparagus spears
(the tinned variety are good for this recipe)
Salt and freshly ground white pepper

Beat together the eggs and cream; season well.

Melt the butter in a heavy-bottomed omelette or frying pan.

Pour the mixture into the pan. You may either set the egg mixture over a low heat, leaving the omelette flat and adding the asparagus tips cut into 1-inch pieces all at the same time, and slide out keeping flat – do not turn it over like a pancake. Alternatively, with the back of a fork gather the omelette together over a good heat, in the French manner, add the spears cut into 1-inch pieces and warmed in a little melted butter, roll the omelette up and turn onto a heated plate.

BACON AND ASPARAGUS FRAZE

The fraze has completely disappeared from our repertoire, for what reason I cannot imagine, as this omelette-cum-pancake is a very tasty first course or a main course for lunch or high tea.

2 eggs
30 g/1 oz flour
Scant 125 ml/¼ pint single cream
Salt and white pepper
100 g/3 oz onion
100 g/3 oz cooked ham or bacon
Asparagus tips (cook fresh asparagus or use tinned)
Butter for frying

Make a batter with the eggs, flour and cream, season and add a little water if it is too thick.

Finely slice the onion and the bacon or ham. Fry these in a little butter until golden brown. Drain away the fat. Drain the asparagus tips if they are tinned.

Make up small pancakes from the batter, adding a mixture of the onion, ham and asparagus tips before turning the fraze over to brown on the other side. Serve as quickly as possible after cooking.

Just how many you make will depend on the generosity of the filling and the size of fraze you like to serve, but each fraze should have an abundant filling. I count on the above quantities to make four.

DRESSED VEGETABLE MARROW

A marrow weighing 1½ kg/3 lb
60 g/2 oz butter
Juice of half a lemon
Salt and freshly ground white pepper
Lettuce

The Dressing

3 parts olive oil
1 part wine vinegar

Dry mustard, salt and pepper to taste
1 heaped tsp chopped gherkins
1 heaped tsp capers
1 heaped tsp finely chopped shallot or onion

Peel and core the marrow and cut into 1-inch cubes.

Melt the butter in a heavy-bottomed pan; put in the marrow, lemon juice and salt and pepper. Cover with a lid and toss over a medium heat until the juices begin to draw. Lower the heat and poach gently until the marrow is just tender.

Drain and cool before putting into the refrigerator to chill.

Mix the dressing ingredients, pour over the marrow and serve on a bed of young lettuce leaves or quartered lettuce hearts.

FRIED CUCUMBER WITH DILL

A large cucumber
Juice of 1 lemon
2 tbsps olive oil
Salt and freshly ground black pepper
1 egg and 1 extra white
Plain flour (see below)
1 tsp baking powder
Oil for frying
Salt

The Sauce

125 ml/¼ pint single cream or yoghurt
125 g/4 oz cream cheese
1 tbsp finely chopped dill
½ tsp castor sugar
1 tsp lemon juice
Salt and pepper

Squeeze the lemon and mix the juice with the oil in a shallow dish or platter; season with salt and pepper.

Cut the cucumber into diagonal slices no more than ⅛ inch thick. Toss them in the oil and lemon.

Make a batter from the beaten whole egg and egg-white, incorporating as much flour as will make a good batter. Add the baking powder and as much cold water as will thin the batter until it just, but only just, adheres to the cucumber pieces. (When it is fried, you should be able to see the green cucumber through the thin crisp batter.)

Have some crumpled absorbent kitchen paper ready on a metal tray at the side of the stove.

Heat the oil in a deep frying pan until it just starts to smoke. Put in the cucumber pieces, a few at a time, making sure that you do not add so many that the oil cools and thus lets out the juices from the cucumber. Fry until golden and crisp. Drain well on kitchen paper.

Serve as soon as possible after frying so that they are still crisp. If you have to keep them warm, leave the oven doors open so that no steam collects to soften the batter.

To make the sauce, finely chop the dill and fork this gently into the cream cheese, together with the lemon juice, sugar and salt and pepper.

Finally gently stir in the cream, adding a little cold water if the sauce appears too thick.

A REGALIA OF CUCUMBERS

To dress cucumbers in this way was known in the seventeenth century, though I have based my recipe on that given by John Middleton, master cook to the Duke of Bolton in the early eighteenth century. Serve either as a vegetable or as a first course.

1 medium-sized cucumber
30 g/1 oz butter
1 small onion
¼ litre/½ pint single cream
1 crushed small clove garlic
2 tbsps chopped chives
2 tbsps freshly chopped parsley
Salt and pepper

Peel the cucumber, cut it in half lengthways and remove the seeds and pulp with a teaspoon. Cut each half into ¼-inch slices. Finely slice the onion. Wash and chop the herbs.

Melt the butter in a fairly wide-based pan. Add the onion and garlic and cook, covered with a lid, for a few minutes. Add the cucumber slices, cover and toss frequently over a low heat for about 3 minutes. Add the cream and season lightly. Cook for a few minutes longer, but take care not to over-cook the cucumbers, which should still be crisp when served.

If the sauce looks oily, add a modicum of water to rectify the consistency. Add the freshly chopped herbs just before serving.

FORC'D TOMATOES

Tomatoes were introduced into England in the late sixteenth century, but it was a further three hundred years before they crept into regular use.

When banks of this delicious spicy-smelling fruit lie invitingly in the food shops and the housekeeping is at an all-time Thursday low, I have looked in vain in my eighteenth-century receipt books for ways of preparing them, but the cooks of that era were far too busy with their skirrets, scorzoneras and trapacons to have turned their minds in the direction of a mere tomato. It was not until the nineteenth century that recipes started to appear for their use.

These stuffed tomatoes may be served as an elaborate vegetable with a roast, or as a main dish for lunch or supper.

8 very large tomatoes
60 g/2 oz lean ham
60 g/2 oz mushrooms
60 g/2 oz white breadcrumbs
1 large onion
1 tbsp freshly chopped parsley or tarragon
¼ tsp cayenne pepper
60 g/2 oz butter
3 egg-yolks
1 crushed large clove garlic
Salt to taste

Cut the thinnest possible slices from the bottom of the tomatoes and reserve them. These lids will then not have the unsightly scar where the stalk has been. Then stand the tomatoes on their stalk ends and they will balance better in the baking dish. Scoop out the seeds and throw them away. Chop up the middles and put them aside in a basin.

Wipe the mushrooms and mince them with the ham, garlic and peeled onion. Melt the butter in a smallish pan and gently fry this mixture for 5 minutes, stirring it regularly.

Add the crumbs and parsley or tarragon to the chopped tomato flesh and combine the two mixtures, seasoning as necessary with salt and cayenne pepper. Bind the mixture with the egg-yolks and re-stuff the tomato shells. One way of ensuring that the tomatoes do not collapse in this, or any other, stuffed tomato recipe, is to make a collar of foil or grease-proof paper, securing it with kitchen thread or piercing the ends with a cocktail stick.

Replace the lids, dot with a little more butter and bake in an oven pre-heated to 150°C/375°F/gas mark 5 for half an hour.

_____

LEEKS IN LEEK SAUCE (Cold)

14 even-sized leeks (reserve 2 for the sauce)
60 g/2 oz butter
Juice of 1 lemon
1 teacup water
Salt and pepper

The Sauce

2 cups olive oil
½ cup white wine vinegar
1 tsp castor sugar
1 heaped tsp mild French mustard
1 tbsp chopped chives
2 tbsps chopped parsley
2 reserved cooked leeks
Salt and freshly ground pepper

The leeks should be of equal size so they will be cooked at the same time. Wash them well and trim off the tough leaves.

Butter an oven-proof dish and lay the leeks in. Dab them all over with the butter, squeeze the lemon juice over and pour the water into the dish.

Lightly salt and pepper, cover closely and bake them until they are cooked but still firm and not collapsed. Cool them in the liquor which you will later strain off and reserve for soup or gravy.

Put all the ingredients for the dressing, including the 2 reserved leeks cut into 1-inch pieces, into a blender or Mouli. When you have a smooth sauce, pour this over the cooled leeks, sprinkle with more chives and parsley and chill before serving.

LEEK PIE

250 g/8 oz shortcrust pastry made with butter
4 good-sized leeks
100 g/3 oz butter
3 eggs
¼ litre/½ pint single cream
1 crushed small clove garlic
1 tbsp freshly chopped chives
Salt and freshly ground black pepper

Line an 8-inch flan ring with the pastry and bake it blind, reserving a small piece of raw pastry to patch up any holes that may appear if the pastry is really short.

Wash the leeks and trim off the darkest green parts, leaving about an inch of green on each. Shred them finely, put into a colander and wash well under cold water; drain well.

Melt the butter in a heavy-bottomed pan, add the leeks and cover with a lid; gently sweat the leeks over a very low heat until they are soft but not browned. Add the garlic, salt and pepper. When the leeks are quite soft, add the chives and leave to cool.

Beat the eggs and add the cream. Season lightly.

Cover the bottom of the flan case with the leeks and pour the cream mixture over them. Bake at 170°C/325°F/gas mark 3 until the filling has set. This will take upwards of half an hour.

ONION TART

250 g/8 oz shortcrust pastry made with butter
4 large onions
100 g/3 oz butter
3 eggs
125 ml/¼ pint single cream
Chopped fresh basil or tarragon
Salt and freshly ground black pepper

Line an 8-inch flan ring with the pastry and bake it blind, reserving a small piece of pastry to patch up any holes that may appear.

Slice the onions very finely. Melt the butter without allowing it to colour and add the sliced onions. Cover with a lid and let them simmer slowly without browning, until they are transparent. Season well with salt and pepper and add basil or tarragon. Leave to cool.

Beat the eggs and add the cream.

Cover the bottom of the flan case with the onions and pour on the cream mixture. Bake for about half an hour, or until the filling has set, at 170°C/325°F/gas mark 3.

PILAF

Rice has been used in this country for longer than most people would like to remember.

The spelling of the word pilaf took many different forms and came out as 'pillow', 'pilau', 'pilow' and even 'pellow'. Whatever it was called, it was used as today, as a carrier for some sauce or other, or with a curry.

2 breakfast cups long-grain rice
4 breakfast cups chicken stock
30 g/1 oz butter
1 small onion
Salt and pepper

Select a suitable casserole or pan that can be used on top of the stove as well as in the oven.

Finely chop the onion. Melt the butter and fry the onion until it is transparent but not coloured. Add the rice and fry it for a minute or so, stirring all the time. Bring the stock to the boil and pour it over the rice.

Season lightly, cover with a tight-fitting lid and put straight into a pre-heated oven at 220°C/425°F/gas mark 7 for exactly 17 minutes. Do not stir the rice after putting the casserole into the oven.

At the end of the *exact* cooking time, remove the lid and you will see that the rice has absorbed all the stock and is loose-grained, cooked, but still moist.

Note: The proportions and method are always the same – double the *volume* (not weight) of stock to rice; bring to the boil and then place in a hot oven for 17 minutes.

RISOTTO

For a risotto, follow the preceding recipe and then add 60 g/2 oz butter and 60 g/2 oz freshly grated Parmesan cheese to the finished pilaf.

You can very simply develop your own variations on this, adding shellfish, diced meats, mushrooms, tomatoes, curry powder, herbs, etc.

RAGOO OF MUSHROOMS

In the eighteenth century this was used as a side dish. Today it makes a good first course or, if served in greater quantity, an adequate and not expensive supper dish.

175 g/6 oz field mushrooms
60 g/2 oz butter
125 g/4 oz onion
125 ml/¼ pint red wine
1 stock cube dissolved in 125 ml/¼ pint water
Scant 15 g/½ oz plain flour
A pinch of powdered rosemary

1 crushed clove garlic
Salt and freshly ground pepper
Hot buttered toast to serve (see below)

Slice the onions and brown them in the butter. Add the garlic and
the rosemary. Add the mushrooms cut into quarters.

Fry everything for a few minutes then sprinkle the flour over and
stir in well. Moisten with the red wine and stock, cook for 10
minutes and adjust the seasoning if necessary.

Serve in individual dishes with hot buttered toast made from a
granary loaf.

WHITE FRICASSEE OF MUSHROOMS

*It doesn't appear to be commonly known that button mushrooms, as we
know the white tight-caps today, did exist in the seventeenth and eighteenth centuries, as John Middleton and Patrick Lamb tell us in their
books on cookery. They were frequently used as a filling for tartlets or
patties and also served as a separate dish.*

*This delicate fricassee can be used to fill individual ramekins or puff
pastry cases and be served either as a first course or as a savoury.*

250 g/8 oz button mushrooms
Juice of half a lemon
125 ml/¼ pint double cream
2 egg-yolks
Salt and cayenne pepper

Wipe the mushrooms clean of all dirt, but do not wash them. Slice
them finely, squeeze the lemon juice over, season lightly and place
in a pan over very low heat.

Toss the mushrooms until they draw and their juices become
sufficient for them to cook. Take care not to over-cook them or
they will become like pieces of leather. Pour over them all but a
tablespoon of the cream. Bring to the boil.

Mix the last tablespoon of cream with the egg-yolks and stir this
briskly into the sauce, but *do not* re-boil. Check the seasoning.

SHAKEN PEAS

There was a time when our vegetables were entities in themselves and served as side or 'corner' dishes. The Continentals, of course, still serve a vegetable in its own right, so to speak. Perhaps this recipe for serving peas will encourage you to try it as a separate dish — only use fresh peas if they are young and tender.

250 g/8 oz frozen baby peas
½ lettuce
1 small onion
30 g/1 oz butter
1 tsp extra butter
1 tsp plain flour
2 tbsps cold water
½ tsp castor sugar
1 tbsp thick cream
4 mint leaves
Salt and freshly ground black pepper

Finely chop the onion and the mint; shred the lettuce very finely.

Work the teaspoon of butter and of flour into a soft paste. Melt the rest of the butter in a heavy-bottomed pan without letting it brown. Add the chopped onion and sweat it without letting it colour. Add the frozen peas, put a lid on the pan and shake well over a low heat until the peas begin to draw.

Add the finely shredded lettuce and the water. Continue to shake the contents of the pan over a low heat. Season lightly with the mint, sugar, salt and pepper.

When the peas are just tender, whisk in a little of the flour and butter mixture, letting the sauce thicken and boil after each addition. Stop adding the mixture when everything is nicely cohered.

Add the cream, re-heat the peas and serve in a heated tureen.

Note: The peas and lettuce should be a good bright-green colour. They will start to go greyish if they have to be kept hot for any length of time and, whilst this will not impair the flavour to any great extent, it will not look so well.

STUFFED VINE LEAVES WITH GRAPES

The 'big' house in England usually had a vinery as well as a peach house and an orangery. The cooks and housekeepers of the eighteenth century in particular went to great lengths with their conserving and preserving, pickling and collaring. The following recipe from the mêlée of their store cupboards is particularly suitable for today's menu if used as a first course, or as a buffet dish when the richer cold meats such as roast duckling or game are also served.

250 g/½ lb black or green grapes
(when muscatel grapes are available,
these are delicious served in this way)
8 vine leaves (fresh or tinned)
1 lemon
2 tbsps white wine vinegar
1 tbsp olive oil
2 tbsps castor sugar
½ tsp rosemary
½ tsp freshly ground black pepper
1 level tsp salt

If the vine leaves are fresh, it is better to choose young ones. Plunge them into salted boiling water for 5 minutes, then wash them well under running cold water and drain. If, as is most probable, you use the tinned variety which are preserved in brine, then rinse them very well in plenty of cold water before draining them. It is even preferable with some brands to let them soak in a sink of cold water for at least an hour.

Split the grapes in half; don't skin them, but remove the pips. Make parcels of clusters of grapes inside each vine leaf and pack these little parcels into a small oven-proof dish.

Bring all the other ingredients to the boil and pour this liquor directly over the stuffed leaves. Cover with foil and cook in the oven at 190°C/375°F/gas mark 5 for ¾ hour. Cool before refrigerating.

Allow 2 stuffed leaves per person.

PRINCIPAL DISHES

Fish

BAKED SEA BASS WITH FENNEL

For those who live near a fishing port there is often the opportunity to have a whole sea bass. If this is not available, any firm-fleshed fish can be prepared in this way. Fillets of Dover sole can be re-formed and held together with wooden cocktail sticks or toothpicks. It is an unusual way of cooking older salmon, and a middle-cut piece lends itself admirably to being baked or roasted.

A bass weighing 3–3½ kg/6–7 lb
2 heads fennel
1 cup olive oil
Juice and rind of 1 lemon
½ tsp fennel seeds
Salt and freshly ground pepper
Butter for roasting
1 sherry glass gin or pastis

Have the bass gutted and decapitated and the tail and fins cut off. Make shallow incisions at 1-inch intervals down both sides of the fish.

Chop a tablespoonful of the feathery top off one of the fennel heads, add to the oil, seeds, lemon juice and rind, and season well with salt and pepper. Place the bass in a shallow dish and pour this marinade over it; turn the fish at frequent intervals and let it soak for at least 4 hours.

Butter an oven-proof dish large enough to contain the fish. Carefully strip down the fennel heads, wash the pieces and pat them dry with a clean towel; arrange a bed of fennel pieces in the dish, sit the fish on top and then cover the fish with more fennel, securing with sticks as and where necessary, but taking care not to pierce the fish too deeply.

Pour the marinade juices over the fish and then put liberal dabs of butter on top. Bake the fish at 200°C/400°F/gas mark 6 for 45 minutes to 1 hour, or until it is cooked through, basting it frequently with the roasting juices.

When the fish is cooked, remove and discard the top fennel pieces, which will probably be too scorched to serve. Manoeuvre the whole fish onto a serving dish and take off the skin.

Strain the juices into a small pan, add the gin or pastis and reduce the sauce until it is rich looking – there should be about 4 tablespoons. Pour it over the fish and serve.

The pieces of fennel which have been underneath the fish will be alright to serve.

FINNAN HADDOCK WITH PARSLEY SAUCE

This gets one away from the piece of smoked haddock afloat in a pint of milk. It retains its delicious favour, and combines it successfully with a version of one of England's most popular sauces. An old aunt of mine always served her haddocks this way and for years I thought she was a very competent 'Continental' cook! She showed me how to make it when I was fourteen. The traditional poached egg can crown the finished dish if you wish.

1½ kg/3 lb smoked haddock
1 litre/2 pints cold water

A squeeze of lemon
A sprig of parsley
Salt and freshly ground white pepper

Parsley Sauce
¼ litre/½ pint fish stock
¼ litre/½ pint single cream
100 g/3 oz butter
30 g/1 oz plain flour
2 heaped tbsps freshly and very finely chopped parsley
A little lemon juice
A pinch of castor sugar
Salt and freshly ground white pepper

Wash the fish; cut into serving pieces.

Lightly oil the bottom of a shallow pan and put in the pieces of fish; cover with the water, season lightly, add parsley and lemon juice and then cover with a circle of oiled paper to fit the surface. Put a lid on the pan and poach slowly (rapid boiling breaks up the flesh), until the fish is just cooked – for about 15 minutes.

Remove the fish, taking out any bones and skin; arrange in a warm serving dish, cover with a damp cloth or wetted paper *and* a lid and keep warm. Reduce the cooking liquor down to half a pint by boiling rapidly.

Melt the butter in a small pan, stir in the flour, strain the fish stock onto this and whisk the sauce until it is smooth. Add the cream and cook for 5 minutes over a very low heat, stirring all the time.

Check the seasoning – there will probably be enough salt. Add a little lemon juice and a pinch of sugar. Stir in the abundance of parsley (I sometimes add a few chopped chives), pour over the waiting fish and serve immediately.

This rich, bright green parsley sauce is a worthy addition to any repertoire. The same technique can be used for any fish which you want to serve in this way.

It is always well to keep a little stock back, just in case the flour you are using is 'stronger' than usual and you wish to thin the sauce down a little.

HADDOCK WITH A PUDDING
IN ITS BELLY

There was a time when this fish dish was made with pike and had the somewhat off-putting title of a 'Pike with a Pudding in his Belly'. As pike are not all that easy to come by these days, a baby haddock stuffed in the following manner makes quite a tasty substitute. I think you will find that the result is far more pleasing than its bizarre though somewhat apt name might well lead you to believe.

A fresh haddock weighing 2–2½ kg/4–5 lb
125 g/4 oz butter
125 g/4 oz fresh white breadcrumbs for the stuffing
Extra breadcrumbs to cover the fish (see below)
2 tbsps freshly chopped parsley
1 tbsp chopped fresh (not dried) sage
1 small onion
Juice and rind of 1 lemon
60 g/2 oz potted shrimps
3 eggs
Butter for roasting
Salt and freshly ground pepper
Melted butter and lemon segments to garnish

Ask your fishmonger to gut and bone the fish, leaving it whole but decapitated and finless.

Melt 1 ounce of the butter in a small pan; chop the onion and soften it in the butter until it is transparent. Make a stuffing with the breadcrumbs, onions, shrimps, parsley, sage, lemon juice and rind and 2 of the eggs.

Stuff the fish with this and sew up the aperture with linen thread, using a slip stitch. Beat the third egg and wash the fish all over with this. Press plenty of fresh breadcrumbs over the top and sides of the fish. Lay the fish in a buttered oven-proof baking dish.

Melt the remaining butter and pour over the whole fish. Bake in the centre of an oven pre-heated to 220°C/425°F/gas mark 7 for 40 minutes, basting frequently, or until the fish gives when pressed at the thickest part. Remove the thread.

If the crumbs start to scorch or brown, reduce the heat appropriately. Serve with extra melted butter and lemon segments.

STUFFED HERRINGS

4 fresh herrings
1 tbsp chopped parsley
2 mushrooms
30 g/1 oz butter
1 crushed clove garlic
3 tbsps fresh white breadcrumbs
2 hard-boiled eggs
1 rasher bacon
A little cream
Salt and freshly ground black pepper
Mustard sauce (p. 230) or lemon segments to garnish

Remove the backbones from the herrings, wash the fish well and pat them dry.

Chop the mushrooms and the hard-boiled eggs. Cut the bacon rasher into dice.

Fry the bacon in the butter and add the mushrooms and the garlic. Combine with the rest of the ingredients, season well and bind with a little cream. Divide the stuffing into 4 portions and stuff each herring with it.

Butter an oven-proof dish well and put the fish into it. Dab the top of each fish with a little more butter and bake them in the oven at 190°C/375°F/gas mark 5 for 20 to 25 minutes or until the herring gives when pressed firmly with the finger.

Serve with a mustard sauce or with lemon segments.

KEDGEREE

I fear tempers would fly and argument ensue if one were to attempt to define just what a true kedgeree is. That it came to us from India, when that great country was part of the British Empire, cannot be denied, but what happened to it after its arrival is anyone's guess.

What do persist through the many versions of this dish are the two basic ingredients – fish and rice. Many say that it can only be made with smoked haddock; others say that eggs are an essential. Curry appears in some recipes, and this would seem logical in the face of its place of origin.

There are those who like it very dry, but I like mine made with salmon (or smoked haddock), eggs, mushrooms and with a very creamy sauce. I have also moved its time of appearance from the breakfast table to the lunch table, unless I indulge in that Americanisation 'brunch', where it fits perfectly.

375 g/¾ lb salmon or smoked haddock
1 small onion
½ litre/1 pint milk
30 g/1 oz plain flour
60 g/2 oz butter
125 g/4 oz button mushrooms
Tip of a teaspoon of curry powder
½ stock cube
Juice of half a lemon
4 hard-boiled eggs
175 g/6 oz rice
Fresh parsley
Salt and freshly ground pepper
125 ml/¼ pint single cream (optional)

Boil the eggs for no more than 10 minutes from cold (they should still have ¼ inch of soft centre). Run them under cold water until they are quite cold and then shell them. Cut them into quarters and then into eighths. Cover with foil until you require them.

Cook the rice in plenty of boiling lightly salted water for 17 minutes exactly, then run it under the cold tap and wash off the starch. Leave to drain in a sieve or colander.

Finely slice the onion and mushrooms.

Melt the butter in a pan which will be large enough to contain all the ingredients. Add the sliced onions and fry until golden brown, then add the mushrooms and fry for a few seconds before stirring in the flour.

Add the touch of curry powder and the piece of stock cube. Gradually work in the cold milk a little at a time, until you have a smooth sauce, and simmer for 5 minutes, stirring to ensure that it doesn't stick or burn.

Correct the seasoning and add lemon juice to acidulate lightly. Skin and flake the fish and fold into the sauce, then fold in the cooked rice and gently allow this to heat through, stirring with a folding action as you do so, so that you do not break up the fish too much.

Finally, just before you are ready to serve the kedgeree, carefully fold in the eggs. Pour the kedgeree into a heated dish, sprinkle with parsley and serve.

If the finished dish is too solid for you, add 125 ml/¼ pint of single cream brought to the boil.

I sometimes serve the rice separately, as it is possible to make it look more attractive this way, particularly if you mould the rice in a buttered ring-mould first, then fill the centre with the salmon or haddock, eggs and mushrooms in their creamy sauce.

SALMON IN CREAM WITH CUCUMBERS

How we cling to our poached salmon or cold salmon with its everlasting cucumber in vinegar! Here are two recipes which show salmon off in a very subtle and unusual way.

1½ kg/3 lb middle-cut salmon or salmon trout
400 ml/¾ pint single cream
125 ml/¼ pint water
1 small onion
A sprig of dill
30 g/1 oz flour
1 cucumber
125 g/4 oz butter
Juice of 1 lemon and a little rind
Salt and freshly ground pepper

Butter an oven-proof dish, finely slice the onion and scatter it over the bottom of the dish.

Rub the salmon all over with half the butter. Season it well and place in the dish. Pour the cream and water round it. Chop the dill and add to the cream.

Cover with foil or a lid and bake at 200°C/400°F/gas mark 6 for 25 to 30 minutes, or until the salmon is cooked. As you are going to skin and fillet the fish, you can legitimately lift the top fillets to see if the fish is cooked through.

When it is cooked, skin and bone the salmon (which will give you 4 fillets), using a teaspoon to scrape away the dark 'cream' which is down the spine. Reserve the liquor. Arrange the 4 pieces of salmon in a serving dish and put to keep warm.

Melt the remaining butter in the bottom of a smaller pan. Stir in the flour, strain the cream liquor onto this and cook slowly, stirring all the time, until you have a delicious creamy sauce. Season to taste with the lemon juice and the lemon rind.

Peel and de-seed the cucumber and cut it into small dice. Add to the sauce. Re-heat and pour over the fish.

Garnish with a little more chopped dill.

A JOLE OF SALMON WITH GINGER

This jole (or jowl) of salmon, or any fish, was usually the head plus a goodly piece of the thick part of the neck. Today there is little need to use this part of the fish. I make this recipe with a piece of middle-cut as the unusualness of the dish warrants a good piece.

750 g/1½ lb middle-cut salmon
2 tbsps oil
1 tbsp lemon juice
Salt and freshly ground black pepper
60 g/2 oz seedless raisins
2 large pieces stem ginger
A little lemon juice
250 g/8 oz puff pastry
1 beaten egg

Get your fishmonger to skin and fillet the piece of salmon. Put the fillets into a shallow dish and pour the oil and lemon juice over them, seasoning lightly with salt and pepper. Let the pieces of fish soak in this liquor for 6 hours, turning them at hourly intervals.

Roll out the pastry into a square large enough to parcel the salmon. Re-form the 4 fillets into their original whole shape and place them near the front edge of the pastry. Finely slice the ginger and put a cushion of these slices over the top of the fish.

Soak the raisins in the remainder of the marinade, plus a little of the ginger syrup, warming them slightly so that they plump up but do not burst. Arrange these in a second cushion on top of the ginger.

Fold over the pastry to meet the front edge, first brushing the bottom edges all round with a little beaten egg, and press the two edges together. Nick at 1-inch intervals with a sharp knife.

Brush over the whole pastry surface with the rest of the beaten egg and sit the jole on a wetted baking sheet. Decorate the top at will with pastry leaves or circles. Make two small slits in the top to let the steam out.

Bake in the centre of an oven pre-heated to 220°C/425°F/gas mark 7 for 20 minutes then for a further 20 minutes at 190°C/375°F/gas mark 5, until the pastry is golden and crisp.

SALMON MOUSSE

Many would argue that the mousse has no place in the English repertoire, but such an argument would of necessity fall flat on its face, for what would be in our kitchen files if we did not beg, borrow or steal, as every country has done since time began?

I cannot think of any cook in this country who does not consider that this dish has a rightful place on his or her menu. I, for one, would always endeavour to serve salmon in some form or another to visitors from abroad. My own recipe for a salmon mousse is as delicate as you will find; it is always successful – light, yet rich, with the true salmon flavour coming through.

750 g/1½ lb middle-cut Scotch salmon
1 small onion
1 carrot
A sprig of dill or parsley
Water, salt and peppercorns
¼ litre/½ pint bland home-made mayonnaise (p. 228)
¼ litre/½ pint aspic, using the fish stock and
30 g/1 oz gelatine (see below)
¼ litre/½ pint double cream
Juice of half a lemon
Salt and freshly ground white pepper
Aspic, tomato, cucumber, etc. to garnish (see below)

Select a pan just large enough to hold the piece of salmon. For a piece as small as this there is little purpose in using a fish–kettle.

Wash and scale the fish and leave it ready to poach. Fill the pan with enough water to just cover the fish. (Stand a small oiled plate on the bottom of the pan to prevent the skin from sticking.)

Peel the onion and the carrot and cut them into quarters. Add these to the water, together with the dill or parsley and a little salt. Bring the liquid to the boil and simmer for 10 minutes before lowering in the piece of salmon.

Poach the salmon for 20 minutes only and leave it to cool in the poaching liquor. Remember that to poach means to cook so slowly that the water is only just moving.

When the fish is cool, lift out the salmon and skin it. Take away the dark band down the spine, using a teaspoon to help you. Carefully remove every bone and then pound the fish flesh in a heavy basin, or a mortar if you possess such a thing.

Put this pounded fish on one side whilst you make the mayonnaise and aspic.

To make the aspic, first measure half a pint of the fish stock; pour through a strainer into a pan and bring to the boil. Add double the usual amount of gelatine, as the aspic has to support quite a lot of ingredients (normal quantities are 30 g per ½ litre or 1 ounce per pint).

Arrange the bowl in a sink of running cold water, making sure that there is no chance of any of the water getting into the aspic! Stir from time to time to ensure even cooling; don't let it set.

Whip the cream until it just starts to ribbon but is not stiff.

Put the salmon into a large bowl and season with a little more salt, a modicum of freshly ground white pepper and a little lemon juice.

Beat in the mayonnaise you have made and add more seasoning if you feel it necessary. Pour in the cold, but not set, aspic and incorporate thoroughly. Fold in the half-whipped cream carefully but thoroughly.

Pour the mixture into a mould or soufflé dish – if you intend to unmould the mousse, the container should be lightly oiled and a circle of grease-proof paper fitted in the bottom. Cover with foil and put into the refrigerator to set.

It is probably much simpler to leave the mousse in its dish where you can decorate the top quite professionally with sections of egg-white, blanched tarragon leaves or sprays of dill, quarters of unpeeled cucumber, strips of skinned and de-seeded tomato, olive rings, etc. First of all make up half a pint of aspic jelly with the normal amount of crystals asked for on the packet, but using half dry white wine and half water.

Let the jelly cool, but not set, then run a thin layer over the top of the mousse and return it to the refrigerator to give the jelly time to set.

Stir the remaining aspic with a warm spoon to ensure that it doesn't suddenly set on you, as it often does when it is 'at the ready'.

Decorate the mousse as you will and then very carefully float a little more jelly on the top to fix the decoration. Put this again in the refrigerator. Finally, float the rest of aspic onto the top. If you follow this method of decorating, the pieces will not float away and leave you frustrated!

Serve the mousse with a home-made mayonnaise seasoned to taste with lemon juice and cream. Use water, not milk, to thin the mayonnaise down if necessary.

An equally delicious mousse can be made with smoked haddock instead of salmon or, even better, with Arbroath smokies.

SALMON IN RED WINE

A game fish long enjoyed in this country but today rarely served in any other way than poached or grilled. The inevitable cucumber, whilst not to be spurned, need by no means be our only way of presenting the king of fish in a national manner. In former years a salmon was treated in a right royal way and cooked with butter and Madeira or with white wine in the 'Rhenish' style.

2 kg/4 lb middle-cut Scotch salmon
500 g/1 lb button mushrooms
1 medium-sized onion
1 clove garlic
1 tsp fresh rosemary
1 bottle Burgundy-type red wine
125 g/4 oz butter
30 g/1 oz flour
Salt and freshly ground black pepper

Chop the onion, slice the mushrooms and crush the garlic. Tie the rosemary in a piece of muslin.

On a plate, work together into a paste 1 ounce of the butter and the flour. Put it on one side in a warm place where it will not harden or set.

Melt the remaining butter in a heavy-bottomed pan or flame-proof casserole just big enough to contain the piece of salmon. Fry the onion until pale golden brown. Add the mushrooms and fry for a minute. Add the garlic, rosemary and seasoning and stir in well.

Wash and skin the salmon and place on this bed of vegetables. Cover with the wine and leave to marinate for 2 hours.

Cut a circle of kitchen paper to fit the inside of the casserole, oil this and lay it on top of the fish. This will help collect any scum. Cover with a lid and gently bring the contents to the boil on top of the stove.

Cook gently for 45 minutes or until the fish gives when pressure is applied with the finger and thumb to the thickest part. When the fish is cooked, carefully remove it from the casserole or pan.

Fillet and bone the salmon, re-forming it on a warm, deepish serving dish. Cover with foil or wetted kitchen paper and keep it hot.

Strain the sauce into an enamel pan and reduce it rapidly, by boiling fast, until only a third of the original quantity is left. Bring the sauce to the consistency of thin cream by adding, little by little, some of the flour and butter paste you have made. Whisk this paste into the sauce carefully, using a balloon whisk to facilitate even mixing of the sauce. Allow the sauce to come to the boil after each little addition, stopping only when you have the consistency you require.

Adjust the seasoning. Remove the rosemary from the mushrooms and onions and return these two vegetables to the sauce. Reheat this, pour over the waiting salmon and serve.

CAVEACHED SOLE

Caveaching was at one time a method of preserving fish. Today it makes an unusual cold first course for a summer dinner party. It also travels well for a picnic, though it is better served chilled.

8 fillets of Dover sole (or any other firm-fleshed fish)
Oil for frying

Salt and freshly ground pepper

The Dressing

1 teacup olive oil
2 tbsps white wine vinegar
2 bay leaves
Finely shredded rind of 1 lemon
1 Spanish onion finely sliced into rings
Salt and freshly ground white pepper
1 tbsp freshly chopped chives, parsley
or basil to garnish

Gently flatten the fish fillets with a wetted rolling pin to stop them curling up. Season lightly with salt and pepper on their insides and fold them over.

Heat the oil in a large frying pan and gently fry the fillets on both sides until they are just cooked. Arrange them, slightly over-lapping, in a long serving dish. Decorate with a spine of onion rings which have been dipped for a second into boiling water.

Make a dressing with ingredients listed and pour this over the fillets whilst they are still hot. Cool the fish and then chill well for 3 hours.

Just before serving, sprinkle with the chives, parsley or basil which have been tossed in olive oil to make them shine.

FRICASSEE OF SOLES WITH MUSSELS

It is often necessary to take a very close look at some of the older recipes for fricassees and stews, for amidst the simpler recipes there will often crop up something quite exquisite. It is only through searching that one discovers that the liquor in which many things were 'stewed' or 'boiled' was often wine or cream, and that deceptive piece of 'butter roll'd in flour' plus the handful of fresh herbs 'strewn in' all went to produce a dish of some delicacy.

4 large fillets of Dover sole (keep the bones)
¼ litre/½ pint fish stock (made with the bones – see below)
1 glass dry white wine
125 g/4 oz mushrooms

1 dessertspoon lemon juice
2 dozen mussels
60 g/2 oz butter
15 g/½ oz flour
1 egg-yolk
2 tbsps thick cream
1 tbsp each chopped parsley and chopped tarragon
Salt and freshly ground white pepper

Wash the fish bones in cold water and break them into pieces; put them into a pan, cover with more cold water, bring to the boil and simmer for 20 minutes. Strain this stock and reduce it, by boiling rapidly, to half a pint.

Butter an oven-proof dish, gently flatten the fillets of sole with a wetted rolling pin, season them lightly, fold them and lay them in the dish. Cover with the wine and the stock. Cover the dish with a lid or a piece of foil and bake the fillets at 190°C/375°F/gas mark 5 for 15 minutes.

Wash the mussels whilst the sole fillets are cooking and open them by steaming them, either in an ordinary steamer or in a large pan with just a little water in the bottom, then take them out and pull away the beards. Stand the mussels in a basin in the steamer to keep them warm until the fish and sauce are ready.

Melt the butter in a small pan, finely slice the mushrooms and fry for a few seconds in the butter.

Sprinkle on the flour and stir in well. When the fillets are cooked, pour the liquor through a strainer onto the melted butter and flour and stir until a smooth sauce is obtained. Season well with lemon juice, salt and pepper and add the freshly chopped herbs.

Finally mix the egg-yolk with the cream and stir this quickly into the hot sauce. Arrange the mussels around the fish fillets, pour the sauce over and serve.

SOLE CREAMS WITH SHRIMP SAUCE

300 g/10 oz fillet of Dover sole
¼ litre/½ pint double cream
2 eggs
Salt and freshly ground white pepper

Shrimp Sauce

125 g/4 oz fresh shrimps
1 small onion
¼ litre/½ pint boiling water
125 ml/¼ pint thick cream
½ clove crushed garlic
15 g/½ oz plain flour
45 g/1½ oz butter
1 tsp lemon juice
½ tsp paprika
Salt and freshly ground white pepper

First prepare the sauce. Shell the shrimps and put them on one side, retaining the heads, shells, etc.

Chop the onion and soften this in the melted butter in a small pan. Sprinkle with the flour and stir well in; add the paprika and garlic. Pour on the boiling water and bring the sauce back to the boil.

Add the cream and simmer for 2 minutes; add the shrimp shells and heads, cover the pan with a lid and, over the lowest possible heat, simmer the sauce for 20 minutes, stirring occasionally to prevent any sticking.

Strain the sauce through a fine sieve into a basin. Wash out the pan and return the sauce to it. Season with lemon juice, salt and pepper (it may be salty enough, so take care). Don't add the shrimps at this stage or they will toughen.

Cover the surface of the sauce with a circle of buttered paper and stand the pan in a larger pan of hot water to keep warm.

Before making the fish creams, make sure that you have a baking dish large enough to contain either castle pudding moulds or individual soufflé dishes. Failing this, small straight-sided coffeecups work very well – or the whole cream can be made in a ring mould. The quantity given will make 8 creams in moulds which are 2½ inches in diameter.

Butter the moulds well.

Beat the eggs. Chill the cream in the refrigerator. Skin and wipe the fillets, put them first through the fine blade of the mincer and then, with the beaten eggs, through a blender or Mouli, making as fine a purée as you can. Chill this well and then gradually beat the cream little by little into the fish purée, adding a little salt if it looks as though it is getting too thin. You will notice that the mixture seizes and thickens when you do this, but take care to be quite modest with the salt. Add a little pepper. When all the cream is incorporated you should have a mixture which is just about dropping consistency.

Pre-heat the oven to 200°C/400°F/gas mark 6. Two-thirds fill the baking dish with hot water and place this on the centre shelf. Two-thirds fill the moulds, stand them in the water bath in the oven and bake for 25 to 30 minutes.

Have heated plates at the ready if you want the creams to be at their lightest.

Quickly run a small palette knife round the side of the creams and turn them onto a dry napkin to absorb quickly any spare butter or moisture. Add the shrimps to the hot sauce. This dish does not like to be kept waiting and two hands are better than one at service time, but it is well worth the extra effort.

Chicken breasts can be served in this way, substituting the same weight of raw breast meat for the fish. In this case make a rich sauce from double-strength chicken stock instead of the water. Poach 60 g/2 oz of finely sliced white mushrooms in a tablespoon of sherry for a garnish.

SOLE WITH ORANGES

If you present this dish to any visitor it is sure to draw comment, as it is unusual for us here in England and virtually unknown outside out shores. This recipe, formerly disguised as 'Boil'd Soles', is one of my favourites.

6 large fillets Dover sole
Dry white wine to cover
Fresh thyme, basil or marjoram
15 g/½ oz butter
Salt and freshly ground black pepper

The Sauce
175 ml/⅓ pint single cream
½ tsp arrowroot
2 egg-yolks

The Garnish

Fresh orange segments
Anchovy fillets
Capers
Freshly chopped parsley

Butter the bottom of a shallow pan just large enough to contain the fillets when folded or rolled. Gently pat the fillets with a wetted rolling pin, season them and fold or roll each one up with a sprig of any one of the fresh herbs inside.

Just cover with the wine; cut a circle of paper large enough to fit the surface of the fish, butter it and lay it on top of the fillets to collect any albumin scum. Put a lid on the pan and poach the fish for 6 to 7 minutes, no more.

Remove the fillets to a clean dry tea-towel to drain and remove all traces of liquor, then arrange them in a long row on a narrow serving dish and keep them warm.

Strain the cooking liquor into a small pan and reduce to exactly 175 ml/⅓ pint. Work the arrowroot into the egg-yolks and add the cream. Stir this cream mixture into the hot liquor and simmer gently, stirring all the time, until it is the thickness of a light custard.

With the arrowroot in the sauce you will be able to bring it just to boiling point, but do not let it boil. Check the seasoning and pour the sauce over the waiting fillets.

Garnish with a cross of anchovy fillets and four orange segments to each piece of fish, sprinkle with capers and a little chopped parsley and serve immediately.

This dish can be served cold, in which case do not cover the fish until the coating sauce has cooled; if you have any bland mayonnaise to hand, add a tablespoon of it to the cold sauce to make it richer. Garnish as above.

TROUT WITH ALMONDS

Our two most famous universities have been responsible in no small way for the preservation of many English recipes, Oxford claiming the rights to this delicious way of preparing trout.

Trout with almonds is extremely popular in the Scandinavian countries where there is a wealth of this fish to be caught.

6 trout weighing at least 175 g/6 oz each
Flour
Oil for frying
125 g/4 oz flaked sweet almonds
60 g/2 oz butter
A squeeze of lemon juice
Salt and freshly ground white pepper

Clean and gut the trout, cutting off their heads behind the gills; take great care not to cut straight across behind the gills or you will lose a great deal of the flesh. There is an obvious diagonal path to follow if you look carefully.

Dredge each trout in flour and season lightly with salt and pepper. Heat some neutrally-flavoured oil in a heavy-bottomed frying pan. When there is a blue haze coming from the oil, gently lower the trout into the pan and fry for 3 or 4 minutes on each side, or until the trout give when firmly pressed with the finger in the thickest part. Remove the trout to a warm serving dish and pour the bulk of the oil into a storage jar, leaving only about 2 tablespoons. Put the butter into the pan over a medium heat, and when it is melted add the almonds. Lower the heat and, stirring all the time with a spatula, carefully let the almonds acquire a pale golden colour. Watch the process carefully at this stage, for almonds scorch very quickly and this would destroy their delicate flavour.

Add a squeeze of lemon juice and a light seasoning of salt and freshly ground white pepper and then pour the almonds and butter over the fried trout. Serve immediately.

ROAST LOBSTER

Roasting in what we now call a Dutch oven was equivalent to today's grilling. Lobsters were abundant and their price was reasonable according to the Star Chamber accounts.

Lobster is at its most delicious when served cold just after boiling, with a sauceboat of good fresh mayonnaise, but grilling or roasting can be attractive, as the flavour is so different. You will need to have live lobsters for this and each should weigh about two pounds.

2 live lobsters
Butter and oil
Lemon juice
Salt and freshly ground pepper
Butter – or Hollandaise Sauce (p. 225)
or Mayonnaise (p. 228)

Look at the black, top shell of the lobster and you will see, near the head, a distinct cross on the shell. Take a pointed heavy-bladed knife and pierce the lobster at the centre of this cross. This will kill it immediately. Bring the knife over, through and down the lobster shell, cutting first the head in half, then, reversing the knife, cutting the body similarly in half.

Remove the 'sack', which is the grey-green bit right at the top of the head. Don't remove any of the 'cream'. Remove also the alimentary canal, which is in the tail meat and looks like a dark tube running right into the tip of the tail.

Also remove the roe, which will appear as black slime before cooking, but which goes red after boiling or grilling. Brush the shell with oil and grill the halves of lobster, shell uppermost under a hot grill for up to 10 minutes. Avoid burning the shell; it will turn red as you apply heat.

Turn the halves, spread with butter and a little lemon juice, and grill the lobster for a further 5 to 10 minutes.

Serve immediately with melted butter or one of the sauces.

It is much better to boil the claws. This is quickly done by putting them into a pan of boiling water for 20 minutes. Crack the shells with a rolling pin, taking care not to crush them. They *can* be grilled, but for the inexperienced cook it is difficult to know just when they are cooked.

A 2-pound lobster should serve 2 people. Anything smaller should be served as 1 portion (2 halves).

―――――――――――

DUBLIN BAY PRAWNS IN CREAM

Often mistaken for scampi, these delicious shellfish used to be served in a very simple manner where they were steamed and then tossed in melted butter and a little lemon juice. I have enlarged on this and added cream, which slots them more easily into our present-day repertoire.

If you are unable to obtain real Dublin Bay prawns, then of course scampi with their nutty flavour will respond very well to this way of preparation.

1½ kg/3 lb Dublin Bay prawns
(or 750 g/1½ lb frozen scampi)
1 small shallot, chopped
60 g/2 oz butter
½ tsp flour
¼ litre/½ pint double cream
¼ litre/½ pint fish stock
Lemon juice
1 crushed clove garlic
Cayenne pepper
Salt and freshly ground white pepper
Long-grain rice to serve

Wash the prawns in cold water and then steam them for 30 minutes over fast-boiling water. Let them cool before shelling them: retain the heads and tail shells.

Melt the butter in a heavy-bottomed pan, add the shallot and let it cook until it is transparent but not coloured. Add the shells and toss them around in the pan. Sprinkle the flour over the shells, add the fish stock, garlic and cream and simmer all these together for 20 minutes.

Strain the sauce away from the shells into a smaller pan and reduce it by boiling rapidly until it is a good creamy consistency. Season with lemon juice and a little salt and pepper. Add the prawns and give them time to heat through, but do not boil them in the sauce or they will toughen.

Pour into a serving dish and sprinkle with a modicum of cayenne. Serve with boiled long-grain rice.

PRAWNS IN JELLY

This dish calls for fish aspic, made as for Chicken in Jelly (p. 114), substituting fish stock for the chicken stock.

Allow at least 30 g/1 oz shelled, cooked prawns
per person (see below)

1 cucumber
Fennel fronds, parsley or dill

The Stock

1½ litres/3 pints cold water
4 sole bones or the equivalent
of turbot bones
A sprig of parsley
Salt

The Aspic Jelly

45 g/1½ oz gelatine crystals
2 tbsps cold water
4 egg-whites
1 wine glass Mosel or other light white wine
For the garnish, see below

Clean the sole bones of all blood and cut off the heads. Cover with cold water, add the salt and parsley and bring to the boil, boiling for 20 minutes.

Strain the stock through a muslin bag into a clean pan and reduce it by boiling rapidly until you have approximately 1 litre/2 pints. Strain again; measure 1 litre/2 pints and put it aside to cool, then make the jelly, remembering to include the wine.

Fill individual glass dishes with the shelled prawns (or defrosted shrimps or prawns). The quantity will depend on the size of your dishes – and purse! Add tiny cubes of peeled and de-seeded cucumber and a sprinkling of fennel fronds, finely chopped. If you do not have fennel, either fresh dill or parsley will do.

When the fish aspic is cold, but not jellied, pour it over the prawns and put to set.

To Serve

Either present in the glass dishes in which you have made them – and do use glass so that the transparency of the jelly looks attractive and appetising – or unmould them and arrange attractively on a little finely shredded lettuce mixed with shredded raw fennel root and a light dressing of oil, lemon juice, a hint of sugar, salt and pepper.

MUSSEL STEW

Perhaps many will say that this is England's answer to the French Moules Marinières — so it should be, for England has some of the world's finest shellfish.

4 dozen fresh mussels
2 large leeks
1 crushed clove garlic
1 medium-sized onion
¼ head celery
100 g/3 oz butter
30 g/1 oz plain flour
¼ litre/½ pint dry white wine or dry cider
½ litre/1 pint single cream
3 tbsps freshly chopped parsley
Salt and freshly ground pepper

Wash the mussels well under plenty of cold running water. Pull the black thread away from the shells and discard it.

Melt 1 ounce of the butter in a large heavy-bottomed pan. Finely shred the leeks, onion and celery and add to the pan together with the garlic. Add the wine or cider.

Put in the washed mussels, cover with a lid and slowly shake the pan continuously over a low heat until all the shells have opened in the steam. Any closed shells must be thrown away. The whole process will take about 15 minutes.

With a strainer lift out the mussels into a sieve which should be covered with a clean cloth and then arranged over a pan of slowly boiling water to keep the mussels warm.

Melt the remaining butter in a small pan and stir in the flour. Pour the cream into the mussel stock and bring to the boil.

Whisk the butter and flour into the stock, bit by bit, letting the sauce thicken each time a little is added. Impatience here will only produce a lumpy sauce.

Season with salt and pepper, return the mussels to the sauce, bring to the boil and stir in plenty of freshly chopped parsley. Serve in soup plates.

Half the shells can be removed for ease of eating; each diner should be provided with a side plate for empty shells.

Poultry

CHICKEN WITH CELERY SAUCE

So many of our superlative dishes have no doubt been overlooked because they had such uninspiring names, and one can hardly be blamed for overlooking this dish which was called quite simply Boiled Chicken with Sellery. Only after having taken a closer look at the receipt does one realise that much is hidden in the recipe to bring it into the range of 'high cooking'.

A capon or roasting chicken weighing 1½–2 kg/3–4 lb
2 small heads celery
1 small onion
1 carrot
A sprig of parsley
A sprig of fresh rosemary
Salt and pepper
60 g/2 oz unsalted butter
30 g/1 oz flour
125 ml/¼ pint double cream
2 egg-yolks
Long-grain rice to serve

Choose a pan just big enough to contain the chicken. If the pan is too big, more water than is necessary will have to be used and this produces a much weaker sauce. Fit the chicken into the pan and cover to within 2 inches of the breast bone with boiling water. Cold water lets out too much of the juices of the chicken. The breasts will cook in the steam.

Wash the celery and cut in half lengthways. Now cut each half crossways into ⅛-inch strips. Wash again and add to the chicken.

Wash and peel the carrot and onion and add them whole, with the herbs tied in a piece of muslin.

Season lightly and then boil gently for 40 minutes, or until the thighs are cooked but still pale pink. (There is a tendency to cook chickens for too long and they end up dry.) Keep the surface of the liquid well skimmed.

When the chicken is cooked, remove it to a serving dish, take out the skewer and string and leave whole to be carved, cut into serving-sized joints, or strip all the meat off the bones. Whichever way you choose, arrange it in an oven-proof dish and keep it warm until the sauce is ready. Take out the onion, carrot and herbs and discard them.

In a second pan, melt the butter and stir in the flour. Strain 400 ml/¾ pint of the hot stock onto this and work into a smooth sauce with a whisk.

At this stage strain the celery from the rest of the stock and arrange it round the chicken, mopping up any surplus liquid with the corner of the clean linen cloth or tea-towel as it draws from the waiting dish.

Just before serving, mix the egg-yolks with the cream. Bring the sauce to the boil, remove from the heat and whisk it gently for a few seconds to let the heat get away from the bottom of the pan. Now briskly stir in the cream and yolks, check the seasoning and pour the sauce over the waiting chicken.

Serve immediately with boiled long-grain rice. There should be an abundance of celery in the sauce and this will serve as your vegetable.

This dish is very good cold, but will *not* re-heat as there are egg-yolks in the sauce.

CHICKEN IN JELLY

A roasting chicken weighing 2–2½ kg/4–5 lb
2 sticks celery
2 carrots
1 leek
1 small onion
Juice of half a lemon
A piece of lemon peel
A sprig of parsley
4 cloves
1 bay leaf
Salt

The Aspic Jelly

1 litre/2 pints ice-cold stock in which
the chicken has been cooked
45 g/1½ oz gelatine crystals
4 egg-whites
1 wine glass Mosel or other light white wine
2 tbsps cold water
2 tbsps freshly chopped parsley and tarragon

Choose a pan which will just take the chicken but with still enough room for 1½ litres/3 pints of water.

Rinse the chicken, wipe it well inside and out and put it into the pan. Wash and peel the celery, carrots and onion, cut them into rough chunks and pack round the chicken. Add lemon peel and juice and cover with 1½ litres/3 pints of cold water.

Split the leek open to the centre lengthways and wash thoroughly, tie the parsley, bay leaf and cloves inside it and add to the pan with a little salt — if a leek is not available, tie the herbs in a piece of muslin.

Bring the liquid to the boil and then simmer the chicken gently for 45 minutes to 1 hour. Remove the bird to a platter and put to cool but do not refrigerate. Strain the stock and check the seasoning at this stage; once the stock is clarified, nothing other than the wine should be added.

Cool the stock and refrigerate and, when it is ice cold, make the aspic jelly as follows.

Soften the gelatine in the cold water. Break up the egg-whites with a fork, but do not whisk them hard.

Put the egg-whites and stock into a pan and stir continually over a low heat until the stock begins to boil. At boiling point, add the softened gelatine and water and reduce the heat until the stock is *just* turning over. Stop stirring at this point and let the egg-whites do their job of clearing any dirt from the stock: this will take about 20 minutes.

As soon as the stock looks absolutely clear, turn the heat off but do not rush to strain the aspic; allow it to cool somewhat, when the scum will form a more solid mass and will be less likely to break up.

Upturn a stool and arrange a jelly bag from the legs. Stand a clean glass bowl underneath to receive the clarified liquid. Carefully pour the jelly through the bag or a double thickness of dry clean tea-towel – which is not impregnated with washing powder! Do not press the liquid through the bag or cloth.

When the jelly is cool, but not set, add the wine.

Take all the skin, fat and gristle off the chicken and take out the bones. Cut the meat into diagonal strips, or leave in attractive large pieces. Arrange these in a mould or glass bowl.

As soon as the aspic starts to thicken, stir in the chopped herbs, pour over the chicken and put to set.

CHICKEN STUFFED WITH SAFFRON RICE

Perhaps because of its cost, saffron is rarely used today, but a little goes a long way, and the aroma is so exotic that it makes the relatively small extra cost well worthwhile in this lovely old English receipt. Saffron usually comes in tiny thimbles and one of these will be sufficient for both stuffing and sauce.

Ideally this dish should be made with a boned chicken (p. 123), but you may feel this is a labour and your poulterer may not be co-operative enough to do it for you.

A roasting chicken weighing 1½ kg/3 lb
60 g/2 oz butter
½ tsp powdered rosemary
3 tbsps olive oil
Salt and freshly ground black pepper

The Stuffng

6 tbsps cooked long-grain rice
1 small onion
30 g/1 oz butter
1 tbsp chopped chives or the
pale green part of spring onions
2 tbsps thick cream
1 crushed clove garlic
½ tsp powdered rosemary
¼ tsp powdered saffron
Salt and freshly ground black pepper

The Sauce

15 g/½ oz plain flour
¼ litre/½ pint chicken stock
125 ml/¼ pint thick cream
1 good glass sherry
¼ tsp powdered saffron
¼ tsp powdered rosemary
Salt and freshly ground pepper

The Stuffing

Finely chop the onion. Melt the butter in a small pan and fry the onion until it is a pale golden colour. Add the garlic but do not fry it. Remove the pan from the heat.

Stir in the cooked rice and chives. Sprinkle over the rosemary and the saffron and stir in well until the colour starts to draw. Bind with the cream and season well.

Fill the bird with this stuffing.

Roasting

Blend half a teaspoon of rosemary and some salt and pepper into the butter. Rub this mixture all over the skin of the chicken and stand the bird on a rack in a roasting tin.

Pour over the olive oil, put a piece of foil over the breasts to prevent scorching and roast at 220°C/425°F/gas mark 7 for 40 minutes or until the thighs are tender but not over-cooked. Baste frequently during the roasting time. Remove the chicken to a warm serving dish, removing any strings, wing tips, etc. for easy carving.

The Sauce

To make the sauce, transfer the fats from the roasting tin to a small pan, sprinkle in the flour, add the chicken stock and bring the sauce to the boil. Add the herbs, spices, salt, pepper and sherry and cook for a few minutes.

Strain the sauce into a clean pan, add the cream, then bring the sauce to the boil and serve, either poured over the whole chicken or in a separate sauceboat.

There is enough rice in the stuffing for 4 people. Extra rice can be passed if more is preferred.

CHICKEN AND TRIPE RAGOO

750 g/1½ lb honeycomb tripe
A jointed roasting chicken weighing 1¼ kg/2½ lb
2 large onions
6 large tomatoes
2 crushed cloves garlic
4 medium-sized carrots
2 teacups water
3 teacups dry white wine
60 g/2 oz butter
½ tsp ground mace
1 level tsp thyme
1 tsp cornflour
2 tbsps single cream or top of the milk
Salt and freshly ground white pepper
3 tbsps freshly chopped chives and parsley to garnish

Wash and dry the tripe and cut it into 2-inch squares. Clean, peel and slice all the vegetables; de-seed and skin the tomatoes.

Melt half of the butter in a heavy-bottomed pan. Fry the vegetables until they are golden brown. Add the garlic and other seasonings and transfer all the contents of this pan to an oven-proof casserole, which should be of a size just large enough to contain all the ingredients with the liquid just covering them.

Quickly brown the chicken pieces in the remaining butter on all sides and put them, together with the squares of tripe, into the casserole. Cover with the wine and water and season lightly.

Make a little flour and water paste and seal the lid of the casserole. Cook in a pre-heated oven at 170°C/325°F/gas mark 3 for 3 hours.

Remove the chicken pieces, strip off the skin and take out the bones. Cut the meat into strips and return to the casserole.

Work the cream into the cornflour and stir this into the sauce; return the dish to the oven for a further 15 to 20 minutes.

Sprinkle liberally with freshly chopped chives and parsley just before serving.

CHICKEN, VEAL AND HAM PIE

A good raised pie is something which can be safely bought in our pork butchers, but it is a treat to have a home-made one now and again.

The Filling

4 full gammon rashers cut ⅓ inch thick
A roasting chicken weighing 1½ kg/3 lb
500 g/1 lb leg veal
1 tsp rubbed sage or 1 tbsp chopped chives
1 sherry glass Madeira or brandy
30 g/1 oz butter
Salt and freshly ground black pepper
A little lemon juice
Gelatine

Hot Water Pastry

(to line a mould or tin 8 inches in diameter, 4 inches deep)
625 g/1¼ lb plain flour
250 g/8 oz lard
175 ml/⅓ pint water
½ tsp salt
¼ tsp icing sugar
¼ tsp ground mace
1 egg-yolk
A little cream or top of the milk

The Filling

Skin and strip all the meat off the chicken, leaving the breasts whole. Put the skin and bones into a pan, cover with cold water and simmer for 30 minutes – this stock is for the jelly.

Mince together the meat from the chicken legs with one of the rashers of ham and half a pound of the veal. Season this with a little sage, salt and pepper and add the brandy. Work this into a forcemeat.

With a thin-bladed, very sharp knife, cut the chicken breasts into long diagonal slices and cut the veal in a similar way. (You will find this easy to do if you cut on a diagonal plane.)

The Pastry

Sieve all the dry ingredients together and put them into a large bowl, making a well in the centre. Melt the lard in the water and bring to the boil. Pour all the liquid, at one fell swoop, into the well made in the flour, then quickly and deftly work this into a soft dough.

Do not over-knead this dough or it will become like elastic and your pastry will be tough, thoughbeit easier to manage! The dough should be warm and soft enough to work with, yet not slide down the sides of the mould or tin. Cut off a third of the dough and put it on one side to make a lid for the pie.

Butter the tin or mould thoroughly. Lightly roll the remaining dough into a circle large enough to fit into the bottom of the tin. You should by now be able to draw the dough up the sides of the tin (as you would do if you were making a somewhat heavier crust and using the technique of moulding outside a jar or block). Pressing and pulling very gently, bring the dough up the sides, making sure there are no cracks. With the forefinger bent, ensure that there is no unnecessary thickness at the angle of the tin where the sides join the base. Continue pressing the dough away and up the sides of the tin, trimming off any surplus at the top. With practice you will arrive at a point where you get a thin crust which is still strong enough to support the filling. Seal any cracks that may appear with bits of left-over pastry.

You may well have quite a bit of pastry left, but this will depend on your dexterity at the lining stage. If you haven't *enough* pastry, then the crust is going to be a mighty thick one! But it won't matter that much and shouldn't deter you from carrying on.

Spread a thin layer of the forcemeat into your pastry-lined mould, pressing this well into the corners. Now cover this with a layer of the ham slices and sprinkle with a modicum of sage or chives. Now cover with second layer of the forcemeat, then some chicken slices, and continue like this until you have used everything up, seasoning as you go along with just a little salt and pepper and sprinkling with sage or chives. Finish with a layer of forcemeat on the top (it is easy to stretch the forcemeat if you work with wet fingers), then dot the top with the ounce of butter.

Roll the lid to fit, wet the edges and fix this. (Depending upon your dexterity at the lining stage and the actual size of mould, the lid may well sit an inch or so inside the pie.)

Cut away any excess pastry and pinch the two layers of pastry together with the finger and thumb. Cut a small hole in the centre of the lid and fit a tiny funnel of foil or grease-proof paper to prevent the hole closing during baking time and to let the steam out. Decorate the top with pastry leaves.

Stand the pie on a baking sheet, lay a piece of foil loosely across the top to prevent undue scorching and bake at 170°C/325°F/gas mark 3 for 2 hours. Remove the pie from the oven and let it cool for half an hour. Take it out of the tin very carefully and stand it on the baking sheet.

Mix the yolk of an egg with a little top of the milk or a spoonful of cream and brush the pie all over with this. Increase the oven heat to 190°C/375°F/gas mark 5 and return the pie to the oven for 15 minutes until it is an appetising golden brown.

Make ½ litre/1 pint of jelly with the strained chicken stock, using the normal quantities of gelatine to set ½ litre/1 pint. Add a little lemon juice.

When the pie is cold and the jelly quite cool but not set, remove the foil funnel and, using a kitchen funnel, fill the pie slowly with the jelly, allowing time for it to work its way to the bottom. Keep in a cool place until the jelly is quite set.

FESTIVAL CHICKEN

No matter what form a festival takes, most people have the urge to do something about it, even if it only means putting on a dinner jacket for a concert, colouring an egg for Easter or just baking a cake — some little move to remind us that it isn't just an ordinary day.

A few years ago the organisers of the Harrogate Festival asked me to create a dish in honour of their now annual event. In this way Festival Chicken was born; in fact there was a competition to name this dish, the winning title being Chicken Fiesta. I tend to favour the more English name, as I was very much influenced in my thinking by an old English dish, Hindlewakes, which was based on chicken, prunes, herbs, brown sugar and spices.

The apricot was growing in my part of Yorkshire in the days of Shakespeare, and probably long before that, and it is for this reason that I chose to use apricots in the dish.

For clarity, I have shown the ingredients and method for the three stages quite separately.

First Stage

A boned-out roasting chicken weighing 2 kg/4 lb (see Note)
750 g/1½ lb fresh apricots
60 ml/2 fl oz Brontë liqueur or brandy
100 g/3 oz soft brown sugar
½ tsp mild curry powder
1 finely chopped clove garlic
½ tsp powdered rosemary
60 g/2 oz butter

Second Stage

1 medium-sized onion
250 g/½ lb button mushrooms
6 tomatoes
1 dessertspoon curry powder
60 ml/2 fl oz Brontë liqueur or brandy
2 tbsps olive oil
Salt and freshly ground black pepper

Third Stage

¼ litre/½ pint double cream
A little salt, sugar and lemon juice
Additional apricots to garnish (optional)
Buttered pasta or long-grain rice to serve

First Stage

Halve and stone the apricots, sprinkle them with the liqueur or brandy, curry powder and sugar and leave to soak for 3 to 4 hours.

Make a paste with the butter, rosemary and garlic. Rub half this over the inside of the boned chicken. Pile the marinated apricots onto the spread-out chicken, re-shape the bird and sew up the openings with linen thread. Rub the remaining savoury butter over the outside skin of the chicken.

Second Stage

Roughly chop the onions and mushrooms. Skin and de-seed the tomatoes.

Heat the oil in a frying pan and fry the onions until they are just golden brown; add the mushrooms and fry them for a minute or so.

Butter an oven-proof casserole just large enough to contain the chicken. Transfer the fried vegetables to make a cushion in the bottom of the casserole, add the tomatoes, sprinkle with the curry powder and season lightly.

Pour over the liqueur or brandy and sit the stuffed chicken on top of the vegetables. Cover with a lid and roast in a pre-heated oven at 230°C/450°F/gas mark 8 for 45 minutes or until the chicken is just tender.

Third Stage

Place the chicken on a heated serving dish and remove the linen thread. Transfer the remaining contents of the casserole to a pan and boil these with the thick cream. Continue to boil until the sauce looks unctuous – if there is any oiling, add a little water and stir in well.

Strain the sauce and check the seasoning, adding a little salt, sugar and lemon juice to suit your palate. Pour the hot sauce over the waiting chicken, garnish if you wish with extra apricot halves and serve with buttered pasta or long-grain rice which has had a suspicion of curry powder and butter stirred into it.

This dish can be made with an unboned chicken, but the flavour is somewhat different.

Note: If you cannot get your poulterer to bone out the chicken for you, it is not a marathon job to tackle and it will open up new horizons for you.

First of all, chop off the wings up to the joint nearest the body. Chop off the drumsticks to a point at least 2 inches above the yellow anklet.

Now you will need a very sharp knife which is thin-spined and has a good point. Turn the bird on its back and cut right down the length of the backbone. Then start calmly and carefully cutting the skin and flesh away from any bones that it adheres to, literally as you come to them.

When you come to a leg, start cutting round the inside of the bone at the top end which is nearest to you and gradually turn the leg inside out as you cut the meat away – as though you were rolling down a stocking! Don't worry if the thing looks somewhat ragged at your first attempts, it doesn't matter and practice makes perfect. Turn what will now be a rather flabby square foot of skin and flesh right side out again and arrange it in some sort of order to resemble the form of the original chicken.

There is a more complicated way of starting at the neck, using the same stocking rolling technique, but this is best left to the professionals and is only needed when you are going to re-form a bird in its original shape.

GREEN FRICASSEE OF CHICKEN

I think this is one of the most delicious and most unusual dishes to come out of the English repertoire. The sauce is beautifully rich and the wine-flavoured chicken is perfect with its partner of green leaf spinach.

A jointed roasting chicken weighing 1½ kg/3 lb
Seasoned flour
100 g/3 oz butter or more
¾ bottle dry Rhine wine
3 egg-yolks
125 ml/¼ pint double cream
2 tbsps freshly picked and finely chopped parsley
1 kg/2 lb leaf spinach (before cooking)
Salt
¼ tsp nutmeg or powdered mace
Buttered green pasta to serve

Thoroughly pick and wash the spinach in an abundance of water, allowing time for the grit to fall to the bottom of the sink.

Put a little water in a pan and press in all the spinach, salt it lightly, cover with a tight-fitting lid and cook for 5 to 10 minutes. Drain well and run plenty of cold water through it. Leave the spinach in a sieve with a plate over it and a weight on top to press out any surplus liquid.

When the spinach has completely drained, arrange it in a mounded bed at the bottom of a serving dish large enough to take the chicken pieces. Dot with 1 ounce of the butter, cover with foil and put into the refrigerator until needed. (This operation can be done a day in advance.)

Put the serving-sized chicken pieces into a large plastic bag with the seasoned flour and shake well until each piece is completely coated.

Melt at least 2 ounces of butter in a heavy-bottomed frying pan until it foams and carefully fry the chicken joints until they are golden brown on all sides. Cover the pieces with the wine, put a lid on the pan and gently simmer the chicken until it is tender.

The breasts will obviously be ready before the thighs, so remove these and keep them warm, covering them so that they do not dry up. When the thighs are tender, take them out and arrange all the pieces on top of the spinach.

Re-cover the dish with foil and put it to warm through for 20 minutes in an oven pre-heated to 170°C/325°F/gas mark 3.

Strain the wine stock, which will be slightly thickened from the flour on the chicken pieces, into another smaller pan and bring to the boil just before you are ready to serve the dish.

Beat the egg-yolks and add the cream. Remove the pan from the heat and whisk in this liaison of cream and yolks. If the sauce does not thicken immediately, return the pan to a *very* low heat and whisk gently until it is the consistency of a real custard sauce. Add the parsley and check the seasoning.

Sprinkle a little more mace or nutmeg over the waiting chicken pieces and then coat with the bright green-yellow sauce.

Serve with buttered green pasta.

HINDLE WAKES

It is not so many lifetimes ago that the North would have been in a ferment at holiday times, as their Wakes Weeks began. In the days when the word 'festival' meant more to the religious than to the artistic members of the community, a 'wake' or 'watch' was the custom in many churches on the eve of a great festival.

'Hen de la Wake' was made frequently in both Yorkshire and Lancashire, ready to sustain those who had to keep watch, night-long, in the local church. Sometimes beer would be used, sometimes cider and sometimes a little wine vinegar.

Prunes, lemons and herbs were an essential part of this Wakes Week chicken. Usually these went into a form of stuffing which I feel gives a flavour none too welcome on the palates of today. I make mine in a rather different way (whilst still retaining the traditional ingredients), and find that it is very acceptable to guests who have tried it.

A roasting chicken weighing 2½ kg/5 lb
500 g/1 lb very large prunes
60 g/2 oz breadcrumbs
100 g/3 oz butter (30 g/1 oz cold and hard)
1 tbsp chopped fresh basil
Juice and grated rind of 2 lemons
1 large carrot
2 small onions
45 g/1½ oz flour
125 ml/¼ pint double cream
1 teacup red wine vinegar
Strong hot tea
Salt and freshly ground pepper
Watercress and extra lemon for garnish

Soak the prunes overnight in the hot tea. Carefully slit them and take out the stones.

Finely chop one of the onions and fry it in a little butter. Add the breadcrumbs, herbs and seasoning and the juice and rind of 1 lemon. Grate the ounce of hard butter on the coarse side of the grater and add this.

Stuff the pitted prunes with the mixture, arrange in a buttered baking dish and cover with foil. Bake at 180°C/350°F/gas mark 4 for 25 minutes. Put to cool and leave on one side to garnish the finished dish.

Fit the trussed bird into a pot just large enough to contain it. Add the vinegar, carrot, onion, salt and pepper and just enough water to cover the thighs of the bird well. (The breasts will cook in the steam.) Cover with a tight-fitting lid and cook gently on top of the stove for about 45 minutes, or until the thighs are tender. Leave to cool for 1 hour in the cooking liquor.

Remove the bird, skin it and cut into nice serving portions, taking out any bones. Arrange the pieces on a dish. Cover with foil so that the meat doesn't dry up, but let it get quite cold. Try not to refrigerate unless absolutely necessary. Skim as much fat as possible from the liquor.

Now make the sauce. Melt the remaining butter in a pan, stir in the flour and gradually work in ½ litre/1 pint of the strained cooking liquor. Cook the sauce for 10 minutes, stirring all the time to prevent lumping and burning.

Strain the sauce into a clean basin and check the seasoning, adding the juice and rind of the second lemon and more salt and pepper if necessary. Cover with oiled paper cut to fit the surface of the sauce and cool completely.

Half-whip the cream and fold into the cold sauce, incorporating it thoroughly. Coat each piece of chicken with this sauce.

Garnish with the stuffed prunes, lemon segments and bunches of watercress.

LEMON STUFFED CHICKEN

A boned-out roasting chicken weighing 1½ kg/3 lb
(see Note on p.123)
375 g/12 oz demi-sel cheese
Grated rind of 1 lemon
1 tbsp chopped chives
60 g/2 oz butter
Salt and freshly ground white pepper

The Sauce

30g/1 oz plain flour
1 stock cube
Juice and rind of 1 lemon
125 ml/¼ pint water
¼ litre/½ pint double cream
Salt and freshly ground white pepper

Mix the cheese with the lemon rind and chives and season with salt and pepper. Lay your boned chicken flat on a board and spread the cheese mixture over this. Roll up the chicken, folding the side bits in as you go along. Make a short fat roll and tie it at 2-inch intervals with linen thread, or make a series of slip knots along its length. Rub the skin all over with the softened butter and lightly season the outside.

Stand the stuffed chicken on a rack in a roasting pan and roast at

220°C/425°F/gas mark 7 for 45 minutes, basting well every 10 minutes. Remove the binding thread and put the chicken onto a serving dish to keep hot whilst you make the sauce.

Work the flour into the juices in the pan and then work in the stock cube. Add the water and bring the sauce to the boil. Add the lemon rind and juice and the cream and cook for a few seconds.

Season with salt and pepper and strain over the waiting chicken.

ROAST DUCKLING

Whilst the now traditional way of serving duck with sage and onion stuffing is rather rigidly established, there were days when many realised that this herb can be quite forceful and preferred their ducks to be dressed with milder things such as gooseberries, apples and red wine, or a delicious combination of sorrel, spinach and gooseberries which they aptly called green sauce.

I prefer not to stuff ducklings at all and unashamedly say that I like roast duckling to be served straight from the oven, all crisp-skinned and well roasted, but not dried out!

Any form of accompaniment I like to serve separately. There is no reason why we shouldn't use the old English way of serving braised red cabbage — which isn't far removed from the Continental method — and marry this with our ducks as the Danes do, or even serve an apple and nut stuffing as they also do, for the apple often appeared on the English table with a duckling and not always as apple sauce.

If you still prefer the established stuffing, in spite of the fact that it clutters up the service, bringing things to a virtual halt when an expert carver is not to hand, then try using a little lemon-thyme or freshly picked marjoram, which is so much milder than sage. Use dried sage — if you must — very sparingly.

A duckling weighing no more than 2–2½ kg/4–5 lb

Savoury Butter
60 g/2 oz butter
1 tsp salt
½ tsp black pepper
½ crushed clove garlic
Flavourings (see below)

Clip off the wing tips up to the first joint. Scrape away any yellow scaling around the drumsticks. Cut away any excess fat at the rear-end of the bird.

Now make the savoury butter. Make the butter into a paste with the salt, black pepper and garlic. Add to this any *one* of the following flavourings: 2 teaspoons grated orange rind, lemon rind, lemon-thyme or fresh chopped sage; ½ teaspoon powdered rosemary or grated nutmeg; 2 tablespoons brandy.

Rub a little of this paste well into the breast skin of the bird and spread the rest inside the cavity.

Stand the bird on a rack in a roasting tin and roast at 200°C/400°F/gas mark 6 for half an hour. Lower the temperature one mark and finish roasting. The bird is cooked when the juices no longer run pink when it is pierced with a roasting fork under the leg and held up to let the juice run out. If you prefer your duckling to be somewhat pink, then test its cooked condition by gently pulling the leg away from the body: if the meat between the legs looks very bloody – and the leg won't give very easily in this case anyway – then it requires more roasting, but if the leg gives nicely and the meat looks a pale pink and is still juicy, but not bloody, then all is well. The leg of a well roast duck will be crisp and come away immediately any pressure is applied. Another way of testing is to press the leg meat between the finger and thumb and judge by the resilience or otherwise, but be sure to press in the thick part of the flesh.

It is quite difficult for a non-professional to tell when a duckling is roasted to his or her liking – it requires a deal of experience which is not readily available when duckling isn't eaten very often, but the above hints should help.

Meat

ALAMODE BEEF

This is one of the dishes which even the French have simplified over the years. Caen is the city where Boeuf à la Mode is possibly best known and I think there can be little doubt that it was from this region that our own recipe came; though the Tudors and Hanoverian cooks themselves have varying methods of preparing beef in this way, as well they ought for that is exactly the licence the name of the dish gives. In Caen it is usually served cold, with the meat and vegetables set in the good strong jelly from the gelatine in the knuckle and calf's foot.

2½ kg/5 lb boned and rolled sirloin
(or a cheaper cut if you choose)
1 gammon rasher
1 calf's foot chopped into 2 or 3 pieces
1 knuckle veal chopped into 2 or 3 pieces
½ bottle dry white wine
½ tsp nutmeg
4 medium-sized carrots
4 onions
250 g/½ lb button mushrooms
½ head celery
8 cloves
Oil for frying
Sprigs of thyme, marjoram and parsley
Salt and freshly ground pepper

Heat a little oil in a heavy frying pan and, when it is smoking hot, brown the sirloin on all sides. (If this is done properly, there will be a deal of smoke and muck spluttering and splashing!) Brown the gammon rasher on both sides.

Select an oven-proof dish just large enough to contain the sirloin with the knuckle and calf's foot tucked round it.

Put the gammon rasher in the bottom of the pot, stand the sirloin on top of it and tuck the knuckle and the foot round it. Pour the wine over the beef and add the seasoning and herbs. Cover with a lid and cook for 2 hours at 140°C/275°F/gas mark 2.

Remove the sprigs of herbs; wash and peel the vegetables and chop them into ½-inch dice, wipe and quarter the mushrooms and add everything to the pot. Return it to the oven and continue cooking for a further 2 hours.

Take out the meat, remove the string and place it in a warm serving dish, discarding the knuckle and foot. Lift out all the vegetables with a strainer and arrange them attractively in the dish. Let the liquor stand for 10 minutes, then skim off all the fat from the surface. Bring this gravy back to the boil and pour over the meat.

BEEF IN BEER

It is often forgotten that, as a beer-drinking country, we naturally used this in our cooking. Today cider is still used in the cider-producing areas, but beer rarely appears other than in the mixing of Christmas pudding, though some people still use it in their batter mixing.

1 kg/2 lb rump steak
2 onions
125 g/4 oz field mushrooms
2 crushed cloves garlic
2 rashers bacon
1 bay leaf
30 g/1 oz butter
30 g/1 oz flour
½ litre/1 pint strong ale
Salt and freshly ground black pepper
1 tbsp red wine vinegar

Trim the meat of all fat and cut it into 1-inch cubes. Cut the bacon into small dice. Slice the onions.

Melt the butter in a large frying pan, brown the cubes of meat and turn these into an oven-proof casserole. Fry the bacon until it is crisp, add the onions and let them acquire a golden colour. Slice and lightly fry the mushrooms; add them to the meat.

Sprinkle the flour over the contents of the casserole, add the seasonings, stir everything together well and cover with the beer. Cook in the oven at 170°C/325°F/gas mark 3 for 2 hours.

Just before serving, check the seasoning and stir in the wine vinegar.

BEEF AND HAM MOULD

Many families have their own special version of this way of cooking beef and ham. In the days when those kind Scots made their marmalade in nice stone jars and these were used as moulds we began to call this dish meat roll, but it matters not what shape it is. What I do think is essential is that it should be steamed and not baked. This way it retains its moist texture and is succulent to eat.

500 g/1 lb rump or best stewing steak
375 g/¾ lb lean raw ham
30 g/1 oz white breadcrumbs (from a day-old loaf)
1 large egg
1 dessertspoon chopped chives
Salt and freshly ground black pepper or nutmeg (not both)

Trim the two meats of all fat, sinew, etc. Mince them together through the coarse blade of a mincer.

Beat the egg and mix all the ingredients together. Season to taste. Butter a basin, mould, jar or what you will and pack the mixture into this. Cover with buttered foil.

Arrange the mould in a lidded pan of boiling water which comes two-thirds of the way up the sides, or use a steamer. Bring the water to the boil and then reduce the temperature until it is simmering well. Cook the mould like this for 2 hours. Leave to cool before refrigerating. Turn out and cut into thin slices.

Note: Try adding two dozen olives stuffed with almonds, anchovies or pimento. They look attractive and are a delicious combination.

BEEF OLIVES

First Stage

8 thin slices topside beef
100 g/3 oz fresh white breadcrumbs
60 g/2 oz minced cooked ham
1 tsp grated lemon rind
60 g/2 oz cold hard butter
1 egg
1 tbsp thin cream or top of the milk
Salt and freshly ground pepper

Second Stage

Oil for frying
1 medium-sized chopped onion
1 carrot, peeled and diced
125 g/4 oz mushrooms, wiped and quartered
½ tsp rubbed thyme

1 crushed clove garlic
30 g/1 oz butter
30 g/1 oz flour
¼ litre/½ pint red wine
¼ litre/½ pint stock
1 wine glass port
Salt and freshly ground black pepper
1 tbsp freshly chopped parsley or other herbs

First Stage

Flatten the slices of meat with a wetted rolling pin to break down the tissue. Trim these of all fat and cut them into pieces of roughly the same size and shape.

Make up a forcemeat from the other ingredients, grating the butter on the coarse side of a grater. Bind with the eggs and cream.

Spread this mixture onto the slices of beef and fold in half an inch at each side before rolling into parcels. Tie across and round with strong linen thread.

Second Stage

Have ready a suitable oven-proof casserole which will just hold the beef olives in one layer.

Heat some oil to smoking point in a heavy frying pan, brown the olives on all sides and transfer them to the casserole; add the butter to the frying pan and brown the onion and carrot, stirring all the time to ensure good even colouring.

Sprinkle with the flour and let this brown slowly over a very low heat. Add the mushrooms, garlic and thyme; keep stirring whilst you add the red wine, incorporating the brown crust which will have formed on the bottom of the pan. Add the stock and bring the sauce to the boil; season well and pour the entire contents of the pan over the waiting olives.

Cover with a lid or foil and cook in the oven at 170°C/325°F/gas mark 3 for 1½ hours. Before serving, remove the olives to a plate and take off the strings.

Skim the sauce of any surplus fat and stir in the port. Transfer the sauce to a pan and boil it rapidly for a few minutes until it looks 'brilliant' and of a good consistency.

Clean the sides of the casserole, return the olives, pour over the sauce, sprinkle liberally with any freshly chopped herbs and serve.

DOBE OF BEEF (DOB'D BEEF)

This manner of cooking beef came to us via the French and the Flemish well over three hundred years ago. There are many different ways of treating this and, as might be expected in England, either port or beer was the principal liquor used in its preparation.

I have always based my recipe on that of Anne Blencowe, who uses port for the marinade — it is very rich and extremely good. It is interesting to note that seventeenth-century Mrs Blencowe uses potatoes as a garnish for her 'dobe', although these were probably sweet potatoes. It is, however, an early mention of the potato used in a savoury dish.

1 kg/2 lb best rump steak
125 g/4 oz fat pork or bacon
2 carrots
2 onions
2 crushed cloves garlic
½ stick celery
½ tsp chopped thyme
½ tsp chopped marjoram
6 cloves
60 g/2 oz butter
½ litre/1 pint port or beer
30 g/1 oz flour
1 tsp grated orange rind
¼ litre/½ pint strong stock
Salt and freshly ground black pepper

The Garnish

125 g/4 oz button mushrooms
8 artichoke bottoms (tinned)
4 cooked new potatoes
1 cooked carrot
1 tbsp freshly chopped parsley
60 g/2 oz butter
Lemon segments

Trim the meat of skin and fat and cut into 1-inch cubes. Cut the bacon or pork into ¼-inch dice. Cut all the vegetables into ½-inch dice. Put the meat and vegetables, together with the garlic, into a dish and cover with the port.

Sprinkle with the freshly chopped herbs; if dried herbs are used, these should be tied in a bag and put into the dobe with the vegetables. Leave the meat to marinate for 4 or 5 hours, or overnight.

Drain the meat cubes and the vegetables, retaining the liquor. Melt the butter in a heavy-bottomed pan and, when it has acquired a nice nutty flavour, brown the bacon in it, add the meat cubes and fry at a high temperature until the meat is sealed. This will be best done if you fry a little at a time.

Add the vegetables and the dried herbs if these are being used. Sprinkle with the flour, stir in well and cover with the marinade and the stock. Lightly salt and pepper, remembering that the sauce will be well reduced and therefore strong.

Transfer all the contents of the pan to an earthenware casserole and cover tightly, sealing the lid with a flour and water paste. Cook in the oven at 180°C/350°F/gas mark 4 for 5 hours.

The finished dish should be a strongly flavoured, cohered mass.

The Garnish

Cut and dice all the vegetables and toss them in the butter until they are thoroughly heated through. Season lightly. Drain and arrange attractively on top of the dobe just before serving.

Sprinkle with freshly chopped parsley and serve with the lemon segments in a side dish.

Plain riced potatoes are perfect with a rich dobe – a potato ricer is a piece of equipment well worth having.

FILLET STEAKS WITH STILTON CHEESE

6 fillet steaks
100 g/3 oz butter
Oil for frying
100 g/3 oz blue Stilton
1 tsp freshly chopped chives
½ crushed clove garlic
1 tbsp port
Watercress
Salt and freshly ground black pepper

Make the Stilton butter first by blending the cheese and butter together and pressing through a hair sieve. Beat in the port. Season well with chives and a little garlic, form into a roll about an inch in diameter, wrap in wet grease-proof paper or foil and chill.

Trim the steaks of all fat and skin; beat them gently with a wetted rolling pin without breaking the meat; re-form into rounds.

Heat the oil in a heavy-bottomed frying pan until it is smoking. Seal and brown the steaks quickly on both sides and then continue to cook them until they are as you would like – rare, medium or well done. Season lightly with salt and freshly ground black pepper, *after* they are fried, as salt draws the blood and impedes the sealing process.

Arrange the steaks on a heated serving dish, cut discs of the Stilton butter and set a piece on top of each steak; place bouquets of washed and lightly salted watercress at the side of each steak.

STUFFED FILLET STEAKS

To arrive at this ostentatious way of serving a steak, I used an idea of Harriet de Salis's from one of her Victorian recipe booklets and combined it with the techniques of crumbing meat.

6 well trimmed fillet steaks
125 g/4 oz button mushrooms
30 g/1 oz butter
15 g/½ oz flour
1 tbsp dry sherry
2 tbsps thick cream
1 tsp made-up English mustard
Salt and freshly ground black pepper

The Coating

1 beaten egg
4 tbsps fresh white breadcrumbs mixed with
2 tbsps freshly grated Parmesan cheese
Oil for frying
Endive, lettuce hearts and watercress to garnish

Insert the sharp point of a knife into the side of each fillet, making a slit large enough for you to manoeuvre the knife inside without enlarging the original aperture.

Prepare the stuffing as follows. Finely chop the mushrooms. Melt the butter in a small pan and fry the mushrooms for a few minutes. Work in the flour and seasonings, add the sherry and work the mixture to a smooth paste, adding the cream a little at a time. Blend in the mustard and let this stuffing cool completely. When it is cold, fill the cavities in the steaks, using a teaspoon to help you do this.

Mix together the crumbs and Parmesan and then dip each steak into the beaten egg and then into this mixture, pressing the crumbs well in.

Heat half an inch of oil in a heavy-bottomed frying pan and, when it is just smoking, fry the stuffed fillets until they are crisp and golden brown, turning them frequently.

Drain the fillets well on crumpled kitchen paper and garnish with crisp curly endive, quartered lettuce hearts and watercress.

There is no need for any further sauce with this dish as the filling acts in this capacity.

STUFFED AND SPICED ROUND (OR BRISKET) OF BEEF

There is no question that a good brisket of beef makes a worthy addition to any cold table, but it looks pretty pale when compared with this old English way of dealing with it.

For the picnic-minded this spiced meat is a boon. It also serves as a very unusual first course at our twentieth-century table, cut into wafer-thin slices and eaten just with a little apple jelly.

A round of beef or brisket weighing 1–1½ kg/2–3 lb
4 calf's kidneys
125 g/4 oz pork fat
A bunch of very fresh parsley
2 sprigs of mint
1 tsp green peppercorns
1 tsp powdered mace
1 dessertspoon sea salt

1 tsp freshly ground black pepper
1 dessertspoon brown sugar
1 carrot
1 onion
Cider

Make deep incisions into the piece of meat at 1-inch intervals with a small sharp pointed knife. Ensure that the knife goes right through to the bottom.

Wash and pick the parsley but do not chop it, likewise the mint leaves.

Skin and trim the kidneys and cut in half lengthways and cut the pork fat into ¼-inch sticks.

Open each cavity with the knife and fill each one with either kidney, fat or plenty of parsley. Push the kidney well down into the cavity and press a stick of pork fat down the side of it. Push a few peppercorns in with the parsley.

The mint leaves will slot nicely between the outside fat and the meat. Now rub the outside with salt, pepper, mace and sugar and fit it into an oven-proof casserole just large enough to contain it.

Peel the onion and carrot and cut each into 1-inch pieces. Pack the vegetables around the meat and add cider up to about the half-way mark.

Cover with a lid and cook in the oven at 190°C/375°F/gas mark 5 for the first hour and then reduce the temperature to 180°C/350°F/gas mark 4 for a further half hour.

Let the meat cool in the liquid before taking out and cooling completely. If you have to store this in your refrigerator, remember to wrap it in clean foil to ensure that the meat doesn't dry out.

The first eating should be unrefrigerated. Cut off the first slice before serving, to reveal the green-white-beige pattern of the parsley, fat and kidney.

STEAK AND KIDNEY PUDDING

You may well ask how this belly-filler can possibly appear under the title of 'fine'. Yet if the crust is made well and with today's products and techniques, there is little reason to condemn as stodge what is really a magnificent dish.

Be inventive when it comes to the crust, giving it nuances of different flavours such as mace, lemon, thyme or bay; keep the lining of the basin as thin as possible or even make the pudding with only a top crust, as there are many attractive basins which can appear at the table; or the traditional cloth, at one time used for covering such a pudding, can be used as a disguise for the basin, for you must use foil to prevent any steam getting into the crust, which is all too often the reason for the top being wet and heavy.

Serve the pudding in its own right, with just a green vegetable or one of the herby medieval salads (p. 244). Of course the meal is going to be solid if the crust is thick, potatoes and carrots are served and there is only an apology for a filling.

I use exactly the same filling for a steak and kidney pudding as I do for a pie. I find that the prolonged cooking where a pudding is made from raw meat is half the cause of the suet crusts in this country being so heavy.

The Filling

1 kg/2 lb rump steak (or best stewing steak)
250 g/8 oz calf's kidneys
250 g/8 oz button mushrooms
1 large onion
1 bay leaf
1 heaped tbsp flour
¼ litre/½ pint red wine
¼ litre/½ pint beef stock
Salt and freshly ground black pepper
Butter for frying
Oysters (optional)

Alternative crusts, each to line a 1½ litre/3 pint basin

Crust 1

250 g/8 oz self-raising flour
1 level tsp baking powder
125 g/4 oz suet
Salt and freshly ground white pepper
A pinch of powdered mace, powdered rosemary
or powdered bay leaf
Cold water to mix

Crust 2

250 g/8 oz self-raising flour
100 g/3 oz suet
60 g/2 oz grated cold hard butter
1 tsp lemon rind
Salt and freshly ground white pepper
Lemon juice and water to mix

First make the filling as follows.

Trim the meat of all fat and skin. Cut the kidneys in half and remove the fat, veins, etc. Cut the meat into 1-inch cubes; slice the kidneys. Quarter the mushrooms and slice the onion.

Mix the flour, salt and pepper in a polythene bag and toss the meats in this until they are completely coated.

Melt about 60 g/2 oz of butter in a heavy-bottomed pan. Fry the onion until golden brown and put this into an oven-proof casserole with a draining spoon. Fry the flour-coated meat until it is brown on all sides. It is as well to do this in two or three batches to ensure good colouring. Transfer the meat to the casserole.

Add a little more butter to the pan and add the mushrooms and toss them around for a few minutes. Add these to the meat. Shake any left-over flour from the bag into the casserole and stir in well. Cover with the wine and stock, season with salt and pepper and add the bay leaf.

Cook in the oven at 180°C/350°F/gas mark 4 for 1 to 1½ hours, or until the meat is just tender and not overdone. Check the seasoning and remove the bay leaf.

Allow the basic steak and kidney mixture to cool. (If you like oysters in your pudding, these – about two dozen – should be added when the mixture is quite cool, just before filling the pudding.)

Sieve the flour, salt and pepper. Lightly toss in the suet and/or grated butter, stir loosely with a fork or rain the dry ingredients through your fingers until they are thoroughly mixed. Make a well in the centre and add the water at one fell swoop.

Gather the ingredients together, kneading as little as possible, until the dough is a workable mass. If you press the finished dough or pastry with the forefinger, the indentation should stay! Like all pastries, if it springs back it is going to shrink and will not be light or short. This is because you have added too much water or over-kneaded it.

The next important thing is to have your steamer or pan ready with boiling water before you put the pudding in to cook.

Dredge a baking board with flour, cut the dough into two pieces. Flour your pin and deftly roll out the first piece as thinly as possible; cut this in half for ease of lining the buttered basin.

Fill the lined basin with the cold steak mixture up to within half an inch of the rim. Roll the second piece of dough into a round, wet the edges of the lining pastry and fit the top on.

Butter a piece of foil at least 4 inches larger in diameter than the top of the basin. Fold this round the rim and leave it slack over the top of the crust, thus allowing it room to rise. Make sure the foil is tightly fitted round the rim so that steam or water cannot enter.

Steam for 1½ to 1¾ hours.

If you use the pan method of cooking the pudding (rather than a steamer), let the water be at least two-thirds to three-quarters up the sides of the basin and keep the water boiling gently, which is just one stage further than simmering. Top up when necessary with boiling water from a kettle.

If you use a steamer, then the water needs to boil at a steady rate and will need constant topping up.

STEAK AND KIDNEY PIE

250 g/8 oz puff pastry
A little beaten egg
Filling (as for the previous recipe)

Roll out the pastry as thinly as possible. Cut strips off this to line the edge of a deep pie-dish.

Fill the pie-dish with the cold steak mixture. Stand a pie-funnel in the centre, cut out a lid, wet the edges of the rim and fit the lid into place. Nick this with a sharp knife at 1-inch intervals. Make attractive decorations with the left-over pieces, but do not knead them again, just lay them on top of each other and roll out in the normal way without folding.

Brush the whole pie with beaten egg and bake at 220°C/425°F/gas mark 7 for 20 minutes, then lower the temperature to 170°C/325°F/gas mark 5 and continue cooking until the pastry is really crisp and golden.

A DISH OF ELIZABETHAN PORK

The idea of fruit with meats seems to belong to this century and for some unknown reason many people think it has crossed the Atlantic from west to east, but any glance at Tudor cookery will soon show that this technique has been around for a very long time.

This pork dish is extremely rich, fruity and spicy and is a must, especially at party time when a dish which can be eaten with a fork is called for.

1½ kg/3 lb leg of pork
1 head celery (or a root of fennel)
2 onions
250 g/8 oz fresh or tinned apricots
125 g/4 oz stoned raisins
1 lemon
1 orange
2 Cox's orange pippins
125 g/4 oz stoned dates
1 tbsp clover honey
30 g/1 oz flour
4 tbsps oil
½ bottle red wine
A large sprig each of fresh marjoram, thyme,
sage and rosemary (if dried herbs are used,
allow 1 level tsp of each, cutting down
rather more on the sage)
3 crushed cloves garlic
1 level tsp powdered mace
1 level tsp black pepper
1 level tsp curry powder
½ tsp fennel seeds
(omit if using fennel root instead of celery)
Salt
Segments of 3 or 4 oranges and
125 g/4 oz halved walnuts to garnish

Trim the pork of bone, rind and any excess fat but leave on a little fat. Cut the meat into 1-inch cubes.

Heat the oil until it is smoking and fry the pork, a little at a time, until it is golden brown, taking each batch out onto a side plate as it is fried. Fry the sliced onions in the fat remaining in the pan.

Return the pork to the pan and sprinkle with the flour, stirring it in well, and then add all the herbs and spices. (If fresh herbs are used, tie them together with linen thread; with dried herbs, tie them in a piece of muslin.)

Shred the celery or fennel root as thinly as possible and add this to the pan. Add the split and stoned apricots and dates and the peeled and sliced apples.

Grate the rind from the citrus fruits and peel them with a knife, divide them into segments and add to the pan together with the rind. Add the raisins. Transfer the whole to an oven-proof casserole and cover with the red wine. Cook in the oven at 140°C/275°F/gas mark 2 for 2½ to 3 hours.

Remove the herbs and serve sprinkled with roughly chopped walnuts and segments of fresh orange.

CROWN OF LAMB

Forming a crown is one of the best ways of presenting the tender, sweet loin-meat of England's young classic. I find that stuffing the lamb with forcemeat or vegetable stuffing after roasting the crown gives a far more acceptable result, in that the meat can be roasted at a higher temperature than when stuffed and it is therefore possible to ensure that the meat is pink while the delicately flavoured fat is crisp and succulent.

I have combined two recipes here, adding to the basic lamb a stuffing for Forc'd Leg of Mutton straight from the Elizabethan kitchen. This stuffing is in fact a lamb dish in itself and can be served as such, but for high days and feast days serve it with the crown and fill the hollow just before serving with a purée of peas, artichokes or mushrooms. It does take quite a quantity of peas to make sufficient purée to be really effective and this could be quite a waste unless you are prepared to make the remains into a soup the following day. Also, the proportions of lamb to stuffing are somewhat irregular and this must be borne in mind. I give quantities for 1 pound of stuffing.

1 crown roast of lamb
125 g/4 oz butter
1 crushed clove garlic
Rind of 1 lemon
½ tsp powdered rosemary
Salt and freshly ground pepper

Stuffing 1 (To Accompany the Crown)
1 kg/2 lb lean leg-meat of lamb
375 g/¾ lb fat pork
2 heaped tbsps mixed fresh herbs (rosemary,
marjoram, thyme, sorrel, parsley, mint and sage –
keep the proportions equal except for the sage, which
should be fairly modest)
2 eggs
Juice and rind of 1 lemon
Salt and freshly ground pepper

Stuffing 2 (To Fill the Crown)
500 g/1 lb frozen peas (better than fresh, for a purée)
60 g/2 oz butter
1 level tbsp freshly chopped mint
A hint of crushed garlic (about ½ clove)
1 tsp castor sugar
A little cream
Salt and freshly ground pepper

The Gravy
1 cup veal or chicken stock
1 cup port
½ tsp potato flour
Salt and pepper
A corner of a stock cube

Make sure that the butcher is good at chining and forming a well
shaped crown – it must be skinned and the heavy saddle bone taken
out.

Make a paste of the other ingredients and rub this all over the
inside of the lamb, putting knobs of it between the cutlets where
they open out. Cover the tips of the bones with foil so that they do

not char. Stand the crown on a rack in a roasting pan. Heat the oven to 230°C/450°F/gas mark 8 and roast the crown for 40 to 45 minutes, lowering the temperature to 220°C/425°F/gas mark 7 after 20 minutes. Baste frequently during the roasting time.

Roasting is an art which one develops and it is extremely difficult to give exact temperatures and timings, as the shape and size of ovens varies and heat comes from different directions with different kinds of cooker. Shapes and sizes of joints also vary. What is essential is to get roasting! If the temperature is too low, the meat doesn't get sealed and true roasting is impaired.

Stuffing 1 (To Accompany the Crown)

Trim the meat of any skin but retain all the fat. Put the meat through the mincer twice. Mix with the herbs, lemon rind and juice. Bind with the eggs. Season well and put into a buttered basin or oven-proof pot.

Cover with foil and either steam for 2 hours or stand the container in a hot water bath and bake in the oven at 190°C/375°F/gas mark 5 for 1¼ to 1½ hours, or until the juices are quite clear.

Serve slices of this with the crown. (It can also be eaten cold as a dish in itself, for picnics or a buffet.)

Stuffing 2 (To Fill the Crown)

Melt the butter in a heavy-bottomed pan, add the peas and toss them over a low heat until they start to draw. Simmer in their own liquid until just tender. Season with a little salt and pepper and the sugar.

Put the whole contents of the pan through a Mouli then beat well. If the purée is too stiff, add a little cream. Season with chopped mint and garlic, and more salt and pepper if needed.

Pile this into the centre of the crown. Attach cutlet frills to each bone and serve as quickly as you can manage. (If the purée is made too far in advance, it will go dark in colour and not look so attractive.)

The Gravy

Pour away any excess of fat from the roasting tin and add the veal or chicken stock and the port. Work all this together and sieve the gravy into a small pan.

Slake the potato flour with a little cold water and whisk just a little of this into the boiling gravy to give a viscous consistency. Season with salt and pepper and the corner of stock cube.

KEBOB'D LAMB

This Middle Eastern way of grilling meat has long been a favourite here to the extent that the name was nearly Anglicised in the sixteenth, seventeenth and eighteenth centuries.

The skewer on which the pieces of meat are pierced is the 'shish' and 'kebab' is the method of cooking — grilling. Lamb is one of the more popular meats for making kebabs, though beef, chicken and firmer-fleshed fish are well in the running. Basically any combination will do if it suits your palate, but if you are not in the habit of serving meat in this way, the following recipe will be a guide until you develop ideas of your own.

It is important to remember not to have the meat and vegetables too close together on the skewer as this prevents effective grilling; for the same reason it is essential to keep the skewers constantly turning, which is not so difficult if you possess a modern rôtisserie with the appropriate attachments, but if you are relying on the more common electric or gas grill it can pose a slight difficulty. A good tip is to ensure that the skewers are suspended in some way so that they do not come into contact with the hot metal of the grill rack, or the meat will stick and tear. If the skewers are long enough it is usually possible to suspend each one across the grill pan, having removed the rack.

1 kg/2 lb lean leg of lamb
1 medium-sized onion
4 firm tomatoes
8 button mushrooms
Peppers would be used today, so include some pieces of
red and green pepper if you wish
Small pieces of bay leaf
Saffron rice to serve

The Marinade

1 teacup olive oil
1 glass red wine

1 crushed clove garlic
A sprig of fresh rosemary
1 tsp fresh basil
Salt and freshly ground black pepper

Mix all the ingredients for the marinade together in a china bowl. Cut the lamb into 1½-inch cubes and pack these into the marinade to soak overnight.

De-seed the tomatoes and cut them and the onion into quarters; also, if you are using them, cut the peppers into quarters.

Select some long skewers (at least 12 inches excluding any handle or decoration they might have – butchers' metal meat skewers are quite favourable for kebabs). Oil the skewers and pierce the meat alternately with pieces of the vegetables and bay leaf onto the skewers and cook under a pre-heated hot grill. Baste the kebabs well with some of the marinade during the cooking time, turning the meat and watching that it does not scorch.

To serve, arrange a bed of saffron rice on each plate and, holding the skewers at the end with a cloth or napkin, carefully but firmly push the grilled meat and vegetables off the skewer with a table fork.

As an alternative, you could try halibut cubes with mushroom, onion and tomato dressed with oil, white wine, parsley, chives, garlic and rosemary or beef cubes with tomato, mushroom, courgette and onion with a more spicy dressing made with oil, red wine, ginger, paprika and cinnamon.

Any of the finished kebabs can be sprinkled with freshly chopped herbs, paprika or a little saffron, when on the plate.

A trickle of freshly made tomato sauce (p. 233) or savoury orange sauce (p. 231) can also be served.

LAMB CUTLETS REFORM

I am lucky enough to possess an original manuscript of Charles Elmé Francatelli's recipe for this world-famous dish which he created for the Reform Club in London. It was written whilst he was still chef to Queen Victoria at Buckingham Palace.

Reform Sauce is uniquely English in that it was designed for an English institution by an Italian who had been a pupil of the greatest of

all French chefs, Carême! At one time the sauce was in two parts: Reform
'chips', which were match-sized striplets of Indian mountain gherkins,
hard-boiled egg-whites, cooked carrots, ham and truffles, were arranged in
the centre of the finished cutlets, which we are instructed to arrange in the
form of a wreath; a brown-type sauce was then served separately. Today
these two accompaniments are brought together and served as one sauce.

Cutlets cut from best end of English lamb (2 per person)
125 g/4 oz cooked ham
60 g/2 oz fresh white breadcrumbs
1 egg
Clarified butter for frying (p. 70)
Salt and pepper

The Sauce
1 medium-sized carrot
2 small onions
60 g/2 oz lean raw ham
30 g/1 oz butter
1 small teacup white wine vinegar
175 g/6 oz redcurrant jelly
½ litre/1 pint beef or chicken stock
2 heaped tsps arrowroot
4 cloves
2 blades mace
1 bay leaf
A sprig of fresh thyme
1 crushed clove garlic
A sprig of fresh parsley

Reform 'Chips'
Equal quantities of:
Cooked lean ham
Hard-boiled egg-whites
Gherkins
Cooked carrots
As many truffles as you can afford (cooked button
mushrooms can be substituted here)
(The ingredients for the 'chips' should
be cut into equal-sized strips)

Mince the ham and mix with the breadcrumbs. Beat the egg and season well with salt and pepper.

Trim and season the cutlets, making sure that they are real cutlets and not chops, because an abundance of fat will not do for this dish. Each cutlet should be trimmed of all but the thinnest layer of fat around it. The bone must be scraped clean to within 1 inch of the nut of meat.

Gently beat each cutlet, without breaking up the meat, with the hilt of a heavy knife or with a wetted rolling pin. Dip them into the beaten egg and then press a good coating of the ham and bread mixture onto each side.

Heat the clarified butter in a frying pan and fry the cutlets over a medium heat, allowing approximately 4 minutes for each side. They should be crisp and golden in colour.

Now make the sauce. Finely dice the carrot, onions and ham into ⅛-inch cubes; melt the butter and fry them until golden brown. Add the wine vinegar and turn up the heat so that the mixture boils rapidly.

The liquor will now reduce quickly. When you have only one-third of the original quantity left, put the pan aside and add the remaining ingredients, with the exception of the arrowroot. Cook very slowly for 30 minutes.

Slake the arrowroot in a small basin or teacup and whisk a little at a time into the pan until you have a bright viscous sauce. The arrowroot thickens the sauce without turning it cloudy.

Strain the finished sauce into a double boiler or into a basin that will stand over a pan of boiling water to keep it hot. Check the seasoning and add the Reform 'chips' just before serving, but long enough to make sure that they are heated through.

ROAST PARSLIED BEST END OF LAMB

Allow 2 'bones' per person, plus 2 extra
For 2 best ends you will need:

60 g/2 oz butter
Salt and freshly ground pepper
½ tsp powdered rosemary
2 crushed cloves garlic

125 g/4 oz fresh white breadcrumbs
2 tbsps chopped fresh parsley
Grated rind of 1 lemon
A little melted butter

The Gravy
1 stock cube
1 tsp potato flour

Get the butcher to skin and chine the lamb. Cut away the first 2 inches of fat from the top of the cutlet bones and scrape these bones clean.

Make a paste with the butter, salt, pepper, rosemary and garlic. Rub this over both sides of the meat.

Stand the best ends on a rack in a roasting tin. This eliminates the possibility of the meat frying and hardening in its own fat, which would happen if the meat lay in the bottom of the tin.

Pre-heat the oven to 230°C/450°F/gas mark 8 and roast the lamb for 30 to 35 minutes. (If your oven elements or burners are placed so that this high temperature causes early scorching, you will have to adjust the placing of the shelf or lower the temperature slightly, but a good keen heat is needed to have lamb which is crisp and brown, but still pink inside.) Baste at frequent intervals.

Ten minutes before the end of the roasting time, cover the lamb with a cushion of breadcrumbs, lemon rind and parsley mixed with the melted butter and seasoned lightly. Press this mixture firmly onto the top of the meat, return it to the oven, lower the temperature to 220°C/425°F/gas mark 7 and continue to complete the roasting time, when the lamb should have a good crisp coating.

To make a quick, clear, tasty gravy, pour away the surplus fat into a storage jar. Add the stock cube to the sediments and a scant teaspoon of potato flour slaked in a breakfast cup of water. Bring the gravy to the boil, check the seasoning, strain into a heated gravyboat and serve.

RAGOO OF LAMB

750 g/1½ lb leg of lamb (cheaper cuts can be
used for family cooking)
1 tbsp seasoned flour

2 large carrots
½ head celery
15 g/½ oz flour
A sprig of rosemary
½ litre/1 pint chicken stock
1 dozen spring onions
¼ tsp cayenne pepper
2 crushed cloves garlic
1 tsp castor sugar
Grated rind of half a lemon
Salt and freshly ground black pepper
15 g/½ oz butter
Oil for frying
4 firm tomatoes and 1 tbsp fresh basil or parsley for garnish

Trim the meat and cut into 1-inch cubes.

Mix the salt, pepper and cayenne with the flour and put this into a polythene bag; toss the meat cubes in this until they are well coated.

Heat a little oil in a heavy-bottomed frying pan and fry the lamb until it is golden brown and evenly coloured. It is as well to fry the lamb in batches to ensure ease of working and effective browning; use a little more oil as and when necessary. Transfer each batch to a casserole when it is finished. Sprinkle the extra half ounce of flour into the casserole, add all the seasonings, garlic, lemon peel and any remains from the polythene bag.

Peel and cut the vegetables into ½-inch dice and brown these in a little oil, adding them to the casserole when they are ready. Pour in the pint of stock and cook at 190°C/375°F/gas mark 5 for 1½ hours, or until the meat is quite tender but not over-cooked.

Half-way through the cooking time, take the spring onions and clean them, leaving on an inch of the green stalk. Brown them in the butter and add the castor sugar, tossing them round in the pan until the sugar caramelises. Add these to the casserole and complete the cooking cycle.

Before serving, skim any fat from the sauce and check the seasoning. Cover with a cushion of diced tomatoes and the freshly chopped basil or very green and very fresh parsley.

To make the diced tomatoes, plunge them into boiling water while you count to ten, take them out (have them in a wire basket

for ease) and plunge them into cold water. Skin them and take out
the stalk stump.

Cut them across 'equatorwise' and gently press out the seeds with
your thumb. Cut the tomato into dice. (If hot tomato dice are
required, just sweat the chopped tomato for a few moments in a
little butter.)

COLLOPS OF VEAL

*This way of serving escalopes of veal was usually known as Scotch
Collops. If the truth were accepted, it can be a deal better than our well
known Austrian friend the Wiener Schnitzel!*

4 escalopes of veal taken from the leg fillet
Fresh white breadcrumbs
1 tbsp parsley
Grated rind of 1 lemon
1 beaten egg
2 tbsps milk
Salt and freshly ground pepper
Butter and oil for frying

Forcemeat Balls

100 g/3 oz raw lean ham
60 g/2 oz refrigerator-hard butter
100 g/3 oz white breadcrumbs
2 tsps freshly chopped parsley
½ tsp fresh thyme
Juice and rind of half a lemon
2 eggs
Salt and freshly ground pepper

The Sauce

1 large glass dryish white wine
or
1 sherry glass medium dry sherry
1 crushed clove garlic
125 ml/¼ pint double cream
1 egg-yolk

A little top of the milk
Salt and freshly ground pepper

Forcemeat Balls

Mince the ham; grate the butter on the coarse side of a grater. Mix all the dry ingredients together and bind them with the beaten egg and lemon juice.

Season well, form into 1-inch diameter balls and dredge with plain flour before gently frying in butter. Keep them warm until the veal escalopes are finished and then arrange them as a garnish.

The Collops

Gently flatten the veal escalopes with a wetted rolling pin, taking care not to tear the flesh.

Mix the fresh breadcrumbs with the chopped parsley, lemon rind, salt and pepper. Beat the egg with the milk. Pass each escalope through the egg-wash and then into the crumb mixture, pressing the crumbs onto the surface of the meat.

Melt half butter and half oil in a heavy-bottomed frying pan large enough to contain at least 2, if not all 4, pieces of veal. When the butter and oil are foaming, carefully lay in the escalopes and fry them on each side until golden brown and tender. Remove the pieces to a warm serving dish and arrange the forcemeat balls down one side of the dish; keep them warm whilst you make the sauce.

The Sauce

If you have done the frying operation carefully, you will not have any burnt sediment in the pan, but a nice brown crust on the bottom. Remove all but 1 tablespoon of the fat and reserve for future use.

Keeping the pan hot but not quite smoking, pour on the wine or sherry and work this with a spatula until the crust is entirely dissolved. Add the garlic and reduce the liquor until you have half the quantity you started with. Pour on the thick cream, stir well and let this sauce boil for a few seconds.

Now pour it through a fine strainer into a small pan and bring back to the boil, check the seasoning and finally take the pan away from the heat (if the sauce appears to be oiling at all, add 1 tablespoon of boiling water and whisk this in well), beat the egg-yolk with a tablespoon of top of the milk and whisk this into the finished sauce.

Pour this over the edges of the cooked veal pieces and serve.

RAGOO OF VEAL KIDNEYS

This ragoo is good as a main dish, as a patty filling or served on buttered toasts; or, if you halve the quantities and chop the kidneys, it makes a superb sauce for veal escalopes or roast veal.

6 calf's kidneys
125 g/4 oz button mushrooms
60 g/2 oz butter
2 tbsps Madeira or medium dry sherry
125 ml/¼ pint double cream
¼ tsp powdered rosemary or ginger
Salt and freshly ground pepper

Skin and trim the kidneys of all fat; slice them thinly. Wash and slice the mushrooms.

Melt the butter in a frying pan until it foams and fry the kidneys until they are tender (if your pan is not very large, it is better to do this in two batches). Season the kidneys lightly with rosemary or ginger, salt and pepper and remove them to a warm serving dish.

Toss the mushrooms in the remaining pan juices, adding a little more butter if necessary. Pour over the Madeira and the cream and cook until the sauce has a good unctuous consistency. Pour over the kidneys and serve.

VEAL OLIVE PIE WITH GREEN PEA PUREE

6 thin veal escalopes
175 g/6 oz good sausagemeat or the same
weight of raw lean ham and leg of veal
minced and bound with beaten egg
1 tbsp freshly chopped parsley

2 tsps freshly chopped chives
60 g/2 oz butter for frying
Salt and freshly ground white pepper
1 finely chopped onion
1 carrot cut into ¼-inch dice
1 crushed clove garlic
1 bouquet fresh herbs
1 tbsp flour
½ tsp made-up English mustard
¼ litre/½ pint veal or chicken stock
125 ml/¼ pint dry white wine or sherry
250 g/8 oz puff pastry
A little beaten egg

The Purée
375 g/12 oz frozen baby peas
60 g/2 oz butter
1 tsp castor sugar
4 mint leaves or 1 crushed clove garlic
Salt and freshly ground white pepper

Gently flatten the escalopes with a wetted rolling pin, stretching them until they are very thin but not broken. The water will prevent the pin dragging the meat. Season each piece with salt and pepper.

Mix the parsley and chives with the sausagemeat or forcemeat and spread this over the veal pieces. Roll each into a parcel, folding in the sides as you go along. Tie each with a piece of strong linen thread.

Melt the butter in a heavy-bottomed pan. Gently fry each 'olive' on all sides until golden brown. Take great care at this stage to ensure even colouring. Remove the olives to a plate.

Put the chopped onion, carrots and garlic into the juices of the pan in which you fried the veal. Gently fry them until they acquire an even golden colour.

Sprinkle on the flour and stir in well; draw the contents of the pan to one side, add the wine and work the crusty residue into this. Add the stock, bouquet and mustard, bring to the boil and stir until a smooth sauce is obtained. Season nicely.

Return the olives to the pan or transfer the whole to a casserole, cover with a lid and braise in the oven for 25 to 30 minutes at 200°C/400°F/gas mark 6. Every 10 minutes baste the olives in their own gravy.

When the veal olives are cooked, remove the bouquet and string and arrange them in an oven-proof dish. Cover with the gravy and put on a top crust of puff pastry; brush with beaten egg. Bake at 220°C/425°F/gas mark 7 for 25 to 30 minutes, until the crust is really crisp and golden.

While the crust is cooking, make the purée of peas: melt the butter in a small pan; add the peas, together with the salt, pepper, mint or garlic and the sugar. Toss the pan continuously until the peas draw their own juices. Cover with a lid and cook over a low heat for 8 minutes. Make the purée in a blender or Mouli, using the cooking liquid. Pile into a dish, dot with butter and keep hot until the pie is ready.

VEAL SWEETBREADS WITH CREAM AND HERBS

Where I come from in Yorkshire it was traditional to serve sweetbreads with treacle! Fortunately other parts of the country had different views on the treatment of these delicacies. They were often served in patty cases, made of either shortcrust or puff pastry, and were known as 'petty patties'.

2 pairs calf's sweetbreads (or 375 g/12 oz frozen)
Chicken stock to cover
1 tbsp white wine vinegar
1 shallot, finely chopped
¼ litre/½ pint cream
45 g/1½ oz butter
1 tsp flour
2 tsps chopped chives
2 tsps chopped parsley
2 tsps chopped chervil
A little lemon juice and rind
Salt and freshly ground white pepper
Patty cases or pastry shells

Soak the sweetbreads in cold water for half an hour, then drain them. Bring them to the boil in the chicken stock and vinegar and cook them gently for 15 minutes. Remove them and wash well under cold water. Take off all the skin and sinew and cut the sweetbreads into ¼-inch thick slices. Discard the cooking liquor.

Melt the butter in a heavy-bottomed frying pan and quickly fry the sweetbreads on each side until tender, letting them acquire a light golden colour.

Remove them to a warm plate, add the chopped shallot to the pan and soften this in the remaining butter; sprinkle with the flour and stir this in well. Add the cream and let the sauce come to the boil.

Return the sweetbreads to the pan and sprinkle with the herbs, salt and pepper and a little lemon juice and rind. Let them simmer in the sauce for 5 minutes and then fill into heated pastry cases.

VEAL CUTLETS IN PASTRY CASES

Cooking in some sort of case whereby the food is completely enclosed, thus retaining all the juices and aromatics which might be with it, is by no means a new venture in English kitchens. The Tudors had their huff crusts, and hams were often baked in this flour and water casing. Fish and meats were also enveloped in brown paper and baked in the oven. It needs no great extension of the imagination to see whence today's popular form of cooking in pastry or foil has come.

When you do bake in paper, particularly if it is good quality grease-proof, there is the added attraction that the case balloons up as the steam is given off and the air inside expands. The French have always made a great feature of this method of presenting certain extravaganza like chicken breasts with truffles, sweetbreads stuffed with foie gras and succulent wedges of salmon delicately flavoured with fresh herbs, cream and butter. But puff pastry has the great advantage of being an integral part of the finished dish.

A further extension of this dish is the French Filet de Boeuf Wellington or, as we call it here, Beef in Shirt Sleeves; this was a great favourite of Edward VII.

Lamb cutlets or chops can be treated in exactly the same way, but instead of the mushroom filling use a well flavoured fresh herb butter (p. 243).

Make sure the butcher chines the loins before cutting the cutlets, leaving only the straight bone on the meat.

6 veal cutlets
Oil for frying
30 g/1 oz butter
1 small onion
60 g/2 oz button mushrooms
60 g/2 oz cooked ham, minced or chopped
1 crushed clove garlic
1 tsp shredded lemon peel
½ tsp powdered rosemary
Thick cream to bind
Salt and freshly ground pepper
375 g/12 oz puff pastry
A little beaten egg

Gently flatten the cutlets with a wetted rolling pin. Trim off any excess fat and trim the bone clean, down to 2 inches.

Heat the oil in a heavy frying pan and seal the chops for 1 minute on each side over a high heat. Put them to cool.

Melt the butter in a small pan. Chop the onion, mushrooms and ham. Add the onion to the butter and let it acquire a golden brown colour. Add the mushrooms and fry them for 3 to 4 minutes, stirring all the time. Add the minced or chopped ham, together with the seasonings, and work the mixture into a cohered mass. Season well with salt and pepper.

Bind with a little cream and cook until the paste is fairly stiff. Let it cool. Spread some of the paste on each side of the sealed cutlets. Roll the puff pastry out as thinly as possible and cut out 6 large circles, 6–8 inches diameter, depending on the size of the cutlets (make a foil template before cutting out the pastry).

Sit a cutlet in the centre of each circle and fold the spare pastry over until the meat is quite enclosed, but leave the bone protruding.

Dampen the edges of the pastry and seal together. With the seam underneath, put the pastry-covered cutlets onto a wetted baking sheet, brush over with a little beaten egg and then bake at 220°C/425°F/gas mark 7 for 20 to 25 minutes, or until the pastry is well-risen, crisp and a good golden brown.

Serve with tomato sauce (p. 233), apple chutney (p. 237) or a creamy mushroom sauce (p. 230).

Game

SADDLES OF HARE
BRAISED IN RED WINE

2 whole saddles of hare
1 large onion
125 g/4 oz mushrooms
60 g/2 oz butter
30 g/1 oz flour
1 bottle red wine
1 level tsp powdered cloves
2 tsps grated horseradish
½ tsp ground mace
Juice and rind of 1 lemon
1 tbsp redcurrant jelly
4 chopped anchovy fillets
A sprig of winter savory or thyme
A pinch of cayenne pepper
Salt and freshly ground black pepper
Oil for frying
Lemon segments and quince or redcurrant jelly to garnish

Have your butcher cut out the 4 whole fillets from the saddles.

Slice the onion and mushrooms.

Dredge the 4 pieces of hare in the flour and brown them on all sides in a little oil. Transfer the fillets to an oven-proof casserole.

Put the butter in the frying pan in which you have browned the hare fillets and fry the sliced onion and mushrooms in it; add the remainder of the flour, the cloves, horseradish, mace, lemon juice and rind, redcurrant jelly, anchovy, thyme or savory and cayenne pepper and the red wine, bring the sauce to the boil and add salt and pepper.

Pour the sauce over the hare and cook in the oven at 180°C/350°F/gas mark 4 for 1 hour, or less if you like the meat under-done.

Remove the hare to a warm dish. Let the sauce settle and skim off any fats that come to the surface. If the sauce is not thick enough, pour it into a pan and add a little butter and flour mixed to a paste, whisked in a little at a time; cook until it looks 'bright'.

Pour the unstrained sauce back over the hare and serve with lemon segments and quince or redcurrant jelly.

Carve the meat lengthways on a broad diagonal plane.

GROUSE MOUSSE

This is a Victorian recipe used a great deal for shooting parties and country house dinners. It is an excellent way of using old or frozen grouse, for they certainly do not roast in an acceptable fashion, and casserole of grouse can pall if one lives in an area where this game is plentiful.

A brace of grouse
The saddle or 2 fillets of hare
1 medium-sized onion
½ tsp powdered cloves
2 egg-yolks
1 tbsp chopped fresh thyme
2 tbsps dry Madeira
2 tbsps brandy
250 g/8 oz unsalted butter
1 level tbsp plain white flour
½ litre/1 pint aspic jelly (see below)
Salt and freshly ground black pepper

If the grouse is frozen, defrost it overnight. Carefully skin the grouse and cut all the meat from them. Skin the hare fillets.

Put all the skin and bones, together with the onion and clove, in just enough water to cover them and simmer for 2 hours, topping up with a little water only if necessary, for a strong stock is required.

Melt 30 g/1 oz of the butter in a small pan and stir in the flour.

Stirring regularly over a low heat, let it acquire a golden brown colour, strain on half a pint of the game stock and make this into a sauce; set aside to cool, having first covered the surface with a circle of oiled paper to prevent a skin forming.

Put all the meat through a fine mincer twice, or through a blender, then mix it with the fresh thyme, softened butter, salt and pepper and the cooled sauce. Beat in the egg-yolks and brandy.

Butter a mould or basin, fill with the mixture, tightly cover it with buttered foil and steam in a pre-heated steamer for 2 hours. When the mousse is cool, turn it onto a serving dish to become completely cold, then put it carefully onto a cooling tray arranged over a dish or metal tray to catch the coating jelly.

Leave this to keep cold in the refrigerator until your jelly is ready to use.

Make up the aspic jelly according to the instructions on the packet, but leave out 125 ml/¼ pint of the water asked for and replace this with the 2 tablespoons of Madeira.

Allow the jelly to cool and then arrange it over a bowl of crushed ice to hasten the setting. Stir it slowly, but continuously, until it starts to gel, then spoon layers of the jelly over the mousse until you have a clear bright coating.

If the jelly sets before you have completed the coating, place the bowl in a sink of lukewarm water and stir slowly until it has re-melted – replace over the ice and repeat the process.

ROAST GROUSE WITH
WILD RASPBERRIES

One of the main problems when preparing and cooking game birds is to keep the flesh moist, hence the hanging technique. This is not only to give the birds the gamey flavour we all love, but to break down the tissues so that the meat needs less cooking and can be roasted quickly. Hang game birds from their necks for about a week in a cool larder or cellar. As soon as the tail feathers are loose to pull, they are ready for plucking.

The grouse used to be stuffed with the raspberries, but this impedes the roasting process as they create too much steam. It is better to serve them separately as a hot fruity sauce.

A brace of young grouse and their livers
250 g/8 oz butter
½ tsp thyme
½ bay leaf
250 g/8 oz wild raspberries or wild strawberries
(the wild are much better for this recipe, but if these
are unobtainable, use the garden variety)
85 ml/⅙ pint port
½ tsp juniper berries
2 tbsps brandy
Salt and freshly ground pepper
6 heaped tbsps fresh white breadcrumbs, coarsely grated

Crush the bay leaf and mix it with the thyme. Grind these in a small mortar and make into a paste with half the butter. Lightly season with salt and a little pepper. Rub this butter mixture all over the birds, both inside and out.

Place the grouse on a grid and roast them at 230°C/450°F/gas mark 8. Twenty to 25 minutes should see them ready for serving. The juices should still run pink when the birds are held up with a fork (take care not to pierce the breasts).

Soak the juniper berries in the port for 2 hours. Bring the port to simmering point in a small pan and simmer for 5 minutes, then remove the berries.

Put the raspberries or strawberries into the flavoured port, toss them carefully and simmer for only a few seconds, then let them stand in the hot liquid until you are ready to serve the grouse.

You can only make a modicum of gravy with small game birds, so pour away any excess fat, but leave a little of this. Splash 2 table-spoons of brandy into the roasting pan and about half a cup of water. Swirl this round and strain into a very small pan. Mash the raw grouse livers with a fork and add to this; simmer for no more than 1 minute. Season and serve in a heated gravyboat.

Serve with fried breadcrumbs. These are often scorned, usually because they are far too dry and often too fine. Make them with rather coarse breadcrumbs as follows: melt the remaining butter in a frying pan, put in the crumbs and fry them over a very low heat until they are a good nutty-flavoured golden brown. It is necessary to move them about in the pan *the whole time* you are frying them or you will get uneven colouring and scorching.

PHEASANT IN CREAM

If you are lucky enough to know people who have a shoot, or you live near a shop where the game is well treated, then a plain roast young pheasant is a dream, but pheasants can be somewhat dry and tough later on in the season. This way of cooking them retains the delicate game flavour of the bird and provides a beautiful sauce. If you can use young birds, the reward is outstanding.

A brace of pheasant and their livers
100 g/3 oz butter
½ crushed clove garlic
2 tbsps olive oil
125 g/4 oz button mushrooms
1 wine glass brandy or Madeira
1 scant tsp flour
Salt and pepper
¼ litre/½ pint double cream

Soften 2 ounces of the butter and mix with the garlic, salt and pepper. Rub this all over the birds, outside and inside.

Heat the oil in a small roasting pan on top of the stove and quickly brown the pheasants all over, using two roasting forks to turn them quickly and deftly so that the breast meat doesn't get 'fried'. Take care not to pierce the skin.

Roast the pheasants for 35 minutes in a very hot oven, 230°C/450°F/gas mark 8, basting frequently. Remove the birds from the roasting tin and put it on one side. Remove the skewers and any trussing strings and carefully detach the legs. Cut the breasts in half, but do *not* take out the breast bones.

Put the pheasants into an uncovered casserole to keep hot. Wipe and slice the mushrooms and quickly fry them in the pan juices. Sprinkle with the flour and stir it in.

Add the brandy and tip the roasting pan to the flame (if you are using gas – if not, use a taper) to ignite any alcohol fumes – this will give you the deep nutty flavour which is so good. Add the cream, bring to the boil and cook for 2 minutes.

Chop the pheasant livers and quickly fry for a few seconds only in the remaining butter; drain the livers and add to the sauce. (This is optional.)

If the sauce looks rather buttery at the edges, add a tablespoon of boiling water and whisk in well. Season lightly, pour over the pheasant and serve.

PHEASANT IN PORT WINE
WITH PRUNES

A brace of young pheasant
2 rashers plain bacon
100 g/3 oz butter
2 tbsps olive oil
125 ml/¼ pint stock
½ bottle tawny port
15 g/½ oz flour
1 small onion
60 g/2 oz button mushrooms
A pinch of cinnamon
A pinch of curry powder
5 or 6 fresh sage leaves
12 giant-sized prunes
Salt and freshly ground black pepper
A little chicken stock or orange juice (optional)

Pack the prunes into a basin and cover with port; soak overnight. Transfer the prunes and port to an oven-proof dish, cover with foil and cook until just tender; remove the prunes with a draining spoon and put on one side; retain the liquor.

Soften 1 ounce of the butter and mix the spices with this, adding a little salt and pepper; rub this mixture over the pheasants. Put a small nut of butter into each bird together with 2 or 3 sage leaves.

Heat the oil in a heavy-bottomed pan that can be transferred to the oven, add the remaining butter and carefully brown the pheasants on all sides.

Cover each bird with a bacon rasher; transfer the pan to the oven and roast the birds at 220°C/425°F/gas mark 7 for 35 to 45 minutes, or until the pheasants are just cooked. Take care not to over-cook the birds or they will be dry; baste two or three times during the roasting time.

Remove the pan from the oven and discard the bacon. Put the pheasants into a serving casserole and remove any string or skewers. Arrange the prunes around the birds and put to keep warm.

Finely chop the onion and add to the pan juices; return the pan to the top of the stove and brown the onion carefully. Add the mushrooms, either quartered or finely sliced, and toss these with the onion over a good heat until they acquire a light golden colour. Sprinkle on the flour and stir in well.

Add the port and stock and carefully bring to the boil; reduce the heat and simmer for 20 minutes; carefully remove any scum or fat, correct the seasoning and strain the sauce over the pheasants and prunes – it should be bright and a rich brown colour. If the sauce should be too thick, add a little chicken stock or even orange juice.

PARTRIDGE IN CHAMPAGNE AND ORANGE SAUCE

2 brace of young partridge
4 thin rashers bacon
6 shallots, finely sliced
2 oranges
2 glasses champagne (or light white wine)
125 g/4 oz butter
4 small sprigs of marjoram
15 g/½ oz flour
Salt and freshly ground pepper
For garnish, see below

Take all the rind off the orange with a potato-peeler, carefully avoiding getting any of the white pith; cut half of this into 4 pieces. Shred the other half as finely as possible and put on one side.

Put a piece of the peel and a sprig of marjoram inside each partridge. Cut half-ounce pieces of butter and put these into the birds.

Lay a bacon rasher and some butter over the breasts, stand the partridge on a wire rack and roast in a very hot oven, 230°C/450°F/gas mark 8, for 30 to 40 minutes. Baste the birds two or three times. Remove the birds to a warm serving dish and discard the bacon.

Strain the juices into a small pan, add the shallots and sweat them until they are golden brown. Stir in the flour; swill the roasting tin with the champagne or white wine and pour into the small pan; bring the contents of the pan to the boil and simmer for 5 minutes, stirring well from time to time.

Add some orange juice and a little stock if the sauce looks too thick. Season lightly and simmer until the sauce looks bright. Strain the sauce before serving.

Boil the orange rind in another small pan for 2 minutes in a little water, and then drain before adding to the sauce. Adjust the seasoning by adding more salt or pepper and perhaps a little sugar; pour into a heated sauceboat.

Serve a whole partridge to each guest with a salad of orange segments, peeled and seeded cucumber pieces and watercress sprigs dressed with a little oil, orange juice and honey.

RICH GAME PIE WITH
A FLAKY CRUST

A brace of pheasant, grouse or other game birds
and their livers
(this is a good opportunity to use older or frozen birds)
1 kg/2 lb rump steak
Half a hare and its liver
1 large onion, finely sliced
250 g/8 oz field mushrooms
2 tbsps tomato purée
1 bottle red wine
Olive oil for frying
60 g/2 oz butter
45 g/1½ oz flour
2 crushed cloves garlic
2 bay leaves
6 sage leaves or ½ tsp dried sage
6 cloves
Juice and rind of 1 orange

2 tbsps redcurrant jelly
Water if necessary
Salt and freshly ground black pepper
Enough puff pastry to cover a large pie-dish
(about 2½ litres/5 pints)
A little beaten egg

Heat some oil in a heavy-bottomed pan and brown the game birds on all sides; remove the birds to a deep oven-proof casserole. Cut the hare into 4 or 5 sections and brown these in the same oil before putting them into the casserole.

Trim the steak of all fat and cut into 1-inch cubes; brown these in the remaining oil and add to the casserole together with any juices from the pan.

Melt the butter in the same pan, heat until it has a nutty flavour and brown the onion in this. Wipe and quarter the mushrooms and add them, with the garlic, to the onion. Stir in the flour and add the seasonings, tied in a piece of muslin; add the wine, orange juice and rind, tomato purée and jelly; bring this sauce to the boil and cook for 2 minutes before pouring over the contents of the casserole. If the liquid doesn't quite cover the meats, add a little water. Cover with a lid and cook in the oven at 170°C/325°F/gas mark 3 for 1½ hours or until the birds are tender. Remove the birds and hare and let them cool sufficiently to handle them. Strip them of all skin. Take off all the meat and cut it into 2-inch pieces and stir back into the contents of the casserole; remove the muslin bag.

Melt a knob of butter in a frying pan, cut the livers into smallish pieces and fry them for a minute or so before adding to the casserole.

Skim off any excess fat, check the seasoning and set aside to cool completely – any steam from a warm filling would impede the rising of the pastry.

Choose a deep pie-dish with a good wide rim; stand a pie-funnel in the centre.

Butter the rim and edge the dish with puff pastry; fill with the cold game pie mixture. Roll out a lid an ⅛-inch thick, brush the pastry with a little cold water and fit the lid carefully; nick at 1-inch intervals all round and decorate with leaves or overlapping small pastry circles. Brush with beaten egg and bake at 230°C/450°F/gas mark 8 for 20 minutes, then reduce the temperature to

200°C/400°F/gas mark 6 for a further 20 minutes or until the pastry is quite crisp and golden.

This type of game pie is best served hot, but it can also be eaten cold.

DOUBLE-CRUSTED PIGEON PIE
(Pigeon Pie in a Huff Crust)

This is such an interesting and unusual recipe for a gorgeous pie that it would be a sin to omit it from any book dealing with English cookery.

6 young pigeons and their giblets
375 g/12 oz grilling steak, cut into 6 very thin slices
4 cloves
1 crushed clove garlic
250 g/8 oz fat bacon
500 g/1 lb button mushrooms
½ litre/1 pint stock made from the bones
and wings of the pigeons
1 teacup sherry
½ litre/1 pint water
A little brown sugar
4 large Cox's orange pippins
12 pitted and cooked prunes
Salt and freshly ground black pepper

Huff Crust
250 g/8 oz self-raising flour
150 g/5 oz suet
Water to mix

Flaky Crust
250 g/8 oz puff pastry
A little beaten egg

Cut the pigeons in half with a cleaver, cut out the backbones and take off the wing tips and the bottom part of the legs, leaving just the thighs attached to the main body of the birds.

Cover these bones, etc., together with the giblets, with water and sherry, add the cloves and a little salt and simmer for 1 hour to make a good stock; this should give you about 1 pint of strained stock.

Trim all the fat from the slices of steak. Wet a rolling pin and gently flatten the steak to break down any sinew.

Butter a very deep, straight-sided pie-dish. Sprinkle the garlic over the bottom of this.

Cut the fat bacon into striplets and fry them until golden brown. Wipe and slice the mushrooms, add them to the frying pan and fry for a further 5 minutes, moving them about to ensure even cooking. Put the bacon and mushrooms into the bottom of the pie-dish and lay the pieces of steak on top. Now pack in the 12 pigeon breasts and cover with half the spiced stock. Season lightly.

Make up a suet crust with the flour, suet and water. Roll this into a circle, about 1 inch thick and just large enough to sit on top of the pigeons, and place it over them. Bake at 180°C/350°F/gas mark 4 for 1½ hours.

Take the dish from the oven and pour the rest of the strained stock *directly over the crust.*

Peel, quarter and core the apples and cut them into slices; pit the prunes. Arrange the fruit on top of the soaked pie crust. Season again lightly with salt and freshly ground black pepper and the merest dredge of brown sugar.

Roll out the puff pastry and cut a piece to fit the top of the pie-dish, making an edge with the remains. Brush the edge of the hot dish with egg; quickly fit the pastry edge, brush again with egg and fit the lid.

Brush all over with egg, make two steam slots, decorate with pastry leaves or what-you-will and return the dish to the oven at 220°C/425°F/gas mark 7 for 25 to 30 minutes, or until the puff pastry is risen, golden and crisp.

PUDDINGS

Hot Puddings

BAKED EGG CUSTARD

This simple little number can be good, provided it doesn't curdle and is sweet enough.

½ litre/1 pint milk
5 eggs
60 g/2 oz castor sugar
A vanilla pod, lemon rind or grated nutmeg to flavour
A little unsalted butter

Select a ring mould or oven-proof dish just large enough to take the quantity being made – the above recipe will amount to about 1½ pints. Lightly butter this with the unsalted butter.

Beat the eggs and sugar together until the sugar has dissolved. Bring the milk to the boil, together with whichever flavouring has been selected (with the lemon, it is only necessary to peel bits of the rind with a potato-peeler; one need not grate or shred it).

Pour the boiling milk over the egg mixture, whisking briskly all the time, then strain it into your mould. Arrange the mould in a baking tin of hot water.

Bake on the middle shelf of the oven, pre-heated to

170°C/325°F/gas mark 3. It will take about 45 minutes for the custard to set. (Test by inserting a knife-blade, which should come out clean; or by gently pressing the edge with your finger – no liquid will come out if the custard is set.)

To unmould, gently ease away the edges with the finger before placing a serving dish over the top and inverting.

BOMBARD'D APPLES

This extraordinarily named dish is in fact a delicious form of baked apple in a pastry case. The finished apple was often iced when served cold.

4–6 Cox's orange pippins
Stuffing (see below)
250 g/8 oz puff pastry
A little beaten egg

Peel and core the apples, leaving them whole, and either stuff them as for Pippin Pie (p. 179), this time chopping the apricots and mixing all the ingredients together, or use a stuffing of your own choice.

Cut large squares of thinly rolled pastry and sit each apple in the centre of a square (see Note); draw up the corners over the apple and dampen the edges before pinching them together, curling back just an inch of each point to reveal the apricot or other stuffing.

Brush with beaten egg all over and bake at 220°C/425°F/gas mark 7 for 20 to 25 minutes, or until the pastry is quite crisp and golden brown.

Note: It is as well to cut a foil template in order to establish the right size of pastry squares to cut, allowing for a ¼-inch seam.

CABINET PUDDING

A little unsalted butter
Boudoir biscuits or sponge fingers
½ litre/1 pint single cream
1 tsp cornflour

6 eggs
A vanilla pod
60 g/2 oz castor sugar
1 tsp grated orange candied peel
1 tsp grated orange rind
1 tbsp brandy

Orange Sauce
125 ml/¼ pint orange juice
Sugar
A little potato flour
½ tsp finely grated orange rind

Soak the grated orange rind and candied peel in the brandy. Grease a straight-sided charlotte mould, seamless cake tin or soufflé dish with unsalted butter. Line this with boudoir biscuits, sugared side to the wall of the container; cut a wedge to lock the last biscuit in place.

Cream the eggs, sugar and cornflour. Bring the cream and vanilla pod to the boil and strain onto the egg, sugar and cornflour mixture. Add the rind and peel to the custard. Carefully fill the mould with this. Stand the mould in a second container of boiling water and poach in the oven at 170°C/325°F/gas mark 3 for 30 minutes, or until the custard is set and firm.

Meanwhile make the accompanying sauce. Bring the orange juice and sugar to the boil. Slake a little potato flour in a tablespoon of cold water, stir this into the boiling juice a little at a time until you have the required consistency. Add the grated orange rind. Dredge with castor sugar to prevent skin forming.

Allow the pudding to cool a little before turning it onto a warm serving dish.

CHOCOLATE PUDDING
WITH RASPBERRY SAUCE

This pudding is rich but very light and is one of those puddings which is 'quiet' when it is cooked, so don't be deceived by a somewhat pale top — lend an ear, and if it isn't murmuring it is cooked.

175 g/6 oz castor sugar
4 eggs
100 g/3 oz self-raising flour
125 g/4 oz plain chocolate
2 tbsps cold water

Raspberry Sauce
250 g/8 oz fresh or frozen raspberries
Juice of 1 lemon
100 g/3 oz castor sugar
2 tbsps gin or water

Put the eggs and sugar into a mixer and whisk them until they are pale and thick and all the sugar crystals have dissolved. (If you don't have an electric mixer, use a round-bottomed bowl arranged over a pan of simmering water just to ease and quicken the whisking process.)

Break the chocolate into small pieces and put it with the *cold* water into a small basin, arranged over a pan of *boiling* water, until it has melted completely. Let it cool a little.

Deftly fold the sifted flour into the egg mixture with a balloon whisk, then quickly but thoroughly incorporate the melted chocolate. Pour the mixture into a papered and buttered loose-bottomed cake tin (8 inches in diameter, 4 inches deep).

Bake at 190°C/375°F/gas mark 5 for about 45 minutes.

Meanwhile make the sauce. Bring all the ingredients to the boil over a very low heat. This will allow the raspberries to draw. Simmer gently for 5 minutes and then very gently press the contents through a fine sieve, applying only a minimum of pressure to the fruit so that the sauce remains clear. (As this way of serving the sauce may seem extraordinarily extravagant, it can be served without sieving.)

Turn the pudding onto a cooling rack, remove the paper and transfer the pudding to a warm serving platter.

Re-heat the sauce and pour into a heated sauceboat; sprinkle the merest dredge of castor sugar over the surface to prevent a skin forming.

CHRISTMAS PUDDING

Everybody has his or her own version of this gorgeous pudding. I am only sorry that we tend to eat it just once in twelve months. I don't suppose we really have to make it a yearly event, but we almost invariably do so.

Here is my own version, which is coarse-textured, nutty, fruity, sticky, dark and oozing with liqueurs – but I warn you, a little goes a long way. It is not a spicy pudding.

To make 2 puddings weighing 2 kg/4 lb:
250 g/½ lb self-raising flour
250 g/½ lb fresh white breadcrumbs
250 g/½ lb ground almonds
375 g/¾ lb sultanas
375 g/¾ lb stoned raisins (muscatels)
375 g/¾ lb whole glacé cherries
60 g/2 oz chopped angelica
125 g/4 oz crystallised apricots
125 g/4 oz whole sweet almonds
125 g/4 oz crystallised chestnuts
500 g/1 lb Barbados sugar
375 g/¾ lb cold, hard, unsalted butter
6 eggs
½ litre/1 pint sweet brown ale such as barley wine
Juice and rind of 1 lemon and 1 orange
6 tbsps Benedictine (2 miniature bottles)

Grate the butter. Beat the eggs. Grate the orange and lemon rind and squeeze the juice and add to the beer and Benedictine.

Combine all the dry ingredients and mix well with the liquids. Put into buttered basins, cover with foil and steam for 5 hours for the first steaming, and then a further 3 hours on the day of eating.

ENGLISH SPONGE PUDDING

For me the secret behind a really good-flavoured sponge pudding is the quality of the butter used. I firmly believe that unsalted butter should be used for all sweets. A sponge pudding is a very personal affair and there are those who have great success with margarine and other cooking media, but the little saved on any other fat than butter cannot be weighed against the elegant flavour which only good fresh butter can produce.

The sponge pudding should be England's answer to the soufflé, but it ought not to be compared with it, for the two things are entirely different and the pudding is essentially a creation of the English over many centuries.

This basic pudding can be sent forth with as many masks and guises as your imagination can conjure up. The range is endless – vanilla, almond, chocolate, coffee, raspberry, orange and lemon: creamy rich custard, dark bitter-sweet chocolate sauce, fresh hot purée of raspberries or redcurrants, warming tones of gingers and treacles. All can be attached to, poured over or give flavour to the steamed sponge pudding, but the success will lie in the pudding itself.

2 eggs
2 tbsp cold water
The weight of the 2 eggs in:
Unsalted butter
Castor sugar
Self-raising flour

Have the butter at room temperature, add the sugar and beat until every granule of sugar has disappeared. Add 1 spoonful of the flour and beat in well.

Beat the eggs with the cold water and gradually beat them into the creamed butter and sugar. Now deftly and thoroughly fold in the rest of the flour.

Spoon into a buttered pudding basin and cover with a circle of buttered foil that is big enough to leave the top slack, to give room for the pudding to rise.

Make sure the foil is well sealed round the brim of the basin so that no steam, which would make the top of the pudding wet, can get in. Have the steamer ready on the stove so that it is good and hot, ready to give the mixture its initial 'push into space'.

Steam for 1½ to 1¾ hours. Remember to top up the steamer with boiling water.

When serving, carefully remove the foil, run a knife around the sides of the basin and invert onto a warm serving dish.

MAIDS OF HONOUR

There can be little doubt that an almighty mix-up has evolved over the centuries between Maids of Honour and Almond Cheesecakes. It is generally accepted that Henry VIII had these delicate cakes served to his various queens during Tudor times. It is also known that Elizabeth I had a penchant for them and would send her ladies-in-waiting into the town of Richmond to buy these delicacies from the local baker who, it is said, invented them. These were no doubt cheesecakes and took their name from the ladies who carried them back to Richmond Palace for the king or queen. To this day there exists a terrace of houses, near to where the palace used to stand, bearing the name of Maids of Honour Row. The Hanoverians spread their fame to many parts of England, even as far as Richmond, Yorkshire, which sometimes lays claim to be the originator of the recipe. No one, however, seems to have noticed the great similarity to the French Gâteau Pithiviers and it is more than likely that the original recipe stems from here.

Whatever argument is put forward as to the original ingredients, I doubt that it will be argued that there is every reason to restore Maids of Honour, in their rich and rightful glory, with yet another version — mine, which I serve as one huge open-faced tart, as a pudding, sometimes hot, sometimes cold.

If you prefer a flaky crust, use 250 g/8 oz puff pastry; or alternatively, make a rich shortcrust.

Shortcrust Pastry

250 g/8 oz plain flour
150 g/5 oz unsalted butter
2 tsps icing sugar
1 egg-yolk beaten with 3 tbsps cold water

The Filling

100 g/3 oz castor sugar
2 egg-yolks
60 g/2 oz unsalted butter
1 heaped tsp self-raising flour
3 tbsps thick cream
Shredded rind of 1 lemon
125 g/4 oz ground almonds
Quince jelly or conserve

First make the pastry. Sieve the sugar and flour together; cut the butter into small pieces and lightly rub into the flour. Make a well in this sandy-textured mixture, add the egg and water all at once and form quickly and deftly into a soft dough.

Leave this to rest for half an hour before rolling out and lining either one large flan ring or smaller deep tartlet tins.

Now make the filling. Cream the butter and sugar thoroughly. Beat in the small quantity of flour. Beat in the egg-yolks. Stir in the ground almonds and lemon rind, incorporating them completely. Finally, slacken the mixture with the cream.

Whether you are making one large tart or individual ones, it is better that they should be deep enough to hold plenty of filling. Put a teaspoon of quince jelly or conserve into each tart case, spread this over the bottom and put a good measure of the almond mixture on top.

Bake in the centre of the oven at 200°C/400°F/gas mark 6 for 20 minutes (a larger tart will take up to 30 minutes). Put onto a cooling tray and dust with icing sugar before serving either warm or cold.

OLD ENGLISH BAKED RICE PUDDING

I wonder how many people realise what an elaborate confection a rice pudding used to be. It is certainly a far cry from the rather wet milk and rice product often served today.

The Georgians would have put a rim of prettily decorated puff pastry round the edge of the dish, though this ought to be baked first in a hot oven should you think of embarking on such an elaboration.

125 g/4 oz pudding rice
½ litre/1 pint milk
60 g/2 oz castor sugar
4 eggs
60 g/2 oz unsalted butter
60 g/2 oz muscatel raisins
60 g/2 oz sultanas
30 g/1 oz chopped peel or glacé cherries
1 sherry glass of brandy
Rind of 1 lemon
Grated nutmeg
Water

Bring plenty of water to the boil in a large pan. Wash the rice, put this into the water and boil for 17 minutes exactly. Rinse the rice in a sieve under running cold water.

Infuse the lemon rind with the milk and sugar in a double boiler. Beat the eggs in a separate basin. Whisk on the hot milk and return the mixture to the pan, stirring all the time until the sauce coats the back of a spoon.

Take the pan away from the heat (off the water, that is), add the butter, fruits, brandy and cold rice. Butter an oven-proof dish and pour the mixture into this.

Stand the dish in a second dish or meat tin containing hot water. Grate a little nutmeg over the top and bake the pudding at 140°C/275°F/gas mark 2 for half an hour or until the pudding is set but not split.

Serve with pouring cream.

PEARS IN RED WINE

Not from France, as many would expect, but from Doncaster, from a recipe dating back to 1740.

½ litre/1 pint Burgundy-type red wine
250 g/8 oz castor sugar
The zest of 1 oily-skinned orange
6 cloves
8 good-sized pears

Remove the zest from the orange with a potato-peeler and shred it as finely as hairs.

Make a syrup from the wine, sugar, cloves and zest by slowly bringing them to the boil and stirring to ensure that all the sugar is dissolved.

Peel the pears and either leave them whole with the stalks still on or quarter them and take out the core; whichever method you choose, select a dish just large enough to pack the pears in. Strain the syrup over them – if they are well packed into the dish, they should be completely covered.

Cook in the oven at 200°C/400°F/gas mark 6 until the pears are tender.

Serve either hot or chilled.

PIPPIN PIE

It is well worth the effort needed to make this Elizabethan apple pie, if only because it will pull you up with a start to realise that this is how today's pie was founded!

For the historians, Cox's orange pippins did not appear on our markets until the early part of the nineteenth century.

Any apple which is reasonably firm will do well for this pie. The pie does not have a pastry bottom, as this would usually go very soggy.

250 g/8 oz puff pastry
1¼ kg/2½ lb Cox's orange pippins, including 6 of even size
Juice and rind of 1 lemon
60 g/2 oz unsalted butter
60 g/2 oz castor sugar
12 fresh apricots (or tinned whole ones)
125 g/4 oz seedless raisins
2 tbsps honey
1 tbsp soft brown sugar
1 heaped tsp mixed spice
Apricot purée or jam
A little beaten egg or top of the milk

Peel and core the 6 even-sized apples and cut them in half 'equator-wise'. Rub them all over with a little lemon juice so that they won't discolour and place on one side ready to receive the stuffed apricots.

Make a purée with the balance of the apples; peel, core and slice them and put them in a pan with 1 tablespoon of water, the juice and grated rind of the lemon, half the butter and enough of the castor sugar to sweeten them. Cover with a tight-fitting lid and let the apples draw over a very low heat, tossing the pan at frequent intervals, until they are soft. Put the pulp through a blender or Mouli and set on one side to cool.

Roll out the puff pastry as thinly as possible and edge a 10-inch diameter shallow dish with this. Cut twelve 2-inch circles with the balance of the pastry.

Split and stone the apricots and make the stuffing: cream the rest of the butter with the brown sugar and honey; add the mixed spice and the raisins. Fill the apricot halves and fit them into the uncooked apple halves. Arrange these on top of the purée in the edged dish and put a teaspoon of apricot glaze or jam on the top of each.

Set a circle of puff pastry on top of each apple and brush the pastry with a little beaten egg (or top of the milk). Bake at 220°C/425°F/gas mark 7 for 25 minutes, or until the pastry is crisp and golden. Five minutes before the end of the baking time dredge a little icing sugar over the pastry; this will give the pie a good shiny finish.

This pie is better served hot, unaccompanied, but can be served cold with thick cream or cold apricot sauce.

An alternative way of making it is to use a long oblong dish; arrange the stuffed apples in two rows and lay pastry strips between the rows, making a lattice top and showing the apples in between.

QUIRE OF PAPER

This method of serving wafer-thin cream pancakes is unusual; in the 1700s Ann Peckham of Leeds dressed hers quite simply by dredging each finished pancake with castor sugar and then laid them one on top of the other until she had the necessary twenty. I suggest you reduce the number of pancakes and spread each one with redcurrant jelly, purée of fresh raspberries, almond buttercream, cinnamon buttercream or sherry buttercream. Sherry or sack was often served with pancakes, along with melted butter, so authenticity has not been tampered with to any great extent. What is to be noted is the quality of the batter.

125 g/4 oz plain white flour
2 eggs and 2 extra yolks
125 ml/¼ pint milk
125 ml/¼ pint single cream
Sherry
30 g/1 oz castor sugar
Unsalted butter for frying

Sieve the flour and sugar into a bowl and make a well in the centre. Beat the whole eggs, yolks, cream and milk together; pour the mixture into the well and gradually incorporate the flour until you have a smooth batter. Use the sherry to arrive at the consistency of thin cream.

Heat a heavy-bottomed pancake pan, brush with melted butter and fry the pancakes in the usual way.

Make a stack of pancakes with fillings as suggested above. To serve, cut into wedges like a cake.

Note: At the hotel school in Switzerland I was taught to melt the butter for frying the pancakes and pour this into the batter. With a hot heavy-bottomed pan there was never any need to grease it and the pancakes were thin and light.

A RICH BAKED CUSTARD PIE

This rich shortcrust pastry used to be known as royal paste.

400 ml/¾ pint single cream
1 level tsp cornflour
60 g/2 oz castor sugar
6 eggs
A vanilla pod or a few drops of essence

Shortcrust Pastry
250 g/8 oz plain flour
150 g/5 oz unsalted butter
15 g/½ oz castor or icing sugar
1 egg-yolk
3 large tbsps cold water

First make the pastry. Deftly rub the butter into the flour. Sift in the sugar, stirring with a large dinner fork. Beat the egg-yolk with the cold water and add at one fell swoop, quickly collecting the dry ingredients into a loose ball with the fork. Do not work the pastry too much.

Roll the pastry out on a floured board to the required size for an

8-inch flan ring. Place the ring on a buttered baking sheet and line it with the pastry, decorating the edges to your fancy. Fit a second lining of foil (shiny side to the pastry) and put the pastry in a cool place to rest for half an hour.

Bake the pastry case at 180°C/350°F/gas mark 4 until it is almost cooked. Take it out of the oven, remove the foil and leave the case on one side until you have made the filling.

Mix together the cornflour and the sugar; add the eggs one at a time, beating until all the sugar has dissolved. Add the vanilla pod to the cream; bring the cream to the boil and pour onto the egg mixture, whisking all the time. Remove the pod.

Fill the flan case and bake in the middle of the oven at 140°C/275°F/gas mark 2 until the custard is set. This will take about 30 to 45 minutes. Let the flan cool somewhat before removing the ring.

The custard pie can be served warm or cold.

SHERRY PUDDING

I don't know where this recipe comes from, but it appeared at frequent intervals for Sunday lunch in my family home and my parents were Victorians, so . . .

125 g/4 oz self-raising flour
125 g/4 oz unsalted butter
125 g/4 oz soft brown sugar
2 eggs
175 ml/⅓ pint sweet brown sherry
175 g/6 oz finely chopped candied peel (see below)
Egg custard to serve

Soak the peel (which *must* be fresh-sticky and not hard) in the sherry for 1 hour.

Cream the butter and sugar until every granule of sugar has dissolved. Beat in the eggs one by one and fold in the sifted flour.

Drain the peel and add just 2 tablespoons of the sherry to the mixture to slacken it.

Butter a pudding basin and two-thirds fill this with alternate layers of pudding mixture and peel. Cover with buttered foil and steam for 2 hours.

Serve with an egg custard (p. 206) in which you have allowed for the balance of the sherry to be used.

Cold Puddings

APPLE TRIFLE

This sweet appears, and is, simple. It is also rich and very effective.

4 large Cox's orange pippins
1 scented rose
1 tbsp castor sugar
3 tbsps cold water
30 g/1 oz unsalted butter
¼ litre/½ pint double cream
Crystallised rose petals (see Note)

The Sauce
4 egg-yolks
¼ litre/½ pint double cream
1 level tsp cornflour
½ tsp rosewater

Peel, quarter and core the apples and cut them into thin slices. Melt the butter in a shallow pan and put in the apples in even layers with the rose petals interspersed between.

Splash with the cold water, cover with a lid and poach over a low heat until tender. Remove the rose petals and put the apples aside to cool.

Make the sauce as for Burn't Creams (p. 184) and put it aside to cool. Arrange the apples in the bottom of a serving dish. Cover with the cold sauce.

Whip the unsweetened cream until it stands in peaks. Fork or pipe this over the apple and cream base. Chill well before serving. Decorate with the rose petals *just* before serving as, if these are the commercial variety, there is a tendency for the colour to run.

Note: It is a simple job to crystallise your own rose petals.

Pick a fresh heavily scented rose. Pull each petal off and carefully paint with gum arabic. Dredge with castor sugar until every fragment of the surface is covered. Cover a cooling tray with a sheet of grease-proof paper and put each petal onto this, making sure they do not touch each other.

Dry in an airing cupboard and store in an air-tight jar until ready for use.

BURN'T CREAMS

Cambridge has sent many great men into the world and Trinity College also carries a reputation for sending us one of the world's most delicious cold sweets. There are endless variations on this creamy pudding; some have lemon rind added, some vanilla or bay leaf. All are unctuous with cream and egg-yolks.

8 egg-yolks
½ litre/1 pint double cream
1 tsp cornflour
60 g/2 oz castor sugar
Half a vanilla pod or the grated rind of half a lemon

It is essential to have everything at the ready when dealing with cookery which involves the mounting of eggs, so first select the dish or dishes (a big pudding always has a better texture) into which you are going to put the finished cream. They must be fire-proof as the dish has to go under a spanking hot grill. Then select a basin which is as near round-bottomed as you can get and make sure that it will fit comfortably into the top of a saucepan which must contain boiling water that can be in contact with the bottom of the basin.

Have a large bowl at the side of the stove half-filled with very cold water and a kitchen towel at the ready for holding the basin and to prevent steam burns.

If you do all this you should never have trouble with this type of cookery.

Cream the egg-yolks, sugar and cornflour until they are quite white.

Rinse the bottom of a pan with cold water, put the vanilla pod or grated lemon rind into the cream and bring this to the boil over a low heat. Remove the pod.

Pour the boiling cream directly onto the yolk mixture, whisking all the time with a balloon whisk.

Now arrange the basin on the top of the pan of boiling water and quite slowly, gently but carefully, stir the cream continuously until it is quite thick and the whisk leaves a definite trail. If you whisk too furiously you will beat too much air into the cream and it will be difficult to see when it has thickened. Keep the whisk moving all the time, clearing the sides and bottom of the basin as you work it.

As soon as the sauce is thick, take hold of the basin with the kitchen cloth and stand it in the cold water to take away that heat, which could just make it curdle. The water is there as a safety measure, so if you see the first signs of the cream curdling it can be saved by this action of plunging the basin into cold water and whisking the heat away.

Pour the cream into the dish, or dishes if you are making individual ones. Allow the cream to cool completely before putting it into the refrigerator for at least 6 hours to set right through.

An hour or so before serving, pre-heat the grill until it is red-hot. With a sugar dredger, coat the top of the cream with castor sugar, wipe clean the edges of the dish and stand it on a metal tray or rack. Slip this under the grill and carefully watch it until the sugar has completely melted and taken on a caramel colour.

Do not put the cream back into the refrigerator as this will soften the crisp top.

BUTTER'D ORANGES

This is possibly my very favourite English recipe. I think it was this that started me off delving into every aspect of the past, looking for other recipes as different as Butter'd Oranges certainly are. Anne Blencowe's book, where I found it, was printed in 1694 (at least the copy that I have was), so it must have been on the go in the seventeenth century. I have yet to discover it in this form in any other recipe book, so maybe it was a speciality of hers. The great ladies of the eighteenth century, Mesdames Glasse, Raffald, Smith, Fraser and others, don't have it in the copies of their books that I possess and Eliza Acton and Mrs Beeton either thought nothing of it (which I can hardly believe is true), or did not know about it (which is more probable).

Over the years since I first discovered the recipe I have developed two versions; there is very little difference in them, except that one is somewhat lighter in texture when finished, and for this reason I have let that become my main one, as guests seem to prefer it to be rather less rich in butter.

6 orange shells
2 large juicy oranges
60 g/2 oz castor sugar
5 egg-yolks
1 tsp rosewater
125 g/4 oz unsalted butter
125 ml/¼ pint double cream
1 large piece soft candied orange
Crystallised rose petals (p. 184)
and extra whipped cream for decorating

First prepare the orange shells.

Reverse the orange so that the stalk or bud is at the base. Holding a small pointed cook's knife at a diagonal angle, insert the tip into the orange an inch down from the apex, cut round and remove a lid. Traditional zig-zag cutting can be used.

Take a teaspoon, if possible an old one which has a worn and rather sharp edge, and, using the palm of your hand as a protective wall, scoop and lever out all the orange flesh until the shell is quite clean. Do likewise with the lid. *Take care not to pierce the skin at any point.* You will be left with a stalk of pith sticking up from the bottom of the shell. Cut this out with a sharp knife or pair of scissors. Clean the edges of the base and lid of any bits of unsightly pith. At this stage fix any decoration to the lid with a cocktail stick. Never use wire where it is likely to come into contact with food. It is quite safe to wire any rosebuds or miniature flowers to the stick before pushing it through the orange peel lid; if you have any gutta-percha, a strip can be wound round any wire for extra protection. At Christmastime it is nice to use baubles, tinsel bows, miniature angels, organza petals or any other notion that takes your fancy.

(The juice and flesh from the emptied oranges can be used as juice for breakfast, making squash or adding to sauces.)

Now prepare the filling. Grate the rind from the 2 oranges, which should give you 1 level tablespoon when pressed down. Squeeze the juice from the oranges.

Select a round-bottomed basin that will fit nicely and firmly into the top of a pan of boiling water.

Mix the orange juice and rind, egg-yolks and sugar together in the basin. Arrange the basin over the water, making sure that the water is in contact with the bottom of it.

Stir the mixture gently, but continuously, with a balloon whisk, until it is thick as a good custard. Take care to scrape the sides of the basin during this operation, but do not whisk too briskly or you will create a foam which will prevent your seeing when the liquid has thickened. When the orange mixture starts to ribbon, remove the basin from the top of the pan and stand it in a large bowl of cold water to cool slightly. Continue stirring and add the rosewater.

Remove the basin from the cold water.

Cut the butter into 1-inch cubes before you begin, so that it is soft but not melted. Whisk these pieces into the mixture, making sure that each one is incorporated before adding the next. Half-whip the cream and fold it into the mixture. Cut the soft candied orange into tiny pieces or shred it on a grater. As the Butter'd Orange starts to set, fold this into it so that it stays suspended and doesn't all sink to the bottom.

Fill the orange shells. Decorate the top of the Butter'd Oranges, when set, with home-made crystallised rose petals pouring from under the lid of the orange.

A simpler decoration is to use a rose piping tube and pipe a band of whipped cream round the rim of the orange base, letting it be somewhat thicker on one side than the other so that the lid stands at an attractive angle.

These oranges look most attractive when nestling in a folded organza napkin, or mounted into a pyramid.

CHEESE PYE (Cheesecake)

This 250-year-old recipe is far too scrumptious to be left at the bottom of any drawer. It must never be forgotten that the Georgians had more kinds of pastry than we tend to use today. Twentieth-century sweet pastry was frequently used for pies which today may well be called flans, and in this recipe for cheesecake yet another name appears. It matters not what's in a name – what is more important is what goes into the making of this dish.

The Pastry

125 g/4 oz plain flour
60 g/2 oz unsalted butter
60 g/2 oz castor sugar
1 egg-yolk
1 tbsp cold water
Icing sugar

The Filling

4 eggs
175 g/6 oz castor sugar
Juice and grated rind of 1 lemon
500 g/1 lb cottage cheese
30 g/1 oz plain flour
60 g/2 oz flaked sweet almonds

First make the pastry. Rub the butter into the flour as lightly as possible. Dredge in the sugar. Beat the egg-yolk with water and deftly mix the paste to a loose dough. Do not over-knead the pastry or it will be tough and shrink from the sides of the flan ring.

Line an 8-inch flan ring with this pastry. Put a large circle of foil (shiny side to the pastry) into the flan ring to hold the sides in place while it is baked in the oven at 190°C/375°F/gas mark 5 for 15 minutes. Remove the foil very carefully.

Now make the filling. Separate the eggs. Beat the yolks with the sugar until the granules are dissolved. Add the rind and lemon juice. Beat in the cheese together with the sifted flour.

Whip the egg-whites until they stand in peaks and fold them into the cheese mixture. Pour the mixture into the baked flan case, sprinkle evenly with the flaked almonds and bake at

170°C/225°F/gas mark 3 for 40 to 45 minutes.

Turn off the heat but leave the cheesecake to cool in the oven for 20 minutes. Remove the flan ring during this last 20 minutes. When cold, dredge the top of the cake with icing sugar.

CHESTNUT CREAMS

As there are many brands of excellent chestnut purées on the market, there is little reason for not making one or two of the old English sweets in which the chestnut was the principle ingredient. Of course the texture of home-made chestnut purée is grander, but it is a deal of labour. (To make your own purée, peel one pound of chestnuts and poach them slowly in vanilla-flavoured milk until tender. Put through the first sieve of a Mouli. Cool before using.)

375 g/¾ lb unsweetened tinned chestnut purée
2 sherry glasses Jamaica rum
125 ml/¼ pint double cream
Juice and rind of 1 orange
60 g/2 oz castor sugar
Cream and crystallised orange for decoration

Dissolve the castor sugar in the rum over a low heat and allow to cool. Beat in the chestnut purée.

Whip the cream together with the orange juice and rind. Fold into the rum-flavoured purée, fill into individual glasses and chill well.

Decorate with lightly sweetened, rum-flavoured whipped cream and a segment of crystallised orange.

CHOCOLATE PYE

One of the many varieties of pastry used by the Georgians was crackling crust, made from almonds and egg-whites. This crisp crust, with a very delectable filling of chocolate and cream, they chose to call quite simply 'chocolate pye'.

If you find the almond pastry too difficult to handle, make a shell of your favourite sweet pastry, but not a lard shortcrust, as its flavour is too crude for the filling.

Crackling Crust
175 g/6 oz ground almonds
60 g/2 oz castor sugar
1 egg-white

The Filling
¼ litre/½ pint single cream
250 g/½ lb plain chocolate
60 g/2 oz whole almonds
¼ litre/½ pint double cream for piping
1 tbsp rum
1 tbsp icing sugar
Chocolate flakes and toasted almonds for decoration

Work the almonds, castor sugar and beaten egg-white into a stiff paste and leave in the refrigerator for half an hour. Form the paste into a ball and roll out to line an 8-inch flan ring. Dredge with flour if it gets too sticky.

If you find the paste very soft, it is quite all right to press it into the ring, where it may have broken. Trim and decorate the edge with your finger and thumb or the prongs of a fork.

There is no need to employ the usual lining of paper and dried beans, etc. – just cut a strip of foil and fit that round the inside edge to prevent it from collapsing.

Bake the flan case at 180°C/350°F/gas mark 4 for 20 to 25 minutes. Take care that the paste doesn't scorch, as almonds tend to burn quickly. Allow to cool before removing the foil and flan ring. Stand the shell on a cooling tray.

Now make the filling. Break the chocolate into small pieces. Put these into a basin and cover them with the cream. Stand the basin in a pan of boiling water and stir until all the chocolate has melted.

Allow the filling to cool, stirring from time to time to ensure even cooling. As it starts to set, gently beat it into a light foam, taking care to note if it starts to split – if it does, stop beating. The chocolate mixture will have become lighter in colour and have increased in volume.

Pour the mixture into the flan case and decorate with swirls of rum-flavoured whipped cream. Stick whole toasted almonds and flakes of chocolate into the whipped cream. This 'pye' should be as exotic as it must have been when the Georgians decorated it with real gold-leafed almonds and crystallised rose petals, and all the frills and furbelows that they could think up.

CLARET JELLY

The English word for red Bordeaux wines used to be clairette – hence the word claret.

The very word jelly smacks of nursery food and school meals, but a wine jelly is a long step from this type of food and it makes a most refreshing finish to any meal. For those with endless patience in their kitchens it can be made with a half-pint of fresh blackcurrant juice, when these berries are in season, but the following recipe using a packet jelly is a very good substitute and will convert many jelly-loathers!

1 packet blackcurrant-flavoured jelly
½ litre/1 pint claret or claret-type wine
The zest of 1 orange
30 g/1 oz castor sugar
Unsweetened whipped cream for decoration

Take the zest of the orange with a potato-peeler – this eliminates getting much of the bitter white pith on the flavoursome orange peel. Finely shred this zest and place in a basin, together with the sugar and jelly cubes.

Bring the claret to just below boiling point and pour it into the basin, stirring until all the jelly is dissolved. Allow to cool, then pour into a wetted mould and put to set.

Decorate with lots of unsweetened whipped cream.

CREAM CAKES

A somewhat odd title for what is virtually England's answer to the meringue. It appeared in many eighteenth-century cookery books, served with a fresh raspberry pulp, which added an unusual dimension.

4 egg-whites
Up to 250 g/8 oz castor sugar (see below)
¼ litre/½ pint whipped cream
250 g/½ lb fresh raspberries
1 tbsp castor sugar
A squeeze of lemon juice

To make the meringues, whip the egg-whites in a scrupulously clean bowl with a fine balloon whisk, whisking by hand.

Whip until the whites are stiff enough not to fall out of the bowl when it is tipped steeply. Add a little of the sugar and whip again, and go on adding the sugar by degrees, whipping after each addition.

The size and condition of egg-whites vary and consequently the amount of sugar needed will also vary. As soon as the sugar appears to be reducing the stiffness of the meringue mixture, stop adding any more.

Drop even amounts of this mixture onto a lightly greased baking sheet with a tablespoon. Bake in a very low oven (120°C/250°F/gas mark ¼) for about 1½ hours. The result should be a creamy-coloured, very light and fragile meringue with a slightly toffee-like centre.

If the meringue cases turn out like plaster of Paris, this will be due to a too dry mixture (often this occurs when an electric machine is used), or too much sugar. Make a rough pulp of the raspberries and sugar, adding a little lemon juice. Sandwich the cream cakes together at the last minute, as otherwise the pulp will soak into the cases and possibly be absorbed, causing the cases to fall. Decorate with the whipped cream.

ETON MESS

The original recipe for this traditional pudding is absurdly simple — chopped strawberries and thick cream! Without fear of divorcing things too far from the original, I think the following recipe is good, easy to prepare and delicious to eat.

500 g/1 lb wild (preferably) or cultivated strawberries
400 ml/¾ pint whipped cream
6 meringue cases (see the preceding recipe)
3 tbsps kirsch (1 miniature bottle)
A little icing sugar

Sprinkle the strawberries with the icing sugar and splash with
the kirsch; chill well. Just before serving, fold in first some
chilled whipped cream and then the roughly crushed meringue
shells.

Pile into a glass bowl or into a large fancy meringue case and
decorate with whole strawberries.

FLOATING ISLANDS

*Sometimes called Snow Eggs, this sweet joined the ranks of other
romantic-sounding things such as Moonshine, A Web of Silver, A Quire
of Paper and Sugar Spun Like Gold, popular with seventeenth- and
eighteenth-century cooks. Though popular in France to this day, it has
never made a full return to stardom here.*

½ litre/1 pint basic cream as for Burn't Creams (p. 184)
4 egg-whites (use the yolks in the cream sauce)
125 g/4 oz castor sugar
Vanilla-flavoured milk for poaching
Single cream (see below)

Make the cream as directed and chill. Stiffly beat the egg-whites
and beat in the castor sugar as though you were making meringues,
stopping when the mixture is wet enough and starts to fall. Bring
the milk (flavoured with either a drop of vanilla essence or a piece
of vanilla pod) to boiling point in a shallow pan, then reduce the
heat so that there is no movement in the pan.

Slip tablespoons of the meringue mixture into the hot milk and
poach the islands on each side for 2 or 3 minutes, until they are
firm. Lift each egg or island with a draining spoon onto a clean
linen cloth to drain and cool.

Arrange the islands in a shallow serving dish, coat with the cold sauce let down with thin cream and serve.

Crystallised rose petals can be added as a decoration, if you have any in your store cupboard (see p. 184).

Note: Some cooks prefer to make the sauce with the poaching liquor, but I find this tastes of albumin and prefer the richer sauce.

FLUMMERY

This delicate pudding has really gone through the mill – I have even seen ground rice given as an ingredient! The original recipe for this old English dish is one of the most delicate you could wish for and simplicity itself to make.

If you don't possess a magnificent Georgian mould for the presentation of flummery, perhaps you do have one of those Victorian affairs in white or brown pottery, with knobs and turrets running riot all over the place. Failing all these things, those custard cups you have never found a use for could well come into their own.

I usually serve flummery quite simply with a boat of thick cream, but my version here goes very well with a fresh orange salad (p. 202).

½ litre/1 pint double cream
30 g/1 oz gelatine dissolved in a little water
60 g/2 oz castor sugar
1 tbsp orange flower water
Juice and grated rind of 1 orange

Put all the ingredients into a double-boiler or into a basin which will fit into the top of a pan of boiling water. Stir gently but continuously until the sugar and gelatine are completely dissolved. Pour into a wetted mould and allow to cool before putting to set into the refrigerator.

There is a version which is made with ground rice, but the result tends to end up as I have mentioned above.

I sometimes omit the orange flower water and the orange rind and juice and substitute 125 g/4 oz of ground almonds which I infuse in the cream.

HONEYCOMB CREAM

This delicately flavoured cream is sometimes called by the unfortunate name of Honeycomb Mould and this could be a possible reason for its slip into disfavour. When flavoured with lemon it is delicious as a sweet in its own right, and when vanilla is used as an aromatic it makes a perfect accompaniment to any of the berry fruits, which can he piled high on a fruit stand as a foil to the cream. When served with a real egg custard into which a little whipped cream has been folded at the last minute, it becomes really exotic. It is best served the day of making.

340 ml/⅔ pint milk
175 ml/⅓ pint single cream
3 large eggs
20 g/⅔ oz gelatine
Juice and rind of 1 lemon or a vanilla pod (see Note)

If using lemon flavouring, carefully grate the yellow rind from the lemon and put it into the cream and milk. Bring these slowly to the boil over a low heat, thus allowing time for the lemon flavour to infuse into the liquid.

Separate the eggs and whisk together the egg-yolks, sugar, lemon juice (if using this flavouring) and gelatine. Whisking briskly, pour on the heated milk and cream.

Now stand the bowl in a sink of cold water, taking care that no water gets into the cream. Stir it from time to time as it cools, keeping the sides well stirred into the rest of the cream, as this is where it will start setting first.

Whilst the cream is still cooling, whisk the egg-whites until they just stand in peaks. Carefully, but fully, incorporate them into the now cold, but not set, cream.

Pour the mixture into a wetted mould or soufflé dish. Leave, until you need it, in a cool place, like a pantry or cellar. Try not to put this pudding into a refrigerator unless the weather, or your kitchen, is very warm. All gelatine sweets are better if they are not refrigerated as this can turn them rubbery if they are left too cold for more than a few hours.

Note: When a vanilla pod is used, this should be put into the milk at least half an hour before you slowly bring the milk to the boil, in order to get the best flavour from the pod. It is removed before the hot liquid is poured onto the egg-yolks etc. (The pod can be rinsed under cold water for re-use at least once.)

ICE-CREAM

There are many ideas as to where ice-creams were first eaten and opinions abound on the subject of their introduction to this country. It is said that Richard the Lion Heart had experience of eating ice-cream, presumably on his crusades, and one theory is that Dr Johnson was the first to mention having eaten this delicate sweet in England. We do know that for centuries ice was cut from English rivers during the winter months and stored in the ice-houses around the countryside, and also that in the seventeenth and eighteenth centuries ice was imported from America in the bottom of ocean-going schooners to supplement stocks in London.

The early cooks were right when they mixed a purée of fresh fruit with good rich cream — nothing more — and chilled this; there is still no better way of making fruit ice-creams. A basic vanilla ice-cream can be used, but this does detract from the delicate and clean flavour of fresh fruit and it is really better as a base for chocolate, coffee, praline, etc. ices. However, as many people will wish to make the less rich fruit ice-cream, I shall give two recipes for this using the basic 'custard'.

An ice-cream maker is a definite possibility for most cooks today, and you can buy a type which slots into the ice-box of a refrigerator, or into a deep-freeze. Many will prefer not to buy the special equipment, but simply to make their ice-cream in either the ice-making compartment of their refrigerator or else in their deep-freeze. If you choose the latter methods, you must be sure to beat the ice-cream two or three times during the freezing process to ensure a smooth and creamy result, taking great care to catch the mixture before ice crystals form, for the latter would ruin the texture of the ice-cream.

BASIC VANILLA ICE-CREAM

This is a very rich ice-cream; for a somewhat plainer, but equally delicious form, substitute milk for cream.

½ litre/1 pint single cream
A vanilla pod
8 egg-yolks
100 g/3 oz castor sugar

Beat the egg-yolks and sugar until they are creamy and thick and all the sugar has dissolved. Bring the cream to the boil, together with the vanilla pod. Remove the pod and pour the cream onto the eggs and sugar, whisking well all the time.

Arrange this bowl over a pan of boiling water and, stirring all the time, thicken the custard until it coats properly the back of a wooden spoon.

Leave the custard to cool completely, then chill. Either follow the instructions for your particular machine, or place in a suitable container in the ice-making compartment of your refrigerator or in the deep-freeze.

The following are some of the variations based on the foregoing recipe.

Brown Bread Ice-Cream

½ litre/1 pint basic ice-cream
2 tbsps Madeira
100 g/3 oz wholemeal breadcrumbs
60 g/2 oz unsalted butter
100 g/3 oz castor sugar

Add the Madeira to the basic ice-cream at the custard stage.

Fry the breadcrumbs in the butter until crisp. Add the sugar and let this caramelise. Cool completely. Crush with a rolling pin. Add to the basic ice-cream as it is beginning to set. Proceed as in the basic recipe.

Ginger Ice-Cream

½ litre/1 pint basic ice-cream
4 large pieces of stem ginger
1 tsp ground ginger

Mix the ground ginger with the sugar and eggs when making the basic custard.

Finely chop the stem ginger; proceed to freeze the ice-cream and add the chopped ginger during the last few minutes of the freezing.

Raspberry and Mint Ice-Cream

½ litre/1 pint basic ice-cream
500 g/1 lb raspberries
4 tbsps castor sugar
4 fresh mint leaves

Using no water, toss the raspberries and mint over a low heat until the juices draw. Simmer with the sugar until the fruit has fallen to a pulp; pass through a hair sieve and cool completely before folding into the basic custard. Proceed as in the basic recipe.

Redcurrant Ice-Cream

½ litre/1 pint basic ice-cream
500 g/1 lb redcurrants
125 g/4 oz castor sugar

Pick the currants and proceed as for raspberry and mint ice-cream.

Walnut Ice-Cream

½ litre/1 pint basic ice-cream
125 g/4 oz shelled walnuts
60 g/2 oz castor sugar

Put the sugar and walnuts into a heavy-bottomed pan and proceed as you would for making almond praline, but once the sugar has turned to a *light* caramel, turn the entire contents of the pan onto a buttered metal baking tray.

When it is cold, crush the walnut mixture. Proceed to chill the ice-cream as in the basic recipe, adding the walnut mixture just as the cream is beginning to thicken.

GOOSEBERRY AND ROSEMARY ICE-CREAM

500 g/1 lb green gooseberries
3 tbsps cold water
4 tbsps castor sugar
Rind of half a lemon

1 level tsp powdered rosemary
¼ litre/½ pint double cream

Top and tail the gooseberries and put them into a pan with all the other ingredients except the cream. Simmer over a low heat, tossing the pan occasionally until all the fruit has fallen to a pulp but is not over-cooked and discoloured.

Cool the fruit and put first through a blender or Mouli and then press the purée through a hair sieve. Cool the purée completely before folding in the cream.

Freeze as in the basic recipe.

TEA ICE-CREAM

As we are a tea-drinking nation, why not have an ice-cream to match!

½ litre/1 pint single cream
25 g/¾ oz Earl Grey tea
8 egg-yolks
125 g/4 oz castor sugar
Jasmine flowers, rosemary, lemon rind, etc. (optional)

Infuse the tea leaves for 10 minutes in the hot cream. Strain through a muslin and proceed as for basic vanilla ice-cream, remembering to bring the cream to the boil again.

Note: Different teas will give different strengths, so it will be necessary to test each tea before use. You will get a rough idea as to its strength if you try it out with water, noting the infusion time.

Aromatic flavourings, such as jasmine, rosemary, mint and so on can be added at will and these should be tested in the same way, i.e. at the infusion stage.

JUNKET WITH GINGER SAUCE

Both seventeenth- and eighteenth-century potteries produced most elegant junket bowls which were often wide and deep enough to hold six or seven pints.

Junket can be a very refreshing sweet to serve after a rich main dish and of course it requires absolutely no effort to produce a simple junket which can be served with a little grated nutmeg sprinkled on at the last minute. Do, however, give it style by serving a huge junket in the most splendid bowl you possess — it is only when it appears in nasty opaque dishes that one thinks of nursing homes!

This version is somewhat richer than ordinary junket and I think it will find a place in your repertoire. An even richer version can be made using Devonshire instead of single cream, which makes a superbly elegant junket, the top of which can be dredged with mixed spice or cinnamon.

¼ litre/½ pint milk
¼ litre/½ pint single cream
45 g/1½ oz castor sugar
1 tsp rennet
A little ground ginger

Ginger Sauce
2 large pieces of stem ginger
1 tbsp castor sugar
1 tbsp Demerara rum
125 ml/¼ pint double cream

Mix the milk and the single cream together and sprinkle in the sugar. Slowly warm this until the sugar is dissolved and the liquid is no more than blood heat.

Stir in the rennet, pour immediately into a large shallow serving dish and leave in the kitchen atmosphere to set. Then make the sauce.

Chop the ginger very finely and mix with the sugar and rum. Stir in the double cream and continue stirring until it ribbons. Chill the sauce.

Sprinkle a little ground ginger on top of the junket before serving, using a dredger to achieve an even coating.

Serve the ginger sauce separately.

MELON AND CASSIA BUD SALAD

A ripe and well-flavoured melon is a delight, but I often wonder how we have come to accept those boat-shaped wedges of this fruit which so often in restaurants in this country appear before us half-ripe and juiceless, with ginger and sugar offered almost apologetically as though they are all that is needed to lift this fruit to gastronomic heights!

That ginger has been served with melon for some time in this country is not in doubt, for we learn from John Farley, chief cook at the London Tavern in the eighteenth century, that he advocated the marrying of the two, but the way he did it is a far cry from that mentioned above. My version is somewhat similar to his.

A ripe honeydew melon
4 good pieces of stem ginger
2 juicy lemons
1 tsp lemon rind
125 g/4 oz castor sugar
1 tsp cassia buds (see below)
or ½ tsp powdered cinnamon

Cut a lid out of the top of the melon and take a thin slice of the bottom so that the melon will balance without toppling over. Take care not to puncture the base when you do this or the juices will run out.

With a large Parisian spoon (the type used for making potato balls) or with a deep-bowled teaspoon, scoop out all the ripe flesh of the melon, taking care not to get too near the outside where it may not be quite ripe.

Put the melon balls into a bowl, together with the ginger, cut into fine slices, and the lemon peeled and segmented as you would an orange for orange salad (p. 202).

Add the teaspoon of grated lemon rind and the cassia buds (these are not unlike cinnamon in flavour, but some people liken them to cloves). Use cinnamon if cassia buds are not available. Sprinkle with the castor sugar and toss carefully together, avoiding breaking the fruits. Fill back into the melon shell and chill well before serving.

An attractive posy of white roses, or some other available decoration, can be wired and attached to the lid which should be tilted to show the fruit piled inside.

ORANGES IN RED WINE

8 navel oranges
375 g/12 oz soft brown sugar
Red Burgundy (see below)
¼ tsp powdered clove
Double cream for serving

Cut the oranges as for orange salad in the following recipe, removing and retaining the rind of at least 3 of them; shred the rind very finely. Measure the juice which will draw from the orange segments. Bring this up to 400 ml/¾ pint *in toto* with Burgundy.

Add the sugar to this wine stock and dissolve it over a low heat. Add the rind and cool the syrup before pouring it over the waiting orange segments. Chill well. Sprinkle with a little powdered clove. Serve with plenty of well chilled double cream.

ORANGE SALAD

8 large fleshy oranges
125 g/4 oz castor sugar
1 small glass gin
Juice of 1 lemon

Finely grate 2 heaped teaspoons of the best part of the rinds. Cut the rind from the oranges with a small sharp knife, having first cut a slice off the top and bottom to reveal the flesh.

Cut off the first slice and then use the white edge of the pith as a guide as you cut 'over-down and under'. Care must be taken not to cut into the orange flesh, and at the same time no pith should remain on the fruit as this is the bitter part of an orange.

Cut out the first segment between the obvious membranes. Put your forefinger into the cavity and use this as a wall against which to work as you cut out the rest of the segments, moving your finger along into a new position as you work. This way you should be able to produce skinless whole segments quite easily.

Carefully arrange the fruit in a dish, in attractive layered circles, sprinkling with sugar and a little rind as you go along. Finally pour over the gin and lemon juice and chill the salad well.

The sugar will dissolve and make its own rich syrup without further liquid or cooking.

PEACH MELBA

If only to help restore this delicious confection nearly back to its original version, I grasp at straws when I claim this as English!

It was created by Escoffier, when he was chef at the Savoy Hotel in London, for Dame Nellie Melba, the glass-shattering Australian soprano. She was herself a British subject and was the inspiration behind other dishes which were to bear her name. The actual Melba sauce was a later creation of Escoffier but today forms an integral part of a Peach Melba.

Vanilla ice-cream (p. 196)
Peaches
Lemon juice
Raspberry sauce (p. 172)
Blanched or green almonds
Whipped cream
Vanilla pod
Castor sugar

Skin the peaches either by 'stroking' them with the back of a knife or by plunging them into boiling water for a few seconds and then into cold water, after which they can easily be skinned. Cut the peaches in half and remove the stones; rub the flesh with fresh lemon juice to prevent discolouring.

Arrange balls of fresh vanilla ice-cream in a large shallow glass bowl. Press half a peach onto the top of each ball, coat each peach with cold raspberry sauce and decorate the dish liberally with vanilla-flavoured whipped cream and almonds.

Note: Have everything ready in the refrigerator – bowl, ice-cream, skinned peaches, whipped cream and almonds. This way you will be able to produce the finished dish quickly and without the ice-cream melting.

PINEAPPLE AND ALMOND SALAD

The pineapple was a symbol of wealth in the eighteenth century and was often glorified even further; sometimes soaked in brandy, at others just chopped and filled back into the shell with bay leaves as an added decoration. The leaves were frequently gilded for splendid occasions. Try my version of serving this fruit.

1 large ripe pineapple
60 g/2 oz nib or split almonds
60 g/2 oz angelica
Juice and rind of 1 lemon
60 g/2 oz preserving sugar
1 wine glass gin

Carefully cut off the skin of the pineapple with a sharp thin-spined knife. Cut the fruit into ⅛-inch slices and arrange overlapping in a row down the centre of a narrow dish.

Dice the angelica as small as possible (it will help here if you wash the angelica in hot water and then use a wetted knife). Mix the angelica with the almonds, sugar, lemon rind and juice.

With a teaspoon make a spine of this mixture down the centre of the pineapple. Pour the gin over, cover the dish with foil and put to chill.

Preserving sugar looks attractive for this dish, but is not essential.

PRINCE OF WALES'S CREAMS
(Lemon Creams)

¼ litre/½ pint double cream
2 eggs and 1 extra yolk
Grated rind of half a lemon
45 g/1½ oz castor sugar
1 tsp rosewater
Cream for decorating

Remove the yellow part only from the skin of the lemon, using the fine side of a grater. Bring the cream to the boil, together with this lemon zest and the rosewater.

Beat the eggs and sugar together until the sugar is dissolved. Pour on the hot cream, whisking all the time.

Fill small custard cups or similar dishes with the cream and stand these in a tin or bath of boiling water. (If the water isn't boiling, this will change the cooking time and process.)

Bake the creams in this receptacle at 180°C/350°F/gas mark 4 for 25 minutes or until set. Wipe the outsides of the cups before cooling and then refrigerating.

Serve topped with whipped cream containing a suspicion of sugar and a few drops of rosewater.

RICE CREAMS

This delicately flavoured creamy-looking sweet looks very attractive when served in individual glasses on white napkins, each one topped with a cluster of fresh raspberries or strawberries when in season.

A different way of presenting them, if you don't choose to serve them on their own, is to make an accompanying jelly of frozen raspberries or some other refreshing fruit. Do not be tempted to use a commercial jelly, for this sweet deserves only the very best of accompaniments and it would be wrong to overpower it with synthetic flavourings.

¼ litre/½ pint milk
60 g/2 oz pudding rice
30 g/1 oz castor sugar
A vanilla pod
2 eggs
¼ litre/½ pint double cream
1 level tsp powdered gelatine

Put the milk and the rice, together with the sugar and vanilla pod, into the top of a double saucepan. Cook over boiling water until the rice is tender; this will take about 45 minutes.

Remove the vanilla pod, wash and dry it and put it away for future use. Sprinkle gelatine into the hot rice and stir until dissolved. There's no need to dissolve the gelatine first.

Separate the eggs and mix the yolks with a tablespoon of the cream. Stir this egg mixture into the rice until it is fully incorporated. Return the pan to its bottom half and continue cooking for a couple of minutes, stirring all the time.

Now stand the pan in a bowl of cold water and stir until it is cool but not set.

Half-whip the remainder of the cream and stiffly whip the egg-whites. Fold the cream into the rice, incorporating thoroughly, then fold in the egg-whites.

Pour into glasses or little pots and put to chill.

––––––––––

A RICH OLD ENGLISH SHERRY TRIFLE

What a mercy that this wonderful pudding properly made can still be found in this country; though, sad to say, there are people about who tamper with an original dish when they would do well to leave it alone. I am not a lover of those trifles in which jelly appears, or even tinned fruits, and where the topping is sometimes nothing more than mean blobs of cream, chocolate vermicelli and the odd bit of angelica, all this usually covering a bright yellow skin of commercial-type custard.

It is a great advantage when a trifle is made with a fatless sponge and not heavy left-over pieces of Victoria sponge cake; a trifle is not the place to use up bits of stale cake and excellent small trifle sponges can be bought if you don't want to make your own.

The Base
2 fatless 7-inch sponge cakes or
1 packet good quality small sponge cakes
Up to 500 g/1 lb apricot purée, apricot jam or quince jelly
Up to ¼ bottle medium dry sherry

The Custard
½ litre/1 pint milk (or half milk and half cream)
5 eggs
1 tsp cornflour
A vanilla pod
45 g/1½ oz castor sugar

The Topping
½ litre/1 pint double cream
125 g/4 oz glacé cherries
125 g/4 oz blanched or toasted almonds
60 g/2 oz of either crystallised apricots,
crystallised pears, Carlsbad plums, etc.
60 g/2 oz crystallised chestnuts
125 g/4 oz ratafia biscuits
Angelica leaves
For fresh fruit trifles, see Variations

First make up the custard. Bring the milk, together with the vanilla pod, to the boil. Mix the sugar with the cornflour, gradually add the eggs and beat the mixture well until it is smooth. Remove the vanilla pod from the saucepan and pour the boiling milk onto the egg mixture, stirring all the time.

Rinse out the pan, leaving a film of cold water in the bottom. Return the custard to the pan and stir it with a wooden spoon over a low heat until it is thick. Plunge the bottom of the pan into a basin of cold water to remove any heat which might curdle the custard. Leave to cool whilst you prepare the base.

Split the sponge cakes in half across their middles; liberally spread them with the purée, jam or jelly, sandwich them together and cut into 1-inch fingers. Arrange these in a shallow trifle dish, some 12 inches across the top and about 3 inches deep.

Sprinkle the sponge fingers with plenty of sherry and pour the waiting custard over them. Cool the trifle base completely. (If the bowl is glass, wipe away any condensation from the sides, as this will look unsightly when the trifle is cold.)

Prepare all the topping ingredients – the actual quantities will depend on the area of trifle to be covered and this is bound to vary slightly. Put each topping ready on a separate plate.

Cut the crystallised apricots or pears and chestnuts and Carlsbad plums into attractive quarters. Cut long spikes of angelica. Empty the packet of ratafias to free them from biscuit crumbs. Make sure that the blanched or toasted almonds are cold or they will melt the cream.

Whip the cream until it just stands in peaks but doesn't look as though it will be cheese at any minute! Spread a thick layer over the trifle.

Starting on the outside edge, put a tight circle of alternate cherries and ratafias round the whole perimeter of the dish. Next fill a piping bag fitted with a large rose tube and make a second circle of round swirls of cream.

Then make a circle of apricot quarters, alternated with an equal-sized swirl of thick rich cream; stick the cream with two or three blanched whole almonds. Next put a circle of cherries and ratafias.

Continue like this until you are within 6 inches of the centre, when you can introduce the more expensive things like the chestnuts, apricots or pears, Carlsbad plums or whatever, all cut into quarters. Arrange these in the centre section with the angelica spikes.

Finish the top by sticking more whole almonds into the first circle of cream swirls if you are feeling in a really luxurious mood.

An attractive and unusual centre can be made if you crystallise a huge, blousy scented rose. Detach the best of the petals, follow the instructions on p. 184 and re-form it attractively in the shape of a 'blown' rose. The petals will keep for weeks in an air-tight storage jar, so can be made well in advance.

Variations

You may prefer to make a fresh fruit trifle and in this case use fresh fruits only for decoration and stick them into the bed of whipped cream at the last moment so that the juices do not draw and spoil the look of the trifle. A purée of the fruit can replace the jam in the sponge cakes. Particularly suitable fruits to use are strawberries or raspberries (wild or garden) and fresh apricots.

A nice alternative is to make an almond trifle. Roughly chop some ratafia biscuits and add these to the cake base. Cover the whipped cream (which in this case should be slightly sweetened) completely with whole blanched almonds and nothing else.

Other acceptable variations are to use Madeira, brandy or rum instead of the sherry. With fresh raspberries, use kirsch in both the base and the whipped cream topping.

STRAWBERRY FLAN

125 g/4 oz plain flour
60 g/2 oz unsalted butter
45 g/1½ oz castor sugar

1 egg-yolk
1 tbsp cold water
Strawberries
Redcurrant jelly
Whipped cream to decorate

Sift the flour directly onto a cold working surface. Lightly but thoroughly rub in the butter until you have a sand-like mixture.

Sift in the sugar, incorporating this by letting it run through your fingers as you lift and rain the flour and butter mixture. Make a well, gathering the mixture high round the sides.

Beat the egg-yolk with the water and pour into the middle of the well. Quickly and deftly work the dry and wet mixtures into a light paste, taking care not to work or knead the dough once the paste is formed.

Put an 8-inch flan ring on a buttered baking sheet. Butter the insides of the ring and line with the pastry. Make a second lining of foil. Fill the flan with dried beans or lentils and bake in the centre of the oven at 190°C/375°F/gas mark 5 for 15 minutes. Remove the beans and foil and ring and return the flan case to the oven for a further 7 to 10 minutes to dry out. Cool the case.

Make up the flan at the last minute in order to keep the pastry crisp. Arrange the picked and cleaned fruits, points upwards, packed in tight circles in the flan case. Melt some redcurrant jelly and, using a teaspoon, coat each strawberry with some of this.

Decorate with swirls of unsweetened whipped cream when the jelly is cold.

SUMMER PUDDING

Of all the deceptively simple sweets ever offered at our dining tables, surely summer pudding is one of the most delicious. I often wonder why our restaurants don't take it up, for you can throw it around, re-mould it, re-chill it, serve it up four days later and it still comes up smiling!

But there are three major 'musts': firstly, it must be served very cold (it deep-freezes admirably); secondly, lashings of thick pouring cream, well chilled, must be offered with it; and thirdly, but not quite so essential, it ought to be made during that short spell when the red berry fruits are in season, as the Danes do with their Röd Gröd.

Also, if you have a good Jewish bakery nearby, it is well worthwhile buying chollah instead of using the industrial bread too readily available nowadays.

White bread to line a 1 litre/2 pint pudding basin (see below)
750 g/1½ lb raspberries
750 g/1½ lb redcurrants
1 small glass gin, vodka or kirsch (optional)
250 g/8 oz castor sugar
¼ litre/½ pint double cream

Put the cleaned fruit into a large basin and sprinkle with the sugar and the spirit or liqueur. Toss the fruit gently until it is well and evenly coated.

This pudding turns out most satisfactorily when it completely fills the basin in which it is made, so it is a good idea to test by piling the fruit into the basin before you line it, allowing for the bread lining.

Cut a circle of bread to fit the bottom of the basin or mould. Cut fingers of bread ¼ inch thick, tapering from 1½ inches at the top to 1 inch at the bottom, and arrange these round the sides of the basin, cutting a final wedge to lock the sides in position. If ordinary bread is used, it would be advisable to cut it ⅜ inch thick. Actual quantities will depend on the ripeness of the fruit, the thickness of the bread and the size of the basin.

Fill the bread-lined mould with the fruit and pile up well over the rim, then press the fruit down with the flat of the hand until it is level with the rim.

From the remaining slices of bread, cut four sections of a circle slightly larger than the top of the basin, so that they can be overlapped by about ¼ inch. (You will save a lot of frustration with all this bread cutting if you make a card template to fit your own particular basin or mould.) If you have miscalculated and haven't enough filling, you will have to trim the sides of the bread down accordingly and reduce the size of the lid.

Choose a plate or cake tin base that will just sit inside the top of the basin. A piece of foil-covered card would do nicely. Put a heavy weight on top and put the basin on a tray and into the refrigerator for at least 8 hours.

To unmould, place your serving dish upside down on top of the pudding, invert the basin and smack it sharply on the sides. The pudding will sag slightly, as the bread will now be completely saturated with the fruity syrup and the fruit will be straining to get out when you cut it, so the unmoulding should be done at the last minute.

Now either decorate with whipped cream, or serve the cream separately.

SYLLABUB

I suppose that the syllabub is England's answer to the Italian zabaglione and the French sabayon, though the name is in fact derived from an old French champagne called Sille. The Tudors and Hanoverians must have actually drunk it, and what we class as syllabub today is perhaps a first cousin of the frothing affair served in its own glass and elegantly placed on its own stand. They did give receipts for A Sillebub to Last a Week as well as one for A Syllabube under the Cow – for the latter, one was instructed to pour the warm milk 'from a great height' when 'no cow was to hand'.

Fortunately this is one of England's great sweets that has made an early return to favour, and already there are many versions.

A syllabub should not be confused with a posset, for the latter was usually a more complete food, often taken by invalids, and could be either hot or cold.

1 orange
¼ litre/½ pint double cream
60 g/2 oz castor sugar
125 ml/¼ pint medium dry Madeira or sherry
Candied fruits for decoration

Finely grate the rind from the orange and squeeze the juice. Put the juice, rind, sugar and Madeira or sherry into a bowl, cover and leave for a few hours to let the oils from the rind impregnate the liquor.

Strain the liquid into a clean bowl and stir in the cream, gradually beating it until it ribbons and nearly stands in peaks (only take it to peak stage if you want to serve the syllabubs immediately).

Fill into the most attractive glasses you have – use custard cups or, if you are lucky, real syllabub glasses. Chill overnight and decorate with striplets of candied fruits.

WALNUT PIE

Sweet Pastry
175 g/6 oz plain white flour
125 g/4 oz unsalted butter
1 tsp lemon juice
60 g/2 oz icing sugar
1 egg
1 tbsp cold water

The Filling
125 g/4 oz ground almonds
125 g/4 oz castor sugar (see Note)
2 eggs
60 g/2 oz walnuts roughly chopped
1 tbsp lemon juice

Lightly rub the butter into the flour until you have a sandy texture. Sift in the sugar, incorporating this by letting it run through your fingers as you lift and rain the flour and butter mixture.

Make a well in the centre of these dry ingredients, beat the egg and add the water and lemon juice to it and pour into the well. Work the mixture quickly and deftly into a dough and leave to rest for half an hour.

Roll out two-thirds of the pastry and line an 8-inch flan ring or loose-bottomed tart tin. Roll out a lid and put on one side whilst you make the filling.

Separate the eggs. Cream the yolks with the sugar until they are white and fluffy. Beat in the ground almonds. Add the chopped walnuts. Stiffly beat the egg-whites and fold into the mixture, adding a tablespoon at first to slacken the walnut mixture.

Fill the lined flan ring, wet the edges, add the lid, seal and pinch or fork round the edge so that it looks attractive. Bake for 40 minutes in the centre of a pre-heated oven at 200°C/400°F/gas mark 6. Dredge with a little castor sugar 10 minutes before the end of the baking time.

Remove the ring and stand the finished pie on a cooling tray. Serve with plenty of whipped cream.

Note: This pie is also good when made with brown sugar.

Sauces, Stuffings, Chutneys *and* Butters

Sauces

APPLE SAUCE

There are two sorts of apple sauce, the watery kind and the rich golden kind. I prefer the latter.

> 4 Cox's orange pippins
> 1 tbsp castor sugar
> About 30 g/1 oz unsalted butter

Peel, quarter and core the apples. Cut into even-sized slices and poach in a modicum of water, plus 30 g/1 oz of unsalted butter per pound of apples, until tender.

Add the sugar and stir well until dissolved. Pass through a blender or Mouli and chill well. This recipe will give you a rich firm sauce.

APRICOT SAUCE

300 g/10 oz apricot jam

125 ml/¼ pint cold water
3 tbsps kirsch

Stir the jam and water in a heavy-bottomed saucepan until the jam is completely melted. Pass this purée through a blender or hair sieve.

Cool, stir in the kirsch and then chill.

Note: For thinning down fruit purées and sauces, keep a small amount of pure sugar syrup in your refrigerator. Make this from 300 g/10 fl oz castor sugar and 300 ml/10 fl oz water; bring to the boil and simmer until the sugar has dissolved – no longer, or the syrup will be cloudy.

BREAD SAUCE

¼ litre/½ pint milk
60 g/2 oz butter
1 small onion, roughly chopped
½ crushed clove garlic
1 bay leaf (or a little nutmeg or 2 cloves)
Salt and freshly ground white pepper
100 g/3 oz fresh white breadcrumbs
125 ml/¼ pint single cream
A little white stock or extra milk

Put the milk, butter, garlic, bay leaf or nutmeg or cloves and onion into the top of a double saucepan and make the mixture as hot as possible. Add the breadcrumbs and let the sauce cook until it is quite thick and smooth. Pass the entire contents of the pan through a blender, Mouli or hair sieve.

Add the cream adjust the seasoning, re-heat and serve.

If the sauce is too thick (this will depend on the kind of bread you use), let it down with a little white stock or milk.

Note: If the sauce has to be kept hot, return it to the double saucepan after sieving and cover with a circle of buttered paper to prevent a skin forming. Keep the water in the bottom pan hot.

BUTTER SAUCE

'Melted butter' is often called for in old cookery books when serving perhaps plain boiled vegetables, poached fish or chicken. This was actually the equivalent of the French Sauce Blanche and it takes very little imagination to see that the two names could easily account for the great misunderstanding that has arisen over the past half century that our vegetables were always served with plain melted butter or white sauce.

The quality of this rich creamy sauce depends entirely on the quality of butter used and under no circumstances must it be left to acquire any other flavour than that of true butter. Great care must therefore be taken to see that it doesn't take on any colour at all.

125 g/4 oz good fresh butter
1 level dessertspoon fine white flour
125 ml/¼ pint milk
1 tbsp lemon juice or white wine vinegar

Cut the butter into small cubes, sprinkle with the flour and work this into a smooth paste with a palette knife on the corner of your kitchen board or on a plate.

Transfer this butter paste to a small pan and, over the lowest heat possible, beat it with a wooden spatula until it starts to melt. Gradually beat in the milk, without raising the heat.

Bring the sauce just to the boil and simmer for 2 minutes, beating all the time, and add the lemon juice or vinegar. The salt in the butter will be adequate and the lemon juice or vinegar will heighten the fresh–butter flavour of the sauce.

CAPER SAUCE

This recipe is based on an eighteenth-century version and is not the creamy or white sauce that is sometimes served. It marries attractively with roast lamb, boiled beef, poached or grilled salmon, and is also good with roast ham.

60 g/2 oz butter
30 g/1 oz plain flour
400 ml/¾ pint stock (taken from the liquor in which you have poached or boiled a piece of meat or fish)

60 g/2 oz roughly chopped capers
Lemon juice
A touch of ground nutmeg or mace
Salt if necessary

Melt the butter in a heavy-bottomed saucepan; stir in the flour; gradually add the stock, stirring all the time, until the sauce is boiling gently.

If there are any specks or lumps, strain the sauce into a clean pan. Mix in the capers, season with salt, lemon juice and a hint of mace or nutmeg.

CELERY SAUCE

Half a head of celery
400 ml/¾ pint chicken stock
60 g/2 oz unsalted butter
30 g/1 oz flour
125 ml/¼ pint double cream
2 egg-yolks
Salt and freshly ground white pepper

Thoroughly wash and finely slice the celery. Melt the butter in a heavy-bottomed pan and soften the celery in it. Sprinkle on the flour and stir it well in; gradually add the stock, stirring all the time, bring to the boil and simmer for 10 minutes. Season lightly and, just before serving, mix the egg-yolks with the cream and stir quickly into the sauce. Re-heat the sauce, but do not boil it again.

CHEESE SAUCE

Depending on which cheese you use, the finished flavour of this sauce will vary enormously, a fact rarely taken into account when making it. I use a mixture of half Gouda, half Edam, for a rich, mild-toned sauce. If I want an edge to it, I use Cheshire and Cheddar. Parmesan gives yet another flavour – very nutty and deep. A light, slightly sour sauce can be made with cream cheese with the addition of a little white Stilton.

60 g/2 oz butter
45 g/1½ oz plain flour (see below)
1 tsp made-up English mustard
125 g/4 oz mixed grated cheese
¼ litre/½ pint milk
¼ litre/½ pint single cream
Salt and freshly ground white pepper
A touch of lemon juice

Melt the butter without letting it get hot. Stir in the flour. The quantity used will depend on the use to which this sauce is being put – pouring, coating, as a base for fish pie, etc. Gradually incorporate the cold milk, stirring the sauce over a low heat and slowly bringing it to the boil; add the mustard. Then add the grated cheese and stir the sauce until this has melted.

Stir in the cream and bring the sauce back to boiling point. Season with salt, ground white pepper and a little lemon juice. Simmer the sauce for 5 minutes, strain and serve.

CHERRY SAUCE

This savoury sauce was a regular accompaniment to a roast haunch of venison. It marries equally well with saddle of hare, roast ham, pork, duckling . . . in fact it can be used wherever a sweet–sour sauce is called for, which is usually when meat is either very dry, as can be the case with game, or when it is unusually fatty.

175 g/6 oz black cherries (fresh, bottled or tinned)
1 small onion
1 tbsp olive oil
2 tbsps redcurrant jelly
¼ litre/½ pint tawny port
125 ml/¼ pint strong game or chicken stock
125 ml/¼ pint orange juice
1 fresh bay leaf
¼ tsp grated lemon rind
A little potato flour
1 tbsp red wine vinegar

A pinch of cayenne pepper
Salt and freshly ground black pepper

Stone the cherries. Slice the onion.

Heat the oil in a small heavy-bottomed pan, add the sliced onion and allow this to brown without burning. Add the stock and simmer for 5 minutes.

Add the port, jelly, orange juice, lemon rind and bay leaf and continue simmering for a further 15 minutes.

Slake about a teaspoon of potato flour in cold water and stir this into the sauce, a little at a time, until it is just viscous. Season and cook the sauce for a further 5 minutes over a very low heat. Remove the bay leaf and strain the sauce through a fine sieve.

Return the sauce to the cleaned pan, add the cherries and cayenne. Simmer gently until the cherries are just plumped up. Stir in just enough of the vinegar to give bite.

CUMBERLAND SAUCE

I have never troubled really to find out why we name this sauce in this way; whether it is after the county of that name or whether a particular Duke of Cumberland had a penchant for it, I don't know. Either would be possible, for the former is a county in the heart of the Lake District and the latter would, no doubt, have had shooting lodges: both would produce game of all types and this sauce is especially good with all kinds of roast game as well as with raised pies and any cold meats. Unknown in other countries except by its British name, but a sauce which is much liked, particularly by the Swiss.

500 g/1 lb good redcurrant jelly
125 ml/¼ pint ruby port (tawny port will not
give such a good colour)
3 oranges
3 lemons
1 level dessertspoon dry mustard
1 small onion very finely chopped
A little salt
Tip of a teaspoon powdered mace
1 sherry glass cider vinegar (*not* malt vinegar)

Using a potato-peeler, remove the rind from all 6 pieces of fruit. Care must be taken to ensure that no white pith is taken off with the rind, as this is the bitter part of citrus fruits.

Collect the strips of rind together into manageable piles and shred the rind as finely as you possibly can with a very sharp, thin-spined knife – try to shred it as fine as a pin, for this will ensure that your sauce is good-looking and elegant. (Patience at this stage will pay dividends.)

Put the shredded peel into a pan and pour over enough water to cover it. Bring the contents of the pan to the boil and immediately pour into a strainer. Cool the peel under cold running water for a minute or so, then put on one side.

Squeeze and strain the juice of 2 of the oranges and 2 of the lemons. Bring this to the boil with all the remaining ingredients and simmer for 15 minutes over a low heat, stirring to ensure that the jelly melts evenly and doesn't catch.

Add the shredded rind and boil for a further 5 to 10 minutes until the sauce starts to thicken. Cool, then refrigerate until the sauce is fully thickened. Serve chilled and do not strain.

CURRY SAUCE

This is a basic curry sauce which can be adapted to all sorts of uses and can be served either hot or cold.

1 onion
1 heaped tsp curry powder
1 tsp tomato purée
15 g/½ oz flour
¼ litre/½ pint chicken stock
1 dessertspoon apricot purée or jam
1 dessertspoon sultanas
4 cloves
½ bay leaf
1 crushed clove garlic
2 tbsps brandy
Salt and freshly ground pepper
Oil for frying

Chop the onion and fry in 2 tablespoons of oil until golden brown. Add the curry powder and cook for 1 minute, stirring well. Add the tomato purée and then the flour.

Reduce the heat and let a crust form on the bottom of the pan – this will give both colour and flavour to the sauce. Remove the mixture from the pan, leaving the crust, and swill the bottom of the pan with the brandy, incorporating the crust. Return the mixture to the pan and add the stock and the other ingredients. Bring to the boil and simmer for 10 minutes.

Strain into a basin and leave to cool, covered with an oiled paper.

If you wish to use the sauce cold for a chicken mayonnaise dish or to use with cold poached fish, add half as much again of thick mayonnaise (p. 228) and stir in well. If the sauce looks too thick, add a little lemon juice and a touch of cold water.

If you want a hot, creamy sauce for boiled chicken with rice or *noisettes* of veal, add 125 ml/¼ pint double cream and bring the sauce back to the boil.

EGG SAUCE

This can be quite dull and it surprises me that with all the pounding and pulping that went on in the past, this sauce didn't undergo that treatment. The mere sieving of the eggs puts it immediately into a very superior class and thus makes it a splendid accompaniment to poached fish or chicken, or even vegetable marrow and cauliflower. In fact, it is a very good all-rounder.

400 ml/¾ pint milk
1 small onion
60 g/2 oz butter
30 g/1 oz flour
125 ml/¼ pint double cream
4 hard-boiled eggs
A little lemon juice
Salt and freshly ground white pepper

Boil the eggs for 8 minutes and no longer. Run cold water over them until they are completely cooled, cracking the shells to allow any sulphur gases which might cause discoloration of the yolks to escape.

Melt the butter in a heavy-bottomed pan and stir in the flour.

Chop the onion roughly, add it to the milk and slowly bring this to the boil.

Whisking briskly, pour the hot milk gradually through a strainer onto the butter and flour, stirring to form a rich smooth sauce. Cook this over a very low heat for a few minutes, stirring all the time to ensure that the flour is completely cooked. Season with salt, pepper and a little lemon juice.

Press the hard-boiled eggs through a hair sieve and fold them into the sauce. Just before serving, half-whip the cream and fold into the sauce to enrich and lighten it.

FENNEL SAUCE

We once had to ignore this most elegant of vegetables on account of its sheer unavailability. The post-war period has, however, brought it back to us and I cannot think of any major town or city that doesn't have a head or two of this aniseed-flavoured vegetable on a stall somewhere.

Tradition has dictated for a long time that this sauce be restricted to fish, and mackerel at that. It fits in where you want it to, and is to be recommended.

A good head of fennel
1 small onion
60 g/2 oz butter
30 g/1 oz flour
1 sherry glass white wine
1 egg-yolk
125 ml/¼ pint double cream
¼ litre/½ pint fish or chicken stock
Salt and freshly ground white pepper

Remove the ferny tops of the fennel and put them on one side to be picked, washed and chopped later. Cut the fennel root in half, then in quarters, and shred this as finely as you can with a very sharp knife, or on the coarse side of the grater.

Chop the onion equally finely. Melt the butter in the bottom of a pan, add the onion and sweat until it is transparent. Add the shredded fennel, cover with a lid and continue to cook the two vegetables together until the fennel is all but cooked. Shake the pan from time to time so that the contents do not acquire any colour and do not burn at the edges.

Dredge on the flour and stir in well. Gradually add the wine and stock (using fish stock if you are serving the sauce with fish), stirring all the time. Bring the sauce to the boil and cook for 10 minutes over a low heat.

Season with salt and pepper, adding a touch of castor sugar if the wine is too sharp.

Half-whip the cream with the yolk and fold into the sauce at the last minute. Finely chop the fennel leaves or fern and sprinkle over the finished sauce.

GREEN GOOSEBERRY SAUCE

This sauce has endless uses; the well known one of coupling it with mackerel comes to mind first, but it is equally good with other fish and with most cold fish dishes; try serving it with salmon, hot or cold. It makes a good alternative to apple sauce and goes very well with duck.

Remember that those delightful creamy, feathery elder blossoms marry very well with the gooseberry, as does lemon, and the two aromatics together show well to advantage with any form of gooseberry dish, adding undertones which enhance the flavour of the green berries.

300 g/10 oz fresh green gooseberries
Juice and rind of 1 lemon
2 sprigs of young elderflower if available
15 g/½ oz butter
1 tsp castor sugar
1 small packet frozen chopped spinach
Water
Salt and freshly ground white pepper

Top, tail and wash the gooseberries. Put them in a pan with the juice and rind of the lemon and the elderflower. Cover with a tight-fitting lid and, without any more water than is already clinging to them after washing, toss the pan over a low heat until the juices draw. Poach the fruit until tender.

Push the fruit through a sieve to give a good purée. This is one of the occasions when a hair sieve is better than a blender, for the latter does not get rid of all the seeds.

Bring 125 ml/¼ pint of water to the boil and cook the spinach quickly until it is just done and still keeps its colour – don't over-cook. Cool this and then squeeze the whole lot hard through the corner of a strong linen cloth. You will need 125 ml/4 fl oz of this bright green essence of spinach.

Add this to the gooseberries and season with a little sugar, salt and pepper. Add the knob of butter and stir in.

If the sauce has to be kept hot, dredge the surface with a little castor sugar. Try not to have to keep it warm for too long as you have gone to great lengths to produce a good bright green sauce and this will darken with prolonged heat and lose its attractive appearance.

If you want a cold sauce, dredge it with sugar and cool in a bowl of cold water before refrigerating.

GREEN SAUCE

¼ litre/½ pint basic mayonnaise (p. 228)
2 tbsps freshly chopped parsley
2 tbsps freshly chopped chervil
1 tbsp freshly chopped tarragon
60 g/2 oz frozen chopped spinach
Lemon juice
Salt and freshly ground white pepper

Defrost and drain the spinach, place it in a sieve and plunge it into boiling water for 2 minutes, then rinse it under cold water and press away all the liquid.

Tie the chopped herbs in a piece of muslin and blanch all these in the same way. Make a purée of the herbs and spinach in a blender or Mouli and stir this into the mayonnaise.

Season with salt, pepper and lemon juice.

HOLLANDAISE SAUCE

The 'rich melted butter' or 'beat butter' called for in many early recipes for boiled asparagus was as near today's Hollandaise Sauce as matters not. It was sometimes known as Dutch Sauce. England has always grown the finest asparagus in the world and its unique favour, and that of other delicately-flavoured vegetables, is complemented by this fine sauce. (See Notes for variations.)

2 tbsps white wine vinegar
3 tbsps water
A small piece of onion
6 peppercorns
A fingernail–sized piece of bay leaf
3 egg-yolks
175 g/6 oz unsalted butter
Lemon juice
Salt if required and freshly ground white pepper

Put the butter into a small pan and stand this in a warm place like the back ledge of an Aga or between the hotplates, or in the grill compartment when the oven is on.

Put the first 5 ingredients into a small pan and boil rapidly until you are left with 1 tablespoon of liquid.

Now add 2 more tablespoons of water. (You require the original quantity of liquid to extract the aromas in the first stage; you then need to replace some of the liquid which has evaporated.)

Select a bowl which has a good round bottom and which will sit in the top of a small pan of boiling water. Put the egg-yolks into the bowl and strain the above reduction onto them, stirring well with a tiny balloon whisk.

Arrange the bowl over the boiling water and whisk gently, but completely, taking care to see that the egg doesn't set on the sides of the bowl.

Continue whisking until the mixture is thick and the whisk leaves a definite trail, but *stop before the eggs scramble.* (Have a container of cold water to hand as a safety precaution; this is useful to dip the base of the bowl into, to remove the heat from it quickly and thus avoid any possibility of the egg over-cooking. It is good moral support to know that you have this first-aid to hand.)

Stand the bowl on a folded damp cloth (this helps keep the bowl steady as you whisk), whisk in a few drops only of the melted butter and gradually, as the sauce thickens, add the butter more quickly until it is all incorporated. (Leave out the milky sediment which will have settled to the bottom of the pan whilst the butter has been slowly melting and getting warm.)

Adjust the seasoning, adding a little lemon juice and salt and pepper if you think it is needed. Squeeze little bits of butter over the surface to prevent a crust forming; this can be whisked briskly into the sauce just before serving. Stand the sauce in a warm, *not hot*, place until you are ready to use it.

As this is a warm sauce, it must not be kept where it is too hot or it will separate, so keep an eye on it. A good place to put it is on top of a plate which in its turn is standing on top of a pan of hot, not even simmering, water.

Notes

1. An easier way of making Hollandaise is to cut the butter into small cubes and whisk them in gradually, but the finished sauce will not be as light in texture as when it is made with warm melted butter.

2. The sauce can quickly be made into Béarnaise sauce by substituting tarragon vinegar in the first stages and then by beating into the finished sauce a tablespoon of meat glaze or half a stock cube, completely melted in 2 tablespoons of boiling water and reduced down to 1 tablespoon; finally, stir in a heaped tablespoon of freshly chopped tarragon or, when this is not readily available, the same amount of good fresh green parsley.

3. Hollandaise is a basic sauce in the classical repertoire and there are plenty of changes to be rung on this theme. The French, rightly or wrongly, gave names to these variations, such as Maltaise, when orange rind and juice are added, and Choron, when the additions are tomato purée and some freshly chopped tarragon. For mousseline sauce, add half the volume of good whipped cream to a well thickened Hollandaise.

Imagination will lead you to interesting results if you don't vary either the original quantity of basics – liquids, yolks and butter – or the method of making the sauce.

HORSERADISH SAUCE (Hot)

Which stock you use will depend on whether you are serving this sauce with boiled beef, poultry or fish.

30 g/1 oz flour
60 g/2 oz butter
¼ litre/½ pint single cream
¼ litre/½ pint strong stock (fish or meat)
3 tbsps freshly grated (or finely minced)
horseradish
2 tsps lemon juice
¼ tsp grated lemon rind
1 tsp castor sugar
1 level tsp dry mustard
Salt and freshly ground white pepper

Melt the butter in a heavy-bottomed pan. Before it gets hot, stir in the flour and the dry mustard. Gradually work in the stock until you have a smooth thick sauce, then add enough of the cream to bring this sauce to a good consistency.

Cook slowly for 5 minutes. Add the grated horseradish, lemon rind and juice, sugar and salt and pepper. Add the remainder of the cream if necessary.

Let this sauce stand in a double pan, or in the pan in which it was made, placed over a second pan of simmering water. Cover the surface of the sauce with a circle of buttered paper and allow the flavour to draw for half an hour.

HORSERADISH SAUCE (Cold)

4 tbsps freshly grated (or finely minced)
horseradish
3 tsps lemon juice
2 tsps castor sugar
½ tsp made-up English mustard
¼ litre/½ pint double cream
Salt and freshly ground white pepper

Mix together all the ingredients, except the cream.

Whip the cream until it ribbons well but is by no means stiff, for it will quickly seize when the other ingredients are folded in, and in any case can quickly be brought up to the right consistency by whipping a little more, but it cannot be let down once it has separated! Fold in the mixture of the other ingredients.

Check the seasoning, remembering that salt helps cream to stiffen quickly. Chill well before serving.

MAYONNAISE

There can be no question that our early cooks had fallen on a method of making mayonnaise when they spoke of 'oil and vinegar beat well together 'til it be thick'. What they didn't realise was that the emulsion they had (inadvertently) made needed a stabilising agent – egg-yolk.

½ litre/1 pint oil (half nut oil, half good
olive oil) at room temperature
6 egg-yolks
1 tsp dry mustard
1 tbsp wine vinegar
Cold water
Salt and freshly ground white pepper

Separate the eggs and put the yolks into a round-bottomed basin. This is an essential as you need to collect and control the yolks within a small area. Add the salt, mustard and a little pepper and work these with a balloon whisk, or more laboriously with a wooden spoon, until they are really thick and sticky.

Have the oil in a jug; then, using a teaspoon, add the first few drops of oil to the egg mixture, whisking vigorously. Beat this in well before adding the next few drops. It is essential to take care in the early stages of mayonnaise making – if you are meticulous at the beginning, you will have no trouble later.

After the first tablespoonful or so has been added slowly, you can start to add the oil more quickly – experience will teach you just when this can be done. As soon as the emulsion starts to reject the oil (this is quite different from curdling), add a little vinegar and beat until it is creamy again. Mayonnaise is curdled when the solid part goes thin and flecky. If this happens, you must start again with a single egg-yolk and work the curdled mayonnaise into it drop by drop. Sometimes a tablespoon of boiling water added to the curdled mayonnaise will do the trick.

Keep the mayonnaise as stiff as your arm will allow. By this I mean that if you have a strong arm you will be able to have mayonnaise as thick as butter, which can virtually be cut with a knife. When a more liquid mayonnaise is needed, thin down with single cream, vinegar or cold water (or a combination of all three); water gives a blander result than vinegar, cream adds richness.

The finished mayonnaise can be flavoured with ketchup, sherry, lemon juice, brandy, Worcester sauce, etc. When next using mayonnaise to make tartar sauce, try adding a few chopped raw gooseberries – this will give a delicious kick to the sauce.

Store mayonnaise in a cool, but not cold, place. It does not keep indefinitely, but will be quite alright for 4 or 5 days. If it begins to look oily, just add a spoonful of boiling water and whisk until it is creamy again.

MINT SAUCE

65 ml/⅛ pint boiling water
A good bunch of young mint leaves
4 tbsps white wine vinegar
2 tsps castor sugar
½ tsp grated lemon rind
Salt and freshly ground pepper

Dissolve the sugar in the boiling water. Wash and chop the mint leaves very finely. Combine all the ingredients.

Chill well.

To make mint jelly, add a level teaspoon gelatine crystals to the hot water, stir until dissolved, together with the sugar. Add the remaining ingredients and chill.

MUSHROOM SAUCE

Serve with poached chicken, poached fish, eggs, fried veal cutlets or as a patty filling.

175 g/6 oz button mushrooms
30 g/1 oz butter
25 g/¾ oz flour
1 small onion
125 ml/¼ pint chicken stock
125 ml/¼ pint double cream
1 tsp lemon juice
1 tbsp Madeira
Salt and freshly ground pepper

Wipe the mushrooms and slice them as finely as possible. Chop the onion very finely.

Melt the butter in a heavy-bottomed saucepan and fry the onion until it is transparent. Add the mushrooms, turn up the heat and toss them for a few minutes until they start to colour.

Sprinkle with the flour and stir this in well; reduce the heat. Gradually add the stock and cream, stirring all the time, bring the sauce to the boil and simmer until it is bright and smooth; this will take about 3 minutes.

Season with salt, pepper, lemon juice and the Madeira.

MUSTARD SAUCE

This sauce is good with boiled chicken, some fish (especially herring and mackerel), cauliflower, celery, spinach and anything else you think it will aid and abet to advantage.

60 g/2 oz butter
30 g/1 oz flour
400 ml/¾ pint milk
1 small onion
2 tsps dry mustard
125 ml/¼ pint double cream

A squeeze of lemon juice
½ tsp castor sugar
Salt and freshly ground black pepper

Rinse a saucepan with cold water, pour in the milk, add the onion cut into small pieces and slowly infuse this over a low heat.

Melt the butter in a second pan and add the flour, stirring until it is completely incorporated and smooth. Remove the pan from the heat, allow to cool a little and stir in the dry mustard. Gradually strain the hot milk into the butter mixture and stir the sauce over a low heat until it is smooth and bright.

Season with salt, pepper, lemon juice and sugar. Just before serving, whip the cream until it ribbons and fold it into the finished sauce to make it light and foamy.

ONION SAUCE

2 Spanish onions
60 g/2 oz butter
25 g/¾ oz flour
A pinch of curry powder
¼ litre/½ pint cold water
125 ml/¼ pint double cream
Salt and freshly ground pepper

Finely slice the onion and cook until transparent in the butter. Season with the curry powder, salt and pepper. Add the flour and stir in well.

Gradually add the water, stirring all the time, and bring the sauce to the boil. Cook for 15 minutes. Pass the sauce through a blender, Mouli or hair sieve.

Add the cream, re-heat, correct the seasoning and serve.

ORANGE SAUCE (Savoury)

For serving with duckling, pork or, as the Tudors did, with lamb!

¼ litre/½ pint stock
1 small onion, finely sliced
1 dessertspoon tomato purée
1 tsp oregano
¼ tsp curry powder
½ crushed clove garlic
¼ tsp powdered rosemary
30 g/1 oz butter
Juice and rind of 2 oranges
1 tsp potato flour
1 tbsp Madeira
Salt and freshly ground pepper

Finely shred the orange rind as for Cumberland Sauce (p. 219). Put the shredded rind in a little water and bring to the boil. Rinse it under cold water, drain and put aside until needed.

Melt the butter in a heavy-bottomed pan and let it acquire a nutty flavour; fry the onion in this until golden brown. Add the seasonings, lower the heat and add the purée, remembering that tomato purée burns very easily, so stir constantly to keep the bottom of the pan clear.

Gradually add the stock, stirring all the time, and simmer for 20 minutes, then add the orange juice and bring the sauce back to the boil.

Slake the potato flour in a little cold water and pour this, a little at a time, into the boiling sauce, stopping when you have a viscous consistency.

Check the seasoning and add the Madeira. Strain the sauce through a fine strainer into a smaller container. Add the orange rind.

If the sauce is not to be used immediately, cut a circle of grease-proof paper, oil it and lay this over the surface of the sauce; stand the pan in a second pan of near boiling water so that further reduction does not take place, as this would make the sauce too strong.

RUM SAUCE

This old recipe for rum sauce has been used in my household ever since I started to cook. It is certainly gilding the lily when served with a rich

Christmas pudding, but what is Christmas dinner if you don't feel considerably over-fed?

¼ litre/½ pint Sauternes (or other sweet white wine)
3 tbsps Jamaica rum
5 egg-yolks
60 g/2 oz castor sugar
Rind of 1 lemon

Cream the egg-yolks and sugar until every granule of sugar has dissolved. Remove the rind of the lemon with a potato-peeler and patiently shred this as fine as hair with a sharp knife. Add to the egg-yolks and stir in the wine and rum.

Arrange the basin over a pan of boiling water, making sure the water is in contact with the bottom of the basin. Whisk the sauce slowly but continuously until it is as thick as double cream. Remove from the heat and continue whisking until the heat has diminished somewhat.

Keep the sauce warm over a pan of hot, but not boiling, water. This time the water must *not* be in contact with the bottom of the basin.

TOMATO SAUCE

This sauce is suitable for grilled meats, fish and poultry and for pasta of all types.

1 kg/2 lb tomatoes
1 tbsp mild tomato purée or ketchup
1 small onion
1 crushed clove garlic
60 g/2 oz green bacon
¼ litre/½ pint chicken stock
15 g/½ oz flour
30 g/1 oz butter
¼ tsp grated lemon rind
¼ tsp dried rosemary
1 tsp lemon juice

1 small glass dry sherry
A little castor sugar
Salt and freshly ground pepper

Finely chop the onion and sweat it in the butter in a heavy-bottomed pan until it is soft and pale golden coloured. Cut the bacon into striplets and add to the pan, frying it until it is cooked and has acquired a little colour. Sprinkle the flour over this and stir in well. Add the purée or ketchup and other seasonings.

Skin and de-seed the tomatoes and add to the pan, together with the sherry, lemon juice and stock. Simmer for 20 minutes or until the sauce is viscous and bright. Press through a hair sieve, add a modicum of castor sugar to taste, re-heat the sauce and serve.

If a creamy sauce is required, add 125 ml/¼ pint double cream after sieving, check the seasoning, re-heat and serve.

Stuffings

DRIED APRICOT AND ALMOND STUFFING
(For Chicken, Duckling and Veal)

250 g/8 oz dried apricots, soaked overnight
60 g/2 oz split almonds
125 g/4 oz seedless raisins
1 large onion
125 g/4 oz fresh white breadcrumbs
1 tsp grated orange rind
1 level tsp allspice
60 g/2 oz butter
2 tbsps sweet sherry or Madeira
1 tsp brown sugar
A little salt and freshly ground pepper

Chop the onion and fry to a golden brown in the butter. Cut the apricots into small pieces and then mix all the ingredients together into a loose stuffing.

BACON AND HERB STUFFING
(Suitable For Almost Anything)

250 g/8 oz fresh white breadcrumbs
60 g/2 oz butter
125 g/4 oz well flavoured bacon
1 medium-sized onion
125 g/4 oz shredded suet
1 tbsp mixed fresh lemon thyme and basil
(or 2 tsps mixed dried herbs)
1 tbsp freshly chopped parsley
1 beaten egg
Salt and freshly ground black pepper

Cut the bacon into striplets and fry these in the butter until golden brown. Add the sliced onions and fry until they are transparent. Mix all the ingredients together, including the butter in which you have been frying the bacon and onions. Season well and bind with the beaten egg.

———————————

EGG, OYSTER AND PARSLEY STUFFING
(For Chicken, Fish and Veal)

175 g/6 oz fresh white breadcrumbs
100 g/3 oz cold hard butter
1 dozen fresh or frozen (chopped) oysters
Juice of half a lemon
1 tbsp freshly chopped parsley
2 chopped hard-boiled eggs
1 beaten egg
Salt and freshly ground white pepper
A little thick cream if needed

Take the butter straight from the refrigerator and grate on the coarse side of the grater. Combine all the ingredients and bind with the beaten egg, plus the oyster liquor and a little cream if necessary.

LIVER AND OLIVE STUFFING
(For Duckling, Goose and Game)

250 g/½ lb good sausagemeat
60 g/2 oz fresh white breadcrumbs
Liver of the appropriate bird
15 g/½ oz butter
12 green olives, stoned and chopped
2 cloves garlic, finely chopped
1 tbsp chopped fresh basil (or 2 tsps dried)
1 beaten egg
Salt and freshly ground black pepper

Lightly fry the liver in the butter. Let it cool and then cut into small dice. Mix all the ingredients together, season well and bind with the beaten egg.

PRUNE AND APPLE STUFFING
(For Duckling, Goose and Pork)

1 sliced large onion
12 large prunes, cooked in tea and then pitted
1 peeled, sliced large baking apple
A little butter
A little dried rosemary
A little sugar
Salt and freshly ground black pepper

Fry the onion lightly in the butter and toss the apple with it for a minute or so. Mix the contents of the frying pan with all the other ingredients into a loose stuffing.

SMOKED OYSTER STUFFING
(For Veal, Chicken and Turkey)

250 g/8 oz cooked long-grain rice
125 g/4 oz smoked oysters

1 small onion, chopped
1 clove garlic, crushed
A little butter
Thick cream to bind
Salt and freshly ground black pepper

Fry the onion lightly in a little butter, then combine all the ingredients and bind with the cream.

Chutneys

CHUTNEY

In spite of chutney having its roots in India − the word is derived from the Hindi 'chatni' − in this country it appears more often as an accompaniment to cold meats, such as brisket or ribs of beef, than as an integral part of the assorted side dishes that appear with curries.

No kitchen store cupboard is complete without it, and there ought to be more than just one kind. Some of the milder chutneys are quite delicious when served with the cheese board, or with fried or grilled fillets of fish in place of the more usual tartar sauce.

It is better to bottle chutney in small quantities, as often only a small amount is needed and it may be some weeks before more is required.

My mother-in-law lived in India for many years; she first introduced me to gooseberry chutney and hers is the recipe I still use.

APPLE CHUTNEY

2½ kg/5 lb apples (half eating and half cooking)
1 kg/2 lb brown sugar
1½ litres/3 pints white wine vinegar
750 g/1½ lb sultanas
30 g/1 oz salt
30 g/1 oz mustard seeds

6 crushed cloves garlic
30 g/1 oz ground ginger
½ tsp cayenne

Peel, core and chop the apples. Put all the ingredients into a preserving pan and boil gently for 2 hours.
Spoon into sterilised warm jars and cover when cool.

APRICOT CHUTNEY

This is delicious with cold duckling or pork.

1½ kg/3 lb fresh apricots
750 g/1½ lb finely chopped onions
250 g/8 oz stoned raisins
500 g/1 lb brown sugar
1 tsp chilli powder
1 dessertspoon salt
1 tbsp mustard seeds
½ litre/1 pint red wine vinegar
1 tsp cinnamon
Juice and grated rind of 1 orange and 1 lemon
60 g/2 oz shelled walnuts

Tie the mustard seeds in a muslin bag. Put all the ingredients, except the walnuts, into a preserving pan. Cook gently for 2 hours, stirring from time to time to ensure that there is no sticking.
Add the walnuts 5 minutes before the end of the cooking time. Spoon into sterilised warm jars and cover when cool.

GOOSEBERRY CHUTNEY

1½ kg/3 lb green gooseberries
875 g/1¾ lb brown sugar
250 g/½ lb stoned raisins
500 g/1 lb finely sliced onions
or

375 g/¾ lb chopped shallots
2 level tbsps salt
5 g/¼ oz mustard seeds
½ tsp cayenne pepper
¾ litre/1½ pints red wine vinegar

Tie the mustard seeds in a piece of thin cotton or muslin. Put all the ingredients to simmer gently for 1½ to 2 hours, stirring from time to time to avoid sticking.

When you have arrived at a soft cohered consistency, spoon the chutney into sterilised warm jars and cover when cool.

MANGO CHUTNEY

If tamarinds are not available, use persimmons, or even tangerines.

25 green mangoes
750 g/1½ lb brown sugar
500 g/1 lb stoned tamarinds
250 g/8 oz stoned raisins
250 g/8 oz sliced green ginger
1½ litres/3 pints white wine vinegar
1 level tsp powdered cinnamon
1 tsp grated nutmeg
100 g/3 oz salt

Peel and slice the mangoes thinly, lay them in a shallow dish, sprinkle with a little of the salt and leave them to draw for 36 hours. Drain them well in a colander.

Dissolve the sugar slowly in half of the vinegar, boil for 5 minutes and set aside. Cook the mangoes in the remaining vinegar for 10 minutes, then add the raisins, tamarinds, ginger, spices and remaining salt.

Simmer gently for 20 minutes, then turn up the heat and gradually add the sugar-vinegar syrup. Stir the chutney vigorously and cook to a well amalgamated mush.

Spoon into sterilised warm jars and cover when cool.

TOMATO CHUTNEY

3 kg/6 lb tomatoes
1½ kg/3 lb cooking apples
125 g/4 oz salt
250 g/8 oz brown sugar
6 crushed cloves garlic
60 g/2 oz powdered ginger
30 g/1 oz mustard seeds
1½ litres/3 pints red wine vinegar

Peel, core and chop the apples.

Place the tomatoes in batches into a saucepan of boiling water, count up to twelve and then plunge the tomatoes into a sink of cold water. Take off the skins, cut out the 'eye', which will now be loose, and slice the tomatoes.

Put the tomatoes with the apples, salt and vinegar into a pan and cook until they are completely pulped. Press this pulp through a hair sieve or pass through a Mouli or blender. Return the purée to the pan, add the ginger, garlic, sugar and mustard seeds tied in a muslin bag. Simmer for 45 minutes.

Spoon into sterilised warm jars and cover when cool.

Butters

BRANDY BUTTER

This can safely be made two or three weeks in advance, and should by no means be restricted to use on Christmas pudding, as it goes well with many other puddings, pies and sweets.

125 g/4 oz unsalted butter
125 g/4 oz castor sugar
4 tbsps brandy
1 tsp lemon juice

½ tsp lemon rind
1 tbsp boiling water

Cut the butter into 1-inch cubes and put with the sugar and lemon rind into a basin. Beat until creamy, add the boiling water and continue to beat until every grain of sugar has dissolved. Add the lemon juice and brandy and beat in well. Put into lidded wax cartons and store in the refrigerator until ready for use.

RUM BUTTER

125 g/4 oz unsalted butter
125 g/4 oz soft brown sugar
4 tbsps Jamaican rum
1 tbsp orange juice
1 tsp orange rind
¼ tsp cinnamon

Proceed as for brandy butter, using very hot orange juice instead of water.

FAIRY BUTTER

The Georgians were very fond of Fairy Butter. I serve it with mince pies at Christmastime and with hot Christmas pudding. It also makes Eccles cakes extra special when the cakes are warmed through and Fairy Butter is offered with them.

125 g/4 oz unsalted butter
The yolks of 3 hard-boiled eggs
60 g/2 oz castor sugar
1 tbsp orange flower water, rum,
lemon juice or brandy

Cream the butter and sugar, beat in the egg-yolks and chosen flavouring. Pass through a fine hair sieve, chill, pile into a bowl and pass with the appropriate dish.

Savoury butters can be used at will with grilled meat, fish and poultry and give an added dimension to liver, sausage, spaghetti and so forth; the best way of serving them is to slice the roll into ⅛-inch discs. Try also serving discs of savoury butter kept hard in a bowl of ice when you next serve a pulse or purée type of soup.

ANCHOVY BUTTER

125 g/4 oz butter
1 crushed clove garlic
12 anchovy fillets
Lemon juice
A touch of cayenne pepper
A few screws of black pepper

Cream the butter, add all the other ingredients, season to taste but do not add any salt. Pass through a blender or Mouli and then a hair sieve.

Form into a roll and fold in wetted grease-proof paper or foil. Refrigerate until needed.

GARLIC BUTTER

125 g/4 oz butter
4 crushed cloves garlic
1 tbsp lemon juice
Salt and freshly ground white pepper
A dash of Tabasco sauce

Cream the butter, add the garlic and season to taste with lemon juice, salt and Tabasco. Form into a roll as in the preceding recipe and refrigerate.

Cut into ½-inch cubes for topping grilled steaks, chops, fish, etc.

HERB BUTTER

125 g/4 oz butter
1 tsp each of freshly picked and finely chopped parsley,
fennel, chervil, basil and chives
½ crushed clove garlic
Lemon juice
Salt and pepper

Cream the butter, beat in the garlic and herbs and season to taste with lemon juice, salt and pepper.

Form into a roll as in preceding recipes and refrigerate.

PARSLEY BUTTER

125 g/4 oz butter
2 tbsps freshly chopped parsley
1 tsp chopped chives
Lemon juice
Salt and freshly ground white pepper

Cream the butter, add the parsley and chives and season with lemon juice, salt and pepper.

Form into a roll as in preceding recipes and refrigerate.

SALADS

One has only to read John Evelyn, the seventeenth-century diarist, on the subject of salads (or sallets, sallids, etc., as they have been called over the years) to see that we used an exotic range of fruits and vegetables, and of salad dressings, with an array of fresh herbs, spices, aromatics and the like. Also included in all of them was oil, an ingredient which in this century went very much out of favour! It is important to recognise from an examination of many old cookery books that when they called for oil and vinegar 'beat well together 'til they be thick', they had arrived at a form of mayonnaise.

My own range of salads has always been very varied, and it would be impossible to decide just where any of my inventions first saw the light of day, as I trained in Denmark, Switzerland, France and England. So, bearing in mind the factors mentioned above, I dubbed them all English! The salad bowl is very much of an artist's medium and I only give you the range of canvases, paints and pigments which I use, for rarely does the same combination appear twice, but I guarantee that it is always interesting and evocative.

I consider the dressings of major importance, so my notes on these come first.

Bases (or carriers for the flavourings): oil, vinegar, bland mayonnaise, yoghurt, sour cream, cream cheese, cottage cheese, pulped avocado, thick cream.

Acidulating agents: red and white wine vinegar (malt vinegar is *very* pungent), any citrus fruit juices, brandy, sherry, gin. (Always add these gradually, stopping when your palate is satisfied.)

Aromatics (to give a primary aroma): onion, shallot, leek, garlic, chives, angostura, *amer picon* (brandy-based orange bitters), relish, fresh flower waters and oils, rinds of citrus fruits.

Herbs: basil, bay leaf, chervil, coriander flower, dill, fennel, lemon thyme, lovage, marjoram, all the mints, oregano, parsley, rosemary, sage, summer and winter savory, tarragon, thyme, verbena. All fresh where possible, otherwise dried or frozen.

Spices: allspice, aniseed, cinnamon, cardamom, clove, coriander, carraway seeds, cumin, curry powder, nutmeg, mace, ginger, paprika, all the peppers, saffron, tumeric.

Sweeteners: scented honeys, brown and white sugar, dark treacle, fruit juices, ketchups, wines, liqueurs.

Oils: olive, peanut, walnut, sesame-seed, sunflower, corn, mustard-seed, almond.

Salad Ingredients

The following are some of my own suggestions for combinations of ingredients. I hope that my ideas will stimulate your imagination and that you will experiment to suit your own tastes.

Ingredients	*Dressings*
Beef, tongue, onions (all cut into striplets)	Oil, vinegar, grated fresh horseradish, mustard
Curd cheese, radishes, hazelnuts	Salt, freshly ground pepper, chives
Peeled and de-seeded cucumber sections, raw fennel root cut into equal-sized pieces	Oil, lemon juice and grated rind, chopped verbena, sugar
Raw fennel root cut into equal-sized pieces, split blanched almonds	Mayonnaise, chopped fennel herb, lemon juice
Grapefruit segments	Oil, white wine vinegar, sugar, curry powder
Lettuce hearts (cleaned and quartered)	Oil, orange juice and grated rind, sour cream, basil, sugar

New potatoes (cooked and quartered), de-seeded cucumber chunks, radishes, spring onions (Don't over-cook the potatoes, which should be firm)	Mayonnaise, chopped dill, lemon juice
Red cabbage (raw, shredded), sultanas	Oil, honey, red wine vinegar
Segmented and skinned oranges, de-seeded tomato quarters in equal proportions	Oil, orange juice and grated rind, mustard
Chopped pear and apple, split blanched almonds	Yoghurt, kirsch, sugar
Cooked long-grain rice, cubes of cream cheese, chopped banana, muscatel raisins	Oil, lemon juice, honey, curry powder, Madeira
Cooked long-grain rice, chopped pineapple, muscatel raisins, brazil nuts	Oil, honey, rum, cinnamon
Boiled shrimps, skinned and de-seeded grapes, cooked long-grain rice	Mayonnaise, ginger, grated lemon rind
Sliced tomatoes	Oil, lemon juice, dried rosemary, quince jelly

Colour plays a very important part in salad-making. Take care to ensure that any foods that would discolour are treated so that they don't. Dip cut fruits such as apples, pears and bananas into lemon juice; see that green vegetables are crisp and green before they are tossed in the dressing; add any flower petals, such as rose or dandelion, to salads at the last minute, as they tend to go black.

Herbs and Spices

Fresh herbs can be grown, or bought, in small pots and these can easily be kept on a kitchen window-sill for immediate cutting. When using dried herbs, as we all have to from time to time, try infusing them in a little boiling water before adding them to your dressings, sauces, ragoos, etc. Deep-freeze fresh herbs when they are in season, ready for winter use. This is a simple process: pick the best parts of the herbs, plunge them into boiling water for just one minute, rinse them well under running cold water, then drain them and seal in appropriate freezer bags.

Herbs and spices do not keep indefinitely and they should be discarded when they look dusty and faded and have lost any smell. Care should also be taken when buying them, as many shops do not keep a fresh stock, for they too tend to think that these things go on for ever.

Dressings

Oil-and-vinegar type dressings should never be added to a green salad until the last minute and must *never* be left overnight. Any left-over dressed salads of this nature must be thrown away.

Cover mayonnaise-dressed salads with a circle of wet grease-proof paper; this will prevent the mayonnaise going dull.

INDEX